THE
Westminster Pulpit

VOLUME VII

THE Westminster Pulpit

VOLUME VII

The Preaching of
G. CAMPBELL MORGAN

WIPF & STOCK · Eugene, Oregon

Wipf and Stock Publishers
199 W 8th Ave, Suite 3
Eugene, OR 97401

The Westminster Pulpit vol. VII
The Preaching of G. Campbell Morgan
By Morgan, G. Campbell
Copyright©1954 by The Morgan Trust
ISBN 13: 978-1-60899-316-1
Publication date 1/15/2012
Previously published by Fleming H. Revell, Co., 1954

G. Campbell Morgan Reprint Series

Foreword

IF IT is true that the measure of a person's greatness is their influence, not only on his own time but on future generations, G. Campbell Morgan must be regarded as a great person. His greatness is seen not only in the wide impact of his ministry on both sides of the Atlantic, but in the fact that his books are still read and studied sixty-five years after his death. Named one of the ten greatest preachers of the twentieth-century by the contributing board of *Preaching* magazine, Morgan made the Bible a new and living book not only to the congregations who listened to him, but the vast multitude of persons who read his books.

Fox sixty-seven years Morgan preached and taught the Scriptures and served churches in England and the United States. What is remarkable is that his commentaries and expositions of the Bible still speak to persons of a new millennium. There have been many changes in the world since he faithfully preached and taught the Scriptures, but the wide appeal of his books testify to the timelessness of his message.

Although he held pastorates in the Congregational and Presbyterian denominations, he had an ecumenical appeal to persons of all denominations and traditions. The mystic

Thomas á Kempis once wrote, "He to whom the eternal word speaks is delivered from many opinions." In one of his sermons, he referred to the words of Amos that there would be a famine for hearing the word of God (Amos 8:11). The timeless work of G. Campbell Morgan addresses that hunger, as his books enable his readers to get beyond opinions to the living Word.

Wipf and Stock Publishers have rendered a great gift to the religious world in reprinting dozens of Morgan's books. This growing collection makes his books more available, so that readers have an option other than searching the internet for used, and often expensive, copies. Among this collection is the classic *The Great Physician* and commentaries on the Gospel of Matthew and John. Persons seeking a living faith and a meaningful encounter with God would profit from reading any of these Morgan books.

Near the end of his ministry, in a sermon entitled "But One Thing," Morgan commented on how Portugal changed the words of a coin after Christopher Columbus discovered America. No longer did the inscription say, *Ne Plus Ultra* (nothing more beyond) but *Plus Ultra* (more beyond). It is the hope of the G. Campbell Morgan Trust that the reprinting of these books will bring readers to the "more beyond," and an even deeper encounter with the Word in Scripture.

THE MORGAN TRUST
Richard L. Morgan
Howard C. Morgan
John C. Morgan

CONTENTS

CHAPTER		PAGE
I	Christ's Call to Courage	9
II	Christ's Next of Kin	22
III	High Purpose, Failing and Fulfilled	34
IV	The Value of Vision	47
V	The Great Confession	60
VI	The Pathway of the Passion	73
VII	The Powers of the Presence	87
VIII	The Pathway to Power	101
IX	The Great Commandments	115
X	The Evangel of Grace	129
XI	Tongues Like as of Fire	142
XII	Men Looking for Their Lord	155
XIII	The Son of Man—Delivered Up	168
XIV	Gethsemane: The Garden of Spices	182
XV	The Darkness of Golgotha	195
XVI	Halting	208
XVII	The Unstraitened Christ	220
XVIII	Burdens: False and True	233
XIX	Like Gods or Godlike	246
XX	The Vine	260
XXI	The Nearness of God Unrecognized	273
XXII	The Nearness of God Discovered	286
XXIII	The Perils of Procrastination	300
XXIV	The Crippling That Crowns	313
XXV	Grace and Law	327
XXVI	God-Governed Life	340

THE
Westminster Pulpit

VOLUME VII

CHAPTER I

CHRIST'S CALL TO COURAGE

Son, be of good cheer; thy sins are forgiven.
MATTHEW 9:2.

Daughter, be of good cheer; thy faith hath made thee whole.
MATTHEW 9:22.

Be of good cheer; it is I; be not afraid.
MATTHEW 14:27.

Be of good cheer; I have overcome the world.
JOHN 16:33.

Be of good cheer; for as thou hast testified concerning Me at Jerusalem, so must thou bear witness also at Rome.
ACTS 23:11.

FIVE FAMILIAR PICTURES OF THE NEW TESTAMENT ARE RE-called by the reading of these words.

The first is that of a man sick of the palsy, carried by his friends into the presence of Jesus; physically trembling and troubled in heart by the consciousness of sin.

The second is that of a woman struggling to reach Him through the movement and pressure of a jostling crowd, troubled by all the suffering of twelve years, twelve years of physical pain, of divorce, of ostracism, of excommunication.

The third is that of a company of disciples in the midst of difficulties which had arisen in the path of duty. The Master had bid them set the prow of their vessel toward the farther shore, and the wind was contrary, and the waves were boisterous. The picture is that of these men suddenly confronted by a new and nameless terror, a specter of the night, moving over the waters toward them.

The fourth is that of a company of disciples face to face with three facts: first, the fact of their Lord's approaching departure by some way they could not understand, and to some bourne about which they knew nothing; second, the fact of the antagonism of the world to Him and to His ideals, and consequently to them also, if in His absence they remained loyal to Him; and, third, the fact of their own appalling weakness. Or briefly, it is a picture of a company of men troubled by the fear of the future.

The last picture is that of a servant of God in prison, rescued from the mob yesterday, threatened by a new conspiracy tomorrow, troubled by the force of circumstances which hindered the progress of his service.

The central fact in these pictures is not that of the troubled souls. The central fact is that of Christ, and of what He said to these people. To the man sick of the palsy He said, "Be of good cheer, child." To the woman broken, bruised, weary, emaciated, and forlorn, He said, "Be of good cheer, daughter." To the disciples in the midst of the storm, terrified by the approach of the phantom, and to the disciples yet more afraid of the future without Him, He said, "Be ye of good cheer." To the man in the prison, hindered in high and holy service, He said, "Be of good cheer." In each case He challenged fear, and uttered a call to courage, and gave His reason for doing so.

These incidents illustrate and illuminate the whole realm of discipleship, and I bring them to you this morning in order, as I may be helped by the Spirit of God, to fasten your attention upon that challenge of Jesus. I bring them to you as a New Year's greeting, not as my word to you, for that would be very worthless, but as the Master's word to you. "Be of good cheer."

Let us then consider, first, the call of Christ itself; second, the arguments of Christ as we find them scattered over these stories; and, finally, let us inquire what is the way of obedience to this call of our Lord.

First, then, the call of Jesus, "Be of good cheer." Now I take up my New Testament, and I find that these are the only occasions on which we have any record of His using these expressions, and no one else is ever recorded to have used exactly the same expression in addressing men. The word is almost peculiar to Christ. It emerges in the writings of Paul in certain applications; but this personal, direct, immediate call was peculiarly that of the Lord Himself. It is therefore important that we should, with all simplicity, inquire what He really did say. In the Revised New Testament from which I read, you will notice that there is uniformity of translation, that on each occasion we have these words, "Be of good cheer." In the Authorized the translation is, "Be of good cheer" in each case except one; in the record of His speech to the woman, the 1611 translators rendered Jesus' words thus, "Be of good comfort."

Now, without any question, there is a fault in this translation, "Be of good cheer." There is something very bright about it, very hopeful about it; and before I am through I shall show you that I have robbed you of nothing by saying that it is not exactly what our Lord said. Indeed, so to translate it is to miss the deepest value of the word. "Be of good cheer" suggests the result rather than the cause. The actual word of which our Lord made use described the cause, and left us to discover the result. There is another word in the New Testament for cheerfulness. When Paul wrote, "The fruit of the Spirit is . . . joy," the thought is that of cheerfulness. But that is not the word here. Cheerfulness will be the outcome of what Christ commanded, but He did not command men to be cheerful. He never dealt with the surface of things. He never told men to smile when they were in agony. He dealt with the underlying agony, and thus called men into such attitude of soul as made cheerfulness possible.

The word employed indicates courage rather than cheerfulness, and, moreover, courage subjectively as a feeling rather than objectively as an enterprise; "Be of good courage" rather than, Do a courageous thing. Our Lord did not say, Forget your trouble by doing something. That may help for the moment, but the agony surges back when the activity ceases. The word that our Lord addressed to the man, to the woman, to the disciples, to the imprisoned apostle, was a word suggestive of that strength of heart which is at once the inspiration of daring and the reason of cheerfulness. The call, then, is to freedom from fear, and to an absolute assurance of safety.

Passing from that attempt to consider the actual meaning of the Lord's word, let us glance at these pictures once more, in order to discover what Christ meant in each case.

There is a conscience troubled by sin; to that man He said, Do not have any fear, be of good courage.

There is a woman's heart trembling through long suffering, which has become destitution; to that woman He said, Have no fear; be full of courage; there is nothing to be afraid of.

Look carefully at those men on board the ship. What was their condition? Intelligence menaced by mystery. I wish I could bring you into real sympathy with those fishermen of blue Galilee. They were men accustomed to the storms that suddenly swept its waters, men who were not often baffled, even when the sea was tossed into fury by Euroclydon. Their chief trouble that night was not that of the storm, but that of the specter moving across the waters. They did not know what it was. Do not, in your superior wisdom, say they ought not to have been frightened at ghosts. That is what you are frightened at this morning! What you are fearing you will find presently to be the Lord Himself! So do not be angry with these men. Try to sympathize with them. Their intelligence was menaced by mystery; and when He came to them, He said, Do not be afraid. There is nothing to be afraid of. Banish panic, establish peace, be of good courage.

Then look at the group of men in that upper room. They were men full of a spiritual aspiration, but threatened by opposition, not merely the opposition of men who were angry with Jesus, and about to crucify Him; but that most subtle and forceful opposition of worldliness in the true and New Testament sense of that word, those materialized ideals for which the enemies of Christ stood, and which had gained so strong a hold upon the heart of the multitudes. That little group of men in the upper room saw Him going. They had been able to believe while He was with them. They had been able, with Him, even though tremblingly, to believe in His philosophy when He said, "Be not afraid of them which kill the body and after that have no more that they can do." But He was going. How were they to be true to that high spiritual ideal, with all the forces of the cosmos as men were interpreting it, against them. To them, thus filled with foreboding, He said, "Be of good courage," there is nothing to fear. Do not be afraid.

And then we come to the picture of Paul, the man of high purpose, and unswerving devotion, who had said, "I must also see Rome," knowing that Rome was the very center of the world, the strategic point from which to proclaim the Gospel and send the messengers of the King along all her highways through the nations. Everything appeared as though he were not going to reach Rome. He was in Jerusalem, and there he had been mobbed, and barely rescued yesterday; and conspirators were planning to murder him to-morrow. Paul was not grieved by reason of his own imprisonment. He was troubled because he was an ambassador in bonds, and his high purpose was being hindered. It was night, when suddenly the Lord spoke to him; and said, "Be of good courage," Paul, there is nothing to be afraid of, neither the mob of yesterday, nor the conspiracy of to-morrow; be of good courage.

Now, I will say the thing some of you are thinking. That is all very well; but if Christ said only that, other men have said it, and it does not help us far. It does mean a little when I am troubled and perplexed, and harassed by fear, and my heart is trembling, to have someone bid me be of good courage. I like the man who comes and says to me, Put on a brave face! I think he helps me for perhaps half an hour. I would rather have such a man than the one who comes and says, I will tell you how you got into this trouble. Put that man out!

But the man who can say to me only, Be of good courage, is not the man I want on this first Sunday as I lift my eyes and try to peer into the mists that lie along the valleys, and wonder what forces are marshaled against my soul. If Christ is going to help me He must give me a reason for courage.

And so I pass to what I think is the central value of the meditation, the arguments of Christ in favor of courage as I find them scattered through these stories.

Inclusively, Christ had one argument with which to confront fear—Himself. There is nothing else to say. To every force which challenges the soul of man He opposes Himself.

In no case does He minimize the antagonistic forces. That is not merely a passing word. That is something to be thought of and remembered. To the man sick of the palsy He did not say, You are quite mistaken about this palsy. You have none. He did not say, There is no such thing as sin, cheer up. Is there anything more deceitful, dastardly, devilish, than to tell that to a man who knows what sin is in his own blood and life? That is not the word of Christ. He was not minimizing the fact of sin; He did not tell the woman who for twelve years had been in the grip of an infirmity that there was no reality in her suffering, that if she would make up her mind there was *nothing* the matter, there *was* nothing the matter. Oh, these utterly foolish, devilish things by which men are being deceived. Jesus did not laugh at His disciples because they were afraid of a ghost. He did not even rebuke them for that fear. He did not tell the men in the upper room that there was nothing in the force of the world as against them. He knew its force, He knew its lure, its subtlety, its insidiousness. He did not tell Paul that the opposition through which he had come was nothing. Christ did not, and does not, minimize the reality of the antagonistic forces which await us and confront us. No, what He did in each case was to place Himself between the assaulted soul and the assaulting foe.

Now let us again pass over our stories. He said to the man sick of the palsy, "Thy sins are forgiven." The rulers immediately objected: "This man blasphemeth. . . . Who can forgive sins but One, even God?" To this objection the Lord replied, "Wherefore think ye evil in your hearts? For whether is easier to say, Thy sins are forgiven, or to say, Arise, and walk? But that ye may know that the Son of man hath power on earth to forgive sins (then saith He to the sick of the palsy), Arise, and take up thy bed, and go unto thy house; and immediately he took up his bed, and departed."

That action on the part of the man was the demonstration of the fact that Christ had dealt with the principle of evil out of which the physical limitation had sprung, that when He said, "Thy sins are forgiven," He had spoken not merely a word of judicial authority but a word of redeeming power. He stood between the sins that assaulted the soul of the man—and righteously assaulted his soul, for had he not been guilty of them?—and the man himself; and therefore He was able to speak the infinite and abiding and perpetual mysterious word of Christianity, the word of forgiveness, the authority and power of which was demonstrated by the new power that appeared in the life of the man.

To the woman He said, "Thy faith hath made thee whole," and before He had said it she was healed. How was she healed? I cannot paint pictures, but there are some I would like to paint, and this is one. Jesus was walking along, with crowds jostling Him; just ahead of Him was Jairus, eager if possible to hasten Him to the house where his little girl lay dying, when, somehow edging her way through the crowd, the woman touched—a better word would be "clutched"—His garment with the grasp of the last, despairing agony of a needy soul. Jesus immediately turned round, "Who touched Me?" His disciples reminded Him that multitudes were thronging Him, and pressing Him; but He said, Someone has touched Me, for I perceive that *dynamite* has gone out of Me. That was the argument of His call, Be of good cheer. His virtue came between her and the assaults of her limitation and pain, canceled them, banished them, lifted her back to life and joy. Daughter, be of good cheer, be of good courage, by My virtue thy need is supplied.

I look at the men as they crossed the sea, and with terror on their faces gazed on the strange, mysterious phantom moving slowly and yet surely toward them over the storm-tossed waters. Christ challenged that fear in the words, "Be of good cheer; *it is I*." If I but knew *how* to say that, I need say no more. "*It*," phantom, ghost, terror, "is *I*." He did not say to them, Never mind, you do not understand it, it will pass presently, and you will forget all about it. No, out of the heart of the infinite mystery He spoke. That is a parable in itself as well as a miracle.

To the men in the upper room, afraid of the forces of the world that would be against them, He said, "Be of good cheer," and His argument for courage was expressed in the words, "I have overcome the world." Over those very forces which they feared He had been victorious through three and thirty years of life; and in His Cross and in His resurrection He perfected His conquest by the reclamation of the cosmos, and the reintroduction of regenerate men to it as having dominion over it instead of being enslaved by it. In fellowship with Him in overcoming life, men find the very cosmos which man's abuse had turned into an enemy, becoming God's minister of light and healing and help and blessing, co-operating with God in all high and holy purposes and enterprise. This, then, was His argument: I have overcome, I have remastered, I have recaptured the very cosmos. Do not be afraid of it. Find in it, in fellowship with Me, that which shall minister to all your need.

And, finally, in the quietness and silence of the prison He stood between His servant and the brutality of the mob and the subtlety of the conspirators, and Himself was the argument for courage. No longer present among His people in bodily form, He appeared to this man as to one born out of due time in a great crisis of need, when the heart was disappointed because service was hindered, and He said, "As thou hast testified concerning Me at Jerusalem, so must thou bear witness also at Rome," and thus He was the argument for courage, the inspiration of cheerfulness.

I think that after that Paul lay down in the prison and had a wonderfully restful sleep till the morning. Be of good courage!

If you will take those stories and go through them again in some half hour when you are alone, I think you will find that there is at least a suggestion of sequence in them. First, be of good courage because thy sins are forgiven by the Redeemer. Then be of good courage because all thy weakness and limitation can be supplied by the virtue that comes from Him. Then, when thy soul is assaulted by some mystery, be of good courage, resting assured that out of the heart of every mystery He will emerge. Then, when the sense of the forces of materialism and of worldliness are opposing thy soul, and thou art conscious of the difficulty of loyalty to Christ and high spiritual ideals, be of good courage, because He has overcome. Then when devoted to high purpose and holy service, thou art baffled, beaten, prevented, hindered, be of good courage, for in the silence of the night He will assure thee that He has made the plan of thy service, and all hell cannot prevent thy coming to Rome if He would have thee there.

Whether this is a sequence or not, it is at least certain that the first is the fundamental word. Christ calls men to courage by dealing first with sin, that deepest reason of trouble, of fear, of panic; and He builds the superstructure of His palace of peace on the purging of the conscience and the putting away of defilement.

Now, how are we to obey Him? That is the final inquiry. The importance and difficulty of this are patent. Intellectually we agree when He says to us, Be of good courage; but actually we so constantly fail.

Suffer me to clear the way by one or two negative considerations. How am I to obey Him when He says to me, Be of good courage? By love? Nay, that fails in my experience. By hope? Nay, on many a day that fades from the sky. By faith? Nay, for in my case faith fears oftentimes; it fears as well as falters.

All this may be confession of weakness. You may say to me, You have no right to have these experiences. Love ought not to fail, hope ought not to fade, faith ought not to fear. Well, if they are confessions of weakness, and they may be, they are certainly statements of fact. What, then, is the condition of courage? Love, hope, and faith are the outcome of the fulfilment of a condition. Love fails, hope fades, and faith fears, when that condition is not being fulfilled. The abiding condition of courage is clear vision of the Lord. Change the word "vision," if you will, and say "definite consciousness of the Lord's nearness." Or better, cancel the preliminary words, *the vision of*, and *the consciousness of*, and leave only this, *the Lord Himself*. I change, He changes not. My love still ebbs and flows. His love can never die. Not my faith, not my hope, not my love, are the final conditions of a real courage, but Himself.

Go back over our illustrations. Did that man, sick of the palsy, lose the sense of fear I think he did. How? Because he made himself believe? No. How, then? Because he believed without being able to help it. How? He saw Jesus, he heard Jesus speak, and he believed. The woman's faith procured her healing without banishing fear, for mark the place in the narrative of the word of Jesus. She touched and was immediately healed. Yet she was full of fear. But when she came in front of Him, and told Him all the truth in trembling; and when those love-lit eyes looked down into her sorrow-dimmed eyes, eyes haunted with the fears of all the years, then fear fled, and courage filled her heart. It did not matter to her that she was excommunicated, ostracized, poor; she had seen Him, and fear folded its raven wings and dropped dead.

I am talking out of my own heart. I am a fearful soul, and I am ashamed of the fact. I have been trying to find out how to be courageous. I have found out! God help me to be true to the revelation! It is to see Him! Looking off unto Jesus, the Author and Perfecter of faith! Consider Him Who endured such contradiction of sinners!

I am speaking to Christian men and women, to those who are familiar with Him in some sense. All our fear and all our panic result from a dimmed vision of the Lord, a dimmed consciousness of Christ. I believe that is the trouble with us all to-day, individually and in Church life, all these tremors, all these fears result from lack of the sense of His presence.

Another word, and I have done. Have you no fear in your heart at all? There are those who are quite without fear. Well, let them suffer me to ask a question. Why not? I believe that there are men and women who answer my inquiry by saying, Because we have seen Him; because we see Him now. I have no more to say to them. Such men and women have found the secret of peace.

But there are others who are not conscious of fear to-day. Let me press upon them the same question. Why not? I charge all such most earnestly to remember in these days, when there may seem in their case to be no cause for fear, no trembling, no panic, weakness, foolishness, that any reason for absence of fear, short of the vision and consciousness of Christ and confidence in Him, is false and your confidence is misplaced, and it may be that before this first Sabbath day of the year be gone to its last hour the crack of doom will come to you, out of the light will come the darkness, and from behind the mountains will rush innumerable foes to assault your soul. There is no refuge for the soul of man other than the Lord Christ.

But now, finally; trembling, terrified, troubled souls, I pray you look and listen! Look to your Lord, and with eyes fastened upon Him listen to His word, "Be of good courage." That means, when He says it, that He puts Himself between thy soul and all the forces in hell and earth that may be against thee.

What shall we say to Him? Well, I am prepared to say that because of what He is my heart is full of courage. I believe, I hope, I love! And having this confidence in my own heart, my message is expressed perhaps most perfectly to my own consciousness by one of those great old hymns of Charles Wesley. Let me conclude with it:

Surrounded by a host of foes,
  Stormed by a host of foes within,
Nor swift to flee, nor strong to oppose,
  Single, against hell, earth, and sin,
Single, yet undismayed, I am;
I dare believe in Jesu's name.

What though a thousand hosts engage
  A thousand worlds, my soul to shake?
I have a shield shall quell their rage,
  And drive the alien armies back;
Portrayed it bears a bleeding Lamb;
I dare believe in Jesu's name.

Me to retrieve from Satan's hands,
  Me from this evil world to free,
To purge my sins, and loose my bands,
  And save from all iniquity,
My Lord and God from heaven He came;
I dare believe in Jesu's name.

Salvation in His name there is,
  Salvation from sin, death, and hell,
Salvation into glorious bliss
  How great salvation, who can tell!
But all He hath for mine I claim;
I dare believe in Jesu's name.

CHAPTER II

CHRIST'S NEXT OF KIN

Whosoever shall do the will of My Father which is in heaven, he is My brother, and sister, and mother.

MATTHEW 12:50.

IN ORDER TO HAVE AN ACCURATE APPRECIATION OF THE MEANing and value of these wonderful words of Jesus we must carefully consider the circumstances in which they were uttered. The story is told in a brief paragraph, of which these are the final words. There is a similar paragraph in the third chapter of Mark's gospel; indeed, the similarity is very remarkable. The story as Mark tells it is hardly changed by sentence or phrase. There is absolutely no difference in any essential matter.

However, in his context, Mark does give some details which Matthew omits. Christ was so pressed with His work, so eagerly sought after by the crowds, so eagerly responding to their seeking, so completely giving Himself up, without stint and without reserve, to the demands that were being made on Him that "when His friends heard it, they went out to lay hold on Him; for they said, He is beside Himself" (Mark 3:21). After recording that fact, Mark goes on to tell the things that were happening in Capernaum, and then, at the thirty-first verse, he resumes the narrative commenced in verse 21, "And there came His mother and His brethren."

Christ, as I have said, was giving Himself without stint, without reserve, to the thronging, pressing multitudes; they followed Him from place to place, came with their criticisms and with their agonies; and with patient courtesy He replied to their criticisms, and with infinite compassion He relieved their agonies. He was so busy that He had not time to eat, was so perpetually occupied that He had no time for rest. That news was conveyed to His mother and to His brethren after the flesh, who evidently were in very close association with Mary, and shared her anxiety and concern for Jesus. His mother heard, and she said, and they said, "He is beside Himself," He is losing His reason. In consequence of this conviction they started on a journey to reach Him, in all probability from Nazareth to Capernaum. When they arrived, they found that He was in a house, surrounded by a crowd of people.

The word was passed to Him that His mother and brethren were without, seeking to speak to Him. He knew why they had come. "He knew all men, . . . He needed not that anyone should bear witness concerning man; for He Himself knew what was in man." His mother had come, full of anxiety for Him, persuaded that He was beside Himself, eager to prevent Him from killing Himself by excess of zeal and toil. She did not understand Him. That is revealed in the gospels from beginning to end. She loved Him with a great mother love; she knew the infinite and appalling mystery of His being; but she never understood Him. When He began His ministry she sought to hurry Him to some demonstration of power, and He had to say to her, "Woman, what have I to do with thee? Mine hour is not yet come." Because she loved Him she would have persuaded Him to take care of Himself.

Knowing this, Jesus said, "Who is My mother? and who are My brethren?" and, pointing to the little group of disciples, exclaimed, "Behold My mother and My brethren! For whosoever shall do the will of My Father which is in heaven, he is My brother, and sister, and mother."

This word was not a slight cast on the natural love of Mary for Him. He was not speaking slightingly of the mother love that had come after Him to stop Him injuring Himself. It was rather a revelation of the fact that there is a closer affinity than that of natural relationship. His word was a declaration that those next of kin to Him are such as share His spiritual conceptions and compulsions. He was revealing to His mother, to His disciples, and to the crowds, the fact that men and women who have fellowship with Him in spiritual vision and spiritual toil are nearer kin to Him than even the woman who had been highly honored as the one who bore Him and gave Him that natural life, through the mystery of which He wrought out into human history God's redeeming purpose.

Let us, then, consider two matters: first, our Lord's teaching in these words concerning the essential nature of that kinship with Him which all those of us who are truly His disciples share; and, second, the particular privileges of kinship which He here described.

First, then, as to the teaching of this declaration concerning the essential nature of our kinship with Jesus. May I ask you to observe negatively that our kinship with Jesus is not that of our humanity; neither is it that of His divinity. I think, perhaps, these things need to be carefully considered and most earnestly stated, for our investigation during recent years, our search, our inquiry, our pressing nearer to the fact of Christ, have resulted in real values, but also they have created grave perils. We have come to a new apprehension of the actuality of the humanity of our Lord. If there are any great artists in the world to-day they will not paint Christ as the great artists of the middle ages painted Him. We have escaped from those conceptions of our Lord which put Him at a distance from the ordinary things of everyday life. The music of the declaration that He was a carpenter is understood as it never has been understood. Whereas I believe there is great value in this rediscovery of the human Christ, I feel that there is peril in the use we may make of the discovery. I hear people perpetually speaking of the Lord Jesus as though He were entirely, absolutely of their own humanity; or speaking of their own humanity as though it were entirely part and parcel of the humanity of Jesus. That is not the case. No man can come to anything like a careful study of the human Jesus without discovering the infinite distance between Him and ourselves. In all the things that demonstrate His nearness we find the supreme evidence of His distance. If you tell me that He was a Man tempted, and therefore of our humanity, I agree. But His attitude under temptation, and his victory over temptation, demonstrate the fact that in His human life He was infinitely removed from any other man. If you suggest that He was a man Who lived on the principle of trust and faith, I perfectly agree; but in that very activity of trust I find Him at infinite distance from myself. His trust never faltered, never wavered; mine has been faltering and wavering all my life. It is when you press on me the fact of His humanity, and I come most perfectly to an apprehension of the truth that He was human, that I am most startled, ashamed, driven back, defeated by the vision of His perfection.

The teaching of the New Testament is that He was not merely of our humanity, but that He was the second Man, the last Adam, the Founder of an entirely new race. As the first race was created in the economy of God by the inbreathing of the Spirit of God to dust, the new race is to be created of that very humanity by a new birth of the Spirit of God. I go back to the Genesis story, and there I see a living creature of the dust, enswathed in Deity, and by that enswathing, inbreathing, created man, differentiated by infinite gulfs from all the creation that lies beneath him. In process of time, out of that human nature, fallen and degraded, in an awe-inspiring mystery the Holy Spirit took of the seed of the woman and made a new Man, the first of a new race, all the members of the succeeding race, to be of fallen humanity but remade, reborn, recreated by the activity of the Holy Spirit. The first Man of the new race was, in an infinite mystery, of the old race, but separated from it by the mystery of His birth. I am not kin of Jesus by virtue of my humanity. That humanity is of the race fallen, and Jesus is the Head of a new race.

Neither is our kinship that of His Divine nature, I am not one with Him in essential spiritual life, for my spiritual life is created, His spirit life is uncreated, His spirit life is of the very life of God, absolutely without beginning. He was in Himself, in a mystery that has for two millenniums defied the analysis and explanation of the schoolmen and theologians, and which will defy them to the end of time, the very *logos* of God, with God, of God, very God from everlasting. To speak of that in man which may be of the Divine nature, that in which He is in the image and the likeness of God, as being kin with the essential mystery of the Deity of Christ, is to show there is no true comprehension of the Christ of the New Testament.

Thus the statement of Christ becomes illuminative and remarkable, for He reveals what kinship with Himself really is, in its deepest and profoundest. Not here does He tell the mystery of its genesis; here, rather, does He reveal the marvel of its expression. What is the expression of our kinship, what is the actuality of it, the nature of it? "Whosoever shall do the will of My Father which is in heaven, he is My brother, and sister, and mother." He is next of kin to Me, that soul who does My Father's will!

Kinship with Christ consists in doing the will of God, doing the will of God, interpreted in the light of His immediate actions, those very actions which His mother had come to hinder, and doing the will of God as interpreted in the light of His perpetual attitudes. If one should inquire what it is to do the will of God, there is but one answer: Behold that Man, and know what it is to do the will of God. Mark well the impulse of His activities; mark well the doing of all the days; observe carefully that the greater part of His life was spent, not in public service, but in private duty. Remember that first there was the naturalness of the child life and its development. Remember that, second, there was the daily round, the common task for eighteen years in the carpenter's shop. Remember that, finally, when the Voice called there was the abandoning of the carpenter's shop without any of that hesitation or modesty which is of the essence of rebellion. He went forward immediately to face the crowds, declaring the will of God, revealing the heart of God in tenderness and compassion. Know what the will of God is by observing Him pouring Himself out in sacrificial service, violating false sanctities in order to establish the true sanctity, breaking the Sabbath to heal a man in order that the man may forevermore find unbroken sabbath of rest in God. Now, said Jesus, whosoever is doing that is next of kin to me, My brother, My sister, My mother. That is the final word.

What lies behind doing the will of God? Knowing the will of God. The man who does the will of God is the man who knows the will of God. The will of God is discovered and must be discovered in a life of personal, direct, immediate communion with God. The will of God must be discovered by persistent and perpetual inquiry as to what the will of God is. All these things are illustrated in the life of our Lord. We hear Him saying such things as these: I speak nothing of Myself; what My Father gives Me that I speak. I do nothing of Myself; what My Father commands Me, that I do. I am not alone, My Father is with Me. He did the will of God because He knew the will of God. He knew the will of God because He lived in communion with God, waited for God, submitted to God, inquired of God. He said, The men who do that are My next of kin.

What, then, is the fundamental thing? What lies at the back of this doing, deeper even than this knowing? Now, we touch not the activities of Life, not even the intelligence of life, we are at the central citadel of human life, the will of man. Once again let the light of the Lord's perfect revelation flash on our thought. We go back, as we so constantly have to do, to the prophetic Scriptures, in order to hear the very keynote of His life:

> In the roll of the book it is written of me:
> I delight to do Thy will, O my God.

The will of God chosen, the will of God inquired after in communion, and consequently known, the will of God done in the actual activity of life—that is the story of Jesus, the whole story, including the stoop from the height to the depth, including the whole mystery of incarnation and the process of the incarnate life and the ultimate darkness of the Cross. Everything is there. The will of God chosen, the will of God known as the result of communion, fellowship, inquiry—the will of God carried out.

Said the Lord: The men who live on that principle, choosing the will of God, inquiring after it in perpetual communion, carrying it out in all the details, in the crises and the commonplaces—these men are next of kin to Me. "Whosoever shall do the will of My Father which is in heaven, he is My brother, and sister, and mother."

Now we turn to what seems to me to be the peculiar and remarkable emphasis and value of this declaration concerning the privileges which He suggested. Let us hear the words again, "Whosoever shall do the will of My Father which is in heaven, he is My brother, and sister, and mother." That declaration emphasizes what we are to Him rather than what He is to us. Again, remember the local circumstances:

His mother and His brethren after the flesh were outside; she was there out of great love for Him, but she stood outside the circle of His own vision, His own passion, His own mission. She did not understand Him; but these men did, and the grace of the declaration is most marvelous when I remember the men, when I remember how they blundered and faltered and failed. Nevertheless, He did say this thing concerning them, and He did say afterwards that they had been with Him through all His temptations. He knew these men, and knew that the choice they had made of discipleship was far finer than the blunders they had made on the way. That is God's attitude towards man. God judges us at last, not by the accidents, but by the motive, the passion that lies underneath. They were twelve valiant saints. I take them at the Lord's measurement rather than at that of any man. They failed and blundered; but He knew them in the deepest of them, and He said, I know all the imperfections, and failings of these men who are with Me, but I know that the central passion, the master passion of their lives is to do the will of God. They supply what I lack in the sympathy of My own mother. She has not yet reached this inner circle; they have, and they are to me all that is suggested by these wonderful words of human relationship, brother, sister, mother.

In that is the exceeding wonder and glory of my text. It does not declare that if I do the will of God Jesus will be Brother to me. That is true, perchance. The text does not declare that if I do the will of God He will be Sister to me in all the sweet suggestiveness of the word. That may be true. That is not what He said. The text does not declare that He will mother me with infinite tenderness. That is true, but that is not what He said.

There He stood, lonely, criticized, misunderstood, and He declared that those blundering, frail souls who nevertheless had chosen the will of God, and who were seeking to know it, and to do it, were by that attitude coming into such affinity with Him that they were to Him brother, sister, mother.

That is the highest, holiest privilege of doing the will of God. Oh, the privileges of doing the will of God! What are they? The perfecting of my own personality presently? The realization of all that is profoundest in my own being by and by? These are privileges; but this is highest—oh that I may say it reverently and yet say it as our Lord said it on this occasion, when He was being misunderstood by everyone—the highest privilege of doing the will of God is that I can minister to the heart of Christ, that I can be His brother, His sister, His mother.

Everyone sees that the words are suggestive, beautifully, exquisitely poetical, chosen by the Master of words and thoughts in order to convey to human hearts that are touched by these human affections great spiritual truths of the possibilities of the influence exerted upon Himself, by the men who do the will of God.

Did you struggle all last week my brother, my sister, to do the will of God in difficult circumstances, in places of temptation, with sorrow wringing your heart and problems pressing on your spirit? Did you steer straight for the goal so far as you were able? Was the passion of your Heart to do His will? Then you were brother, sister, mother, to Jesus.

What do these words suggest? Now, you must use your own faculty of imagination and interpretation. Imagination and interpretation never succeed save as they are love-inspired. You must begin with human love. What is a brother? "A brother is born for adversity." Yes, that is it! Those two boys live together; they are often terribly rude to each other; yes, they are brothers, but wait till one of them has been hit by sorrow, by sin, then you will discover that the other is his brother. "A brother is born for adversity." I love the Hebrew word there: A brother is born for a tight place! "Whosoever shall do the will of My Father which is in heaven, he is My brother." God help us to see this thing. The words of Jesus can touch to heavenly music only chords that are already in our hearts. Is Jesus ever in a difficulty? Yes, in London He is in difficulty, in a tight place. Men are still buffeting Him, bruising Him, crucifying Him. Will you be His brother, standing up for Him, helping to bear His burden? I would like to be. We may be if we will do the will of God.

Not His brother only; His sister. Sometimes I think I could speak better of this. I never had a brother, but I had a sister. When I was getting this sermon ready I was greatly impressed to notice that there is no tender reference to a sister in the Old Testament, except, perhaps, the references to Rebekah and to Miriam. When I come into the New Testament, every reference to a sister is thrilling with tenderness. You are quite welcome to charge me with imagination—I believe in imagination—but I wondered why this was. Among other things, I noticed a story which said, "A certain woman named Martha received Him into her house. And she had *a sister* called Mary." That is how Mary was known, as Martha's sister. John, in writing of them, put it the other way, "Mary and her sister Martha"; yet even he, in the course of a few sentences, was saying "Martha and her sister." Mary was a sister. When Jesus said, "My sister," I wonder whether He was not thinking about Mary. If the courage that stands by you when you are in a tight place is the peculiar quality of a brother, what is the peculiar quality of a sister? That you confide in her because she understands. There have been hours in the lives of many men when they had some confidence, tragic confidence; they could not tell father or mother, but they told their sisters. When, presently, the priests seemed to be winning, and Judas was plotting, Mary made her way to Jesus and violated all the economies by pouring costly nard on His feet. What did it mean? She knew His secret. She was doing it to His burying. I would like to be able to hear His secret. I would like to have some little part in the reception of His confidence in the hour when He needs someone to tell His secret to. Is it possible? Yes, "whosoever shall do the will of My Father which is in heaven, the same is My sister."

We come to the last word, and it is the greatest word of all, "mother." What does "mother" stand for? There is but one answer. If brother is a synonym for courage, and sister for confidence, mother is the synonym for comfort. "As one whom his mother comforteth, so will I comfort you." Comfort: the heart of Christ comforted! Yes, said Paul, "To you it hath been granted in the behalf of Christ, not only to believe on Him, but also to suffer in His behalf." We can comfort the heart of the Lord.

How shall I comfort Him, the sorrowful One, for He is still sorrowful in the presence of the world's sin and agony and sorrow—how can I comfort Him? By doing the will of God. Every life conformed to the Divine will, conditioned within it, devoted to it, busy about the Divine will, ministers comfort to His sacred heart.

"Whosoever shall do the will of My Father which is in heaven, he is My brother, and sister, and mother."

Notice that the figures end there. He did not say the same is My father. Other than of God, He never spoke of any in that relation to Him. When at twelve years of age His mother came to Jerusalem looking for Him, having missed Him from the company, she said, "Thy father and I sought thee sorrowing." He answered her, "How is it that ye sought Me? wist ye not that I must be in My Father's house?" That inquiry was a revelation of His recognition of the fact that God alone was His Father. The figures made use of in my text were all on the human level. We can never be to Him in the place of His Father. When we apply these relations as implying what He is to us, He is brother, sister, mother, and all because He is able to look into our eyes and souls and say, "He that hath seen Me hath seen the Father."

Those who do the will of God enter into the sacred possibilities of ministering to Him. Does not that make it supremely worth while to do that will? How have I sought to appeal to some of you to do the will of God for the saving of your own souls, for the sake of the influences you can exert upon other men for their healing and help. I reach a higher level of appeal now: I pray you choose the will of God as the principle of your life, find your way into fellowship therewith, and seek to do it, not merely for the sake of your own soul, not alone in order that you may help others, but that you may minister to the need of the heart of Christ. I feel that is the highest motive. Oh, if in a life of service, by suffering and by sacrifice I might place another gem in the Redeemer's diadem, weave another garland wherewith to deck His brow; if by devotion to the will of God, and service expressive of that devotion, I can stand up for Him in a tight place, can receive the confidence of His sorrow, and break upon His feet some alabaster box of ointment; if I can only comfort the sorrowing Heart of Christ, then, so help me God, as I know it and am able, I desire to do the will of God.

The final word of the message is this. He made the assertion of my text not only with regard to those disciples who were there, but as a proclamation, and He introduced it with the greatest of all the words of the New Testament, in some senses, "*Whosoever* shall do the will of My Father."

If my name had been written there, I would have thought some other man had borne my name and that it did not mean me; but "whosoever" includes me, includes you. That is my appeal to-night. For Christ's sake, because He needs brothers, and sisters, and mothers, for courage, for confidence, for comfort, seek, and do the will of God.

CHAPTER III

HIGH PURPOSE, FAILING AND FULFILLED

And Peter answered Him and said, Lord, if it be Thou, bid me come unto Thee upon the waters. And He said, Come. And Peter went down from the boat, and walked upon the waters, to come to Jesus. But when he saw the wind, he was afraid; and beginning to sink, he cried out, saying, Lord, save me. And immediately Jesus stretched forth His hand, and took hold of him, and saith unto him, O thou of little faith, wherefore didst thou doubt? And when they were gone up into the boat the wind ceased. And they that were in the boat worshipped Him, saying, Of a truth Thou art the Son of God.

MATTHEW 14:28-33.

THIS IS THE STORY OF ONE OF THE MOST WONDERFUL PRE-Pentecostal experiences of Peter. While it reveals an element of failure, that is not its only quality, neither is it its chief one. That element of failure, however, has so impressed us that we are in danger of failing to observe that it was failure on a singularly high level, failure in an hour of exalted and Christ-honoring experience. While we must not ignore the failure, we ought to consider it in the light of the whole story, for it is a story full of bright and tender light.

In the paragraph there are two sequences, separated by a very definite break. Matthew made use of a well-known Hebrew literary form in writing this story. It is called polysyndeton, and consists of the linking of event to event by the repetition of the word "and" in order to indicate a sequence. You will bear with me if I draw your attention to it by a somewhat grotesque emphasis in reading. The first sequence is found in verses twenty-eight and twenty-nine:

"*And* Peter answered Him and said, Lord, if it be Thou, bid me come unto Thee upon the waters. *And* He said, Come. *And* Peter went down from the boat, *and* walked upon the waters, to come to Jesus."

The sequence is quite as evident, and even more marked in the second part of the story, beginning in the middle of verse thirty:

"*And* beginning to sink, he cried out, saying, Lord save me. *And* immediately Jesus stretched forth His hand, *and* took hold of him, *and* saith unto him, O thou of little faith, wherefore didst thou doubt? *And* when they were gone up into the boat, the wind ceased. *And* they that were in the boat worshipped Him, saying, Of a truth Thou art the Son of God."

Between these two parts of the one story, constituting two sequences, there is a sudden break introduced by the opposite word "but": "But when he saw the wind, he was afraid." Immediately we are brought into a new set of circumstances. Then as suddenly we come to the next "*and*," which is not so much the beginning of a new sequence as the resumption of the first, and the process to the climax which was at first intended. By that process we discover our divisions for this evening's meditation.

Let us consider, first, what this story reveals of an exalted experience, that of Peter, chronicled in the first sequence; second, what the story reveals of sudden defeat recorded in the break that interrupts for a moment the movement of the sequence; and, finally, what the story reveals of fulfilled purpose in the second sequence. Briefly: an exalted experience, a sudden defeat, a fulfilled purpose.

I particularly desire to lay emphasis on the first part of this story, that of the exalted experience of Peter. Over and over again it has been affirmed that his desire was one of presumption. The answer to that charge is that when he expressed his desire his Master said, Come, and He never encouraged mere presumption. We must look carefully at the story and attempt to understand it a little more particularly if we would gather its full value.

In that first sequence we have the record of a great venture, of the Divine warrant for that venture, and of the great adventure which resulted therefrom.

The great venture is recorded for us in these first words: "And Peter answered Him and said, Lord, if it be Thou, bid me come unto Thee upon the waters." We are immediately arrested by the fact that our story begins with this word "and," and therefore cannot be considered complete in itself. We must go back, then, in order to seek the inspiration of the request of Peter. Here we need not tarry, for the whole story is very familiar. The disciples had been sent by the Lord across the sea. In obedience to His command, they had set the prow of the vessel toward the opposite shore; and when the wind was contrary, instead of doing that which would have been comparatively easy, tacking, and so finding the wind helpful instead of a hindrance, because loyal to the Lord, they kept the prow of the vessel toward the shore which He had indicated; therefore the wind was contrary, and the waves threatened to engulf the boat. Suddenly there was added to the terrors of the storm the nameless terror of the approaching phantom, and quite as suddenly the phantom, with all its terror, had merged into the Presence and the infinite music of the Master's voice, "It is I; be of good courage."

It was then that Peter said, "Lord, if it be Thou, bid me come unto Thee upon the waters." If we are at all to appreciate the value of this story, we must attempt to discover the mood of the soul of Peter when he made that request. Imaginatively I am with him in the boat. With him I have been conscious of the rising of the waves, the beating of the wind, and the threatening perils. With him I have lost the fear of the storm itself, the fury of the elements, in the new, fresh fear of the approaching phantom. Suddenly with him I have known all fear banished by the consciousness of the Master's presence and the sound of His voice.

By coming thus into sympathy with Peter in those previous experiences we discover that when he said, "Lord, if it be Thou, bid me come unto Thee upon the waters," he was expressing a desire for fellowship with his Lord in an activity beyond that which is possible to human weakness. It was a high hour of spiritual experience. The mood of his soul was an exalted one. He asked that he might be permitted to make a great venture in fellowship with his Lord in those powers that made Him superior to the forces and perils which had threatened to engulf their frail bark. Observe, moreover, that the method of the venture was that of absolute obedience. The very request was obedience on the part of Peter to the command of the Master, "Be of good courage." Let me be courageous indeed; let me prove my courage; let me enter into all the possibilities of courage by walking on these waters; let me climb the higher heights and prove superior to the forces which filled my soul with terror not an hour ago. It was a high and exalted hour of spiritual desire and vision, and he waited for orders: "If it be Thou, bid me come." It was not a venture inspired by pride or presumption; it was a venture under the authority of Christ, waiting for His command. I wonder whether we really can follow Peter in his experience at this moment. It was such an hour as comes not often to a human soul; it was such an hour as, ever and anon, comes assuredly to every follower of the Lord, an hour when a new vision of the Lord's power produces in the soul a great aspiration after closer fellowship with Him in the exercise of that power, an hour when the Lord, having broken upon the spiritual consciousness in new glory, the heart desires to share His mastery over the forces that threaten to engulf the life. It was a high and holy aspiration, a passionate desire to do exactly what he saw his Lord was doing.

I think that even that attempted analysis of the mood of the man's soul and understanding of his request would not help us, and would hardly carry conviction, unless we had that word which follows, the word of Jesus, that answer that came across the storm-tossed waters, and was heard by the man who made the request, the single, quiet word, "*Come*." That was admission of the possibility of the impossible. It was a call to Peter to prove in actual experience both his Lord's own challenge, "It is I; be of good courage," and Peter's answering challenge, "Lord, if it be Thou, bid me come unto Thee." "Come," said the Lord; the impossible is possible in that mood of the soul, in that attitude of the heart, in that consent of the will.

Yet we have the whole story before us, and we know there was more than that in our Lord's word. He knew perfectly well that within a few minutes that man would be floundering in the waves, and yet He said, "Come." By that "Come" He called Peter to the discovery of weakness in himself of which he was unaware, and that in order to make a new discovery of the power of his Lord in the victory and realization of the very desire that first prompted his request. "Come," said Jesus, the impossible is possible in that mood of the soul. "Come," said Jesus, and prove the challenge of My word, "It is I," and answer the inquiry of thy word, "If it be Thou." "Come," said Jesus, and discover the weakness that lurks within your own heart in order that I may bring you to a new realization of My power, and that through proof of weakness you may find mastery, that in fellowship with Me you may fulfil the high aspiration of the soul which asks to do the impossible.

That call of the Master was immediately followed by the

great adventure. Here I ask you to notice with what particular care the evangelist records the fact: "Peter went down from the boat, and walked upon the waters, to come to Jesus." He did the impossible thing. It is not the story of a man who, foolhardy and impulsive, ventures over the side of a boat who, immediately sinks. It is the story of a man who, suddenly lifted to a wonderful height, saw the possibility of the impossible in fellowship with Christ; asked for permission, waited for orders, and, having received them, obeyed and actually walked on the waters just as his Lord had been walking on the waters. His Lord said "Come," and without hesitation Peter yielded his will to the will of his Lord. With what result? He placed the frail, feeble foot of his humanity on the wave, and he did not sink; he was upheld; he did the impossible thing under the authority of his Master; his will was yielded to his Lord, his body was yielded to his yielded will, and between the frail man and the Lord Christ a union was established so that as he touched the waves Peter did not sink beneath them. He "walked upon the waters, to come to Jesus."

That was a great moment. Whatever follows cannot undo that experience. Within a very few minutes the waves were threatening to engulf Peter! Yes, but he had walked on them! However much I fail and falter to-day, and the waters buffet me, I have walked on them. Whatever follows cannot undo the experience. Nay, rather, the experience will have its effect on anything that follows. As presently we see this man when the waves are engulfing him, and hear his cry for help as he sinks, we know that the cry is the result of the demonstration of his Master's power which he received when he accomplished the impossible.

Now we turn to the second stage of the story, the account of a sudden defeat. Because this part of the story is the best known, we need not tarry with it. On the other hand, because it is here in spite of the exalted experience, we must not omit it. There are three things I shall ask you to note.

First, the reason of the defeat, "He saw the wind"; that was the assault of sense. The sensual and the spiritual are close together; but they are forever antagonistic. One must always reign, and whichever reigns masters the other. If the sensual reigns, the spiritual is dwarfed and imprisoned. If the spiritual reigns, the sensual is kept within true bounds and never allowed the mastery of the life. Suddenly, while Peter walked on the waters, his soul was assaulted through the senses, he became conscious of the fierceness of the wind, and the anger of the waves; and with his eye removed from the Master he became conscious of that assault, he felt its power. What next? Not immediately the sinking, but first the spiritual experience. "He was afraid." As the spiritual and sensual are always close together and forever antagonistic, so also are faith and fear; but they are mutually exclusive. Where faith reigns, fear has no place; where fear reigns, faith is driven forth. In the moment when Peter yielded to the assault of the senses and, taking his eyes from the Lord, looked at the waves and became conscious of the winds, fear dispossessed faith. The failure of faith came when he became conscious of self as opposed to winds and waves. Then he knew the actuality of his humanity, its weakness and its inability to walk in the difficult and impossible place.

Immediately following came the material, physical expression of that spiritual experience of the failure of faith, "beginning to sink." Paralysis of power followed when the wavering of faith failed to make connection with the Lord. He found the waves too weak to hold him, strong enough to drown him, and he began to sink.

That was a sad experience, but it was not the final one. The sadness of the failure does not for a single moment prove that the adventure of faith was unwarranted. The fact that a man to-day is failing, faltering, sinking, engulfed by waves on which he ought to be walking, does not call in question the fineness of the heroism, the splendor of the high hour of vision, when he made his adventure of faith. The sinking is not the inevitable sequence of the walking. The sinking is the outcome of failure to keep in close connection with the Lord, resulting from the assault of the senses, so that fear takes the place of faith, paralysis the place of power, and he is back again on the ordinary level of human life.

So we come to the second sequence, which tells the story of fulfilled purpose. Once again in Peter we have a great venture of faith, "Lord save me," as great a venture of faith as that in which he had said, "Lord, if it be Thou, bid me come unto Thee upon the waters"; but the mood of the soul was different. The mood of the soul when Peter asked to walk on the waters was that of high vision, holy ecstasy, a new aspiration after power. Now the mood of the soul was that of a sense of defeat. The high possibility was passing in paralysis, the sense of strength that came to him as he walked on the waters was ebbing away. Out of the depths and sense of helplessness, in the agony of conscious weakness, he made another venture of faith. It was no longer a request that he might be permitted to make some high adventure, it was no longer a request that he might be permitted to do anything; it was rather a request, helpless, direct, urgent, agonizing, to the Lord to do everything; but it was the request of faith. I believe you will discover its inspiration in the fact that Peter, in that hour of sinking, when the waves were engulfing him, saw the Lord still superior to wind and waves. With that vision of the Lord still victorious, where he was failing, faith expressed itself again, and made a new venture, "Lord, save me."

What followed? "And immediately Jesus stretched forth His hand, and took hold of him." That was the first thing, the hand of power. Closely following came the word of love, rebuking Peter, and revealing the secret of his failure. "O thou of little faith, wherefore didst thou doubt?" Little-faith is one word in the Greek; old Trappe the Puritan translated it *petty-fidiam,* small-faith. Jesus revealed the secret of failure in the question, "Wherefore didst thou doubt?" What does "doubt" mean here? I shall seem to rob it of its significance if I am literal. Why didst thou *duplicate?* That is the root significance, not the final interpretation. Why didst thou think twice? Surely not that, you say! Yes, just that. But is it not wise to think twice? It depends on what the first thought was. Dwight Lyman Moody once told me that the only mistakes he ever made in his life were when he took time to think twice.

Little-faith—it was a beautiful, gentle word, but a rebuking word. Little faith: do not accuse me of irreverence when I say it was a nickname, such a name as love will invent when it desires to rebuke. Peter was Little-faith because he thought twice. "One thing I do" is better. If that had been true of Peter he would never have sunk. It was the thinking back on the decision of a high resolve, it was pausing to question the resolution formed in a high mood of soul, that caused his failure.

Jesus did not say that to Peter until He had saved him. He did not bend over Peter in the waters and say to him: You see what you have done for yourself; if you will confess it I will help you out. No, first the hand was outstretched, and the mighty power of Jesus lifted him; then when Jesus had placed him back on the waves He looked at Peter, and with a smile of tenderness and that sweet tone of which no other friend is capable, said, Little-faith, why did you think twice?

And now Peter walked on the water again. He did the very thing he wanted to do at first. First, he did it; second, he failed to do it; but, third, he did it, he walked back with his Lord on the water to the boat.

I like to look at these two sequences and see how they balance each other; there were three movements in the first, and there were three in the second, and they stand over against each other.

"Lord, if it be Thou, bid me come unto Thee upon the waters." That is the first movement in the first sequence. "Lord, save me." That is the first movement in the second sequence. The second movement in the first sequence is this: Jesus said, "Come." The second movement in the second sequence is this: "Jesus stretched forth His hand, and took hold of him, and saith unto him, O thou of little faith, wherefore didst thou doubt?" The third movement in the first sequence is this: "Peter went down from the boat, and walked upon the waters, to come to Jesus." The third in the second sequence is this: They walked on the waters and went back into the boat. It was a high hour for Peter when he suddenly thought that if indeed it were Jesus it would be possible to do the impossible thing; it was a high and glorious hour of light and vision and power in which he rose superior to the forces that master and trammel and limit. Then came the defeat, the wind and the waves, and paralysis, and sinking. But that is not the last thing. The last thing is, he walked back with his Lord over the waters.

Where did Jesus take him? Back to the boat, to the commonplace, to the everyday. High hours are given to us, and they all have their value, and if we will but answer their lure, their call in the strength of our Lord we shall have marvelous experiences of power to do impossible things; but He will take us back to the boat, we must cross the sea in the ordinary way.

Yes, but there is still something more. Jesus went with Peter into the boat. He is not only the Lord Who Himself is able, and Who enables others, to do impossible things—He is the Lord Who can walk the sea from shore to shore, yet He will stay in the boat with His people as they take the commonplace way. Matthew tells us that so they crossed over to the other side. I turn to the story in John. He does not tell us about Peter's heroic attempt and failure; he tells about the storm, and he tells us that when Jesus came on board, immediately they were at the land whither they went. Was that a miracle? Oh, no, that was the canceling of distance in the comradeship of love. Matthew says, We crossed over; we had all the distance to do, and we did it and worshiped as we did it, for He was with us. John says, We were there at once, because the Lord was with us in the commonplace boat.

Hours of exalted aspiration are to be prized, and they are to be acted upon. They will surely come to us. To every child of God, to every man and woman of faith there are sure to come hours when suddenly some new possibility of power is seen. Such hours are to be prized, and they are to be acted upon; and they are to be acted upon as Peter acted, in obedience to the Lord, waiting His word, seeking to know His will. The impossible is possible to faith, and there is no need to sink. Here, as I have often had to say, I am speaking of things that are in advance of my own actual experience; but I know the truth of them. Peter need not have sunk, and I need never sink in such circumstances. The life triumphant over storms and waves and billows is possible.

But we do sink. We also know the assault of sense, the hour in which we see the waves and the wind in its effect on the waves. Some of us are seeing that to-night, children of God, believers on the Lord Jesus Christ, men and women who have known high hours of vision, glorious hours of victory, but who came up to the service in the house of God this evening discouraged, frightened about to-morrow. They are conscious of the assault of the senses. They are looking at the waves, listening to the howling of the wind; they are calculating the number of the demons from the standpoint of their own personal life and power. Faith is giving way to fear, power is being paralyzed. What shall they do? Let them do exactly what Peter did; cry out, "Lord, save me." But yesterday we said, Lord help us to do this thing, let us do this in Thy strength, energize us for high activity, nerve us for victory. But we cannot say that now; buffeted, bruised, and broken, the billows are overwhelming us. What then shall we say? It is no use asking Him to help us do anything; *we* are falling, sinking. Then what shall we do? Let each cry, "Lord, save me," do everything, undertake for me.

I am after the man who is buffeted by the waves, I do not know who he is; and let those of you who cannot follow me be patient, I am talking to some buffeted soul. Let any man or woman thus buffeted, cry out, Lord save me. That is the cry of faith, and as surely as it is made, that hand will be outstretched to grip and hold you; and He will look at you presently, when He has saved you, and He is quite sure He has gripped you, and He will say, O Little-faith, why did you doubt? He never rebukes the soul in whom the principle of faith is found, however much it waver, until He has restored that soul to the place of power. You will find that all through the Bible. You will find it in the parable which we call the parable of the Prodigal Son. Have you ever thought how unwise a thing it was, from the standpoint of worldly wisdom, for that father to go and meet the boy? Imagine him running to meet the boy, running to meet him in his dirt, embracing him in his rags. Is not that all wrong? Is not the proper thing first to induce the young man to recognize what he has done, and to hold him aloof until he confesses his sin? That is what you and I would do—unless the boy were our own; but that is not what God does. He takes the sinner in his rags and sin and filth, and wraps round him His arms of love; then the boy can confess. Hold him aloof and demand from him a confession of his guilt, and you harden him—or you would if I were the boy. Let me lay my proud head on the bosom of God, and my heart is broken, and I will sob out all the story of my sin. "Immediately Jesus stretched forth His hand, and took hold of him," and then He rebuked Peter; but never until He was walking on the waters with Peter. That is our Lord. That is our Master.

The final word is that at last in comradeship with the

Master our highest aspirations are fulfilled. Do not miss that from the story. Do not look on that early sequence as a high dream of faith that was utterly defeated. Do not think of Peter in that moment as being on some altitude which he never reached again. He reached it again. He reached it by the way of defeat. The Lord brought him to His side, and walked back with him over the waters to the boat. That is what Jesus did to the very end. That is what He meant when He said to Peter, The cock shall not crow, till thou hast denied Me thrice. Let not your heart be troubled: ye believe in God, believe also in Me. You have asked Me where I am going. I am going to prepare a place for you, and in spite of your denial of Me I will come again and take you to the place I am getting ready for you.

Fainting, failing, faltering hearts, take courage! That high moment of soul when you saw the possibility of doing the impossible is yet to be realized, and even though you say I started on the way and was victorious for a week, a month, a year, but I am down again, and the waves are beating me and the wind is mastering me, the Master Himself is at hand. Cry out to Him, and His hand will be on you in power, and the sweet rebuke of His love will be in your ears; then He will walk with you on the waters for a little way, and then He will take you back to the boat—from Sunday to Monday, from the hill to the valley, from ecstasy to everyday experience; but He will be there with you, and the memory of the hour of vision and of triumph will be to you a perpetual inspiration. So may we take heart and be filled with new faith, and in comradeship with our Lord go forward through the storms until He brings us to the desired haven.

CHAPTER IV

THE VALUE OF VISION

Where there is no vision, the people cast off restraint.
PROVERBS 29:18.

THIS IS AMONG THE "PROVERBS OF SOLOMON WHICH THE men of Hezekiah king of Judah copied out." It is the crystallization into a brief sentence of a national principle of the first importance. It must be interpreted in the atmosphere in which it was written, and its terms must be explained therefore by what they signified to those who made use of them.

The central word is most evidently the word "vision." The word means, quite simply and literally, sight, and refers both to the thing seen and to the power to see it. "Where there is no vision," the thing seen; "Where there is no vision," the power to see, "the people cast off restraint."

But the word had a particular value in the Hebrew economy, referring perpetually to a definite and specific revelation of God to the people. In the days of Samuel's childhood "there was no frequent vision." The word of God was precious in the sense of being rare, and the declaration that the word of God was rare is immediately explained by the affirmation that there was no frequent vision, and it is thus evident that the word was used of some definite revelation of God made to His people. Let us bear in mind that value.

The Hebrew word which is translated "cast off restraint"

in the Revised Version, and "perish" in the Authorized Version, means very literally to loosen, to dissolve, to separate, to break up, or as I like to say, using a very simple colloquialism, to go to pieces. "Where there is no vision the people *go to pieces.*" The Revised Version has simply given us a symptom of the disease, not the malady itself. One of the symptoms of the disease assuredly is anarchy, "The people cast off restraint." That which causes anarchy is that the people themselves are dissolved, loosened, broken up, have gone to pieces.

If we take these words in the atmosphere of the times in which they were written, with all reverence we may change our text into words far less beautiful, and used only for the sake of interpretation: Where there is no direct revelation of God to men, the people go to pieces, break up, perish. Where the people lack clear vision of God, that is, are ignorant of His revelation, unacquainted with His will as it is declared, they lack the principle of cohesion and continuity, they are dissolved, they go to pieces.

That conception is central to the history of the Hebrew people as given in the Scriptures. The text itself is among the words of Solomon, a man in whose reign the vision faded. There was no more disastrous failure in the history of Israel than that of Solomon, a man who was punctilious in his observance of externals and neglected the essential, the spiritual verities; who attempted to solace a great people by ostentation and material magnificence, and undermined the kingdom. The vision faded, and the moment the spell created by the presence of the magnificent King Solomon was broken, the people went to pieces: Jeroboam and Rehoboam, the divided kingdom, with all the appalling sequence of the terrible years. That is the man who wrote these words, "Where there is no vision, the people *go to pieces.*"

To go back in history, the graphic description of the condition out of which the mistake of clamoring for a king arose is found in these words: "There was no frequent vision." Men did not hear the word of God, it was rare; there was no continuous traffic with heaven, there was no commerce with the spiritual, no listening for God and to Him. With what result? The people went to pieces; they lost their high ideal of the theocracy and clamored for a king. That was the beginning of the ruin of the kingdom itself.

The same thing is graphically described as the condition preceding the reformation under Asa. Israel had not known the true God, there was no "teaching priest," an arresting phase in itself.

Then we have those wonderful words of the prophet who was neither a prophet nor the son of the prophet, by which he meant to say he was not ordained, not recognized by the schools of the prophets, the herdman of Tekoa who broke upon the people in thunder with a great message. He described the condition as that of "famine for the Word of God." With what result? The young men and maidens thirsted and were weary; they went to pieces, because there was no vision, no dealing with God.

My purpose this evening is to take that principle and see what it means in the case of the great continent of South America, which we are trying during the course of the winter months to understand in order that we may know our responsibility. In previous sermons I have spoken of the geography and the peoples of South America. Its geographical situation and conditions are attracting the attention of the whole world. Its peoples are presenting grave problems to missionary enterprise because of their past history. Moreover, I have declared in passing that the supreme need of the people of South America is twofold: moral dynamic, and spiritual vision.

The text which I have taken puts these two things into their proper relationship. Moral dynamic is always the outcome of spiritual vision. In this sense also the text is true. When there is no spiritual vision morality goes to pieces. That, unless I sadly mistake, is what Harold Begbie has tried to put before us in his last novel, *The Challenge*, a significant title. I am not going to describe the novel. I have read it, and advise you to read it. If I may summarize its teaching in a few words, this is it: *the only challenge to immorality is religion.*

That is the message of my text concerning men and concerning the nation. If these great peoples of South America are to be made strong nationally, they must be made strong individually; and if they are to be made strong individually, it must be by vision in the Old Testament sense of the word, by revelation.

In this fact we have the sanction and compulsion of Christian missions. Let us say it boldly: We have the true vision of God, we have His final revelation, for "God, having of old time spoken unto the fathers in the prophets by divers portions and in divers manners, hath at the end of these days spoken unto us in the Son," in the Son Who is "the effulgence of His glory, and the very image of His substance." Vision through the Son is our greatest possession. It is in the light of that vision that we are assembled for worship in this hour. It is in the light of that vision that we live our lives as Christian men and women. It is in the light of that vision that we are ready and prepared to carry our burdens, to endure restraint, to win victories, to enjoy the high and holy ecstasy of our fellowship. We are, therefore, humanly responsible for those who lack our vision. "Humanly," you say. What do you mean? I could understand it if you argued that it is a Divine compulsion that is laid upon us. It is a Divine compulsion, but I choose to stay on the lower level, the level of human responsibility. Is there any man in God's world more despicable than the man who tells you he has invented a cure for cancer, and then proceeds to make profit out of it and does not give it to the world? If any man has discovered that which will touch the dire disease with sure healing, he owes it to humanity to tell humanity the secret, even at loss to himself. That is the human sanction; it is Divine at last, I grant, for all high human sanctions are at last Divine; but that is a sanction which will be recognized by the man who denies our Christ. Therefore I say that we Christian men and women who have indeed seen the vision, and who have found it to be a vision that heals and helps, our bounden human duty is to see to it that that light is given, so far as we are able to give it, to all people who sit in darkness.

That conception of the sanction and compulsion of missionary endeavor is at the same time a revelation of the sphere of our operations. Where are we to take the light? Wherever people are in darkness. Yes, but South America is not a heathen country. I am told I must not so speak of it. Are the people in darkness? If they are, that is a sphere for missionary operations. That is what we have to discover. That is what the Church of God in the homeland is compelled to consider. It is to that subject I ask your attention from this moment forward.

There are two things I want to do in as few words as possible: first, to state the conditions of the people, and then to apply the principle of the text.

How shall I describe the condition of the people in South America? I am speaking for the moment, not of the Indian tribes, but of the people of Latin America. I know the difficulty of the task; yet there are certain outstanding facts from which there can be no escape.

There exists among these peoples a certain courtliness of manner under appropriate conditions, and an absolute absence of it under other conditions, a courtliness of manner which is conditioned by the etiquette of social, civic, or national functions, but which passes directly when no such claim is set up. The people are rapidly increasing in wealth, and are preeminently lovers of pleasure and display. They are—and the descriptive phrase I use is in some senses an ugly one because of its apparent flippancy—a people characterized by a jovial disregard of truth, a disregard of truth that is easy and careless. They are noted for a lack of conscience, and consequently for widespread distrust and deceit; abounding intemperance, most appalling looseness in all matters of the sexes, widespread indecency of language, and such indecency of action that if you visit the great cities you will never permit your daughters to walk in the streets alone.

In family life there is a very low standard of social purity, and consequently a low standard of homelife; homelife is lacking in sanctity, and therefore lacking in comfort, and appallingly lacking in discipline.

In the social conditions there are things that cannot be named in the assembly of the saints: the loosest of marriage customs, an appalling condition of illegitimacy, so that it has been declared that the percentage of illegitimate births is sometimes thirty, fifty, or even greater.

Politically, there is perpetual unrest; while they now have greatly improved constitutions, for all have been modeled on that of the United States of America, there is lack of administration—the machine lacks the true motive power.

Inclusively, because there is no vision, the people are dissolved; the principle of cohesion and strength in the national life is missing.

That leads us naturally, necessarily, to the lack of vision. Two mistakes are constantly made about South America in speaking of it in this respect. First of all, it is described as a Christian country, and it was because it was so described that it was shut out from consideration by the great meetings of the Edinburgh Missionary Conference. In the second place, it is affirmed that it is a Roman Catholic country. That is not wholly true, for there are still to be found vast numbers of Indians untouched by Roman Catholic influence. Alan Ewbank said, "If you start away at the north and go right down to the south of the continent, you can travel in heathen lands, among people who do not know Who God is. The whole of that Southern continent, except the fringes around the edge, should be colored heathen." About that section of the population there is no question: they lack vision. Here Romanists and Protestants agree. In paganism there is no true vision of God. It will at once be agreed that among these people there is room and demand for our evangelism.

I turn then to the countries where Romanism is without any question the dominant religion. I cannot touch on this subject without recognizing that our campaign—I think I may so describe it now—for quickening interest in that continent is stirring up a good deal of criticism in England. I am receiving a good many letters of protest. I was speaking in Liverpool recently, and after the meeting received a long letter in which the writer charged me with historic ignorance. The only comfort I obtained from the letter was in the last sentence, "You ought to know better, seeing you are a clergyman of the Church of England"! I have had sent to me only this week newspaper cuttings criticizing certain things I have said, and an extract from a book that was published in 1911, called *Peru of the Twentieth Century*, by Percy F. Martin, F.R.G.S., in which he protests against all Protestant work in the country, and affirms that he has "no religious prejudices whatever," which it is quite easy to believe. I have received with this cutting a letter written from this neighborhood by a Roman Catholic, ten pages in length, kindly, courteous, Christly in spirit, but protesting, declaring that we are ignorant of what the Church of Rome has done in South America, and charging me—and that is the special reference I make in regard to this letter—with lack of charity and with slandering the clergy of the Roman Catholic church.

In speaking in public on this subject I have been very careful to distinguish between Roman Catholicism as it is in South America and as it is in England. I believe that underneath they are one; but I quite recognize that there is a vast difference. Moreover, I have always been careful, and shall ever remain careful, to distinguish most particularly between individuals and the system. I am perfectly sure that in the Roman communion there are saints of God; I have known them personally; I have numbered them among my closest friends; and far be it from me to say anything to wound them in the matter of their personal relationship to Jesus Christ.

But it is impossible to be blind to the influence which Rome has exerted in Latin America. I want to say with regard to that one charge, and I want you to hear me very carefully, when we are charged with slandering the Roman clergy in these countries, our appeal will be from Protestantism to Rome itself. I have another letter here, and in it are a few words that have come from Brazil, written by a Roman Catholic lady there, after hearing what was said at our Mundesley Bible Conference about our new work. She writes: "We shall welcome the English church out here, and I hope *many earnest* workers will come out, for my Church has not sent of its best, nor enough, and *its worst side is largely seen in every town.*" But I appeal even from that letter written by a devout Roman Catholic in Brazil itself. I appeal to Pope Leo XIII, and I shall ask you to remember that nothing I have said, nothing any of us has said, as we are attempting to draw the attention of Christian people to this country, is stronger than this. In his encyclical on the point these words occur:

> In every diocese ecclesiastics break all bounds and deliver themselves up to manifold forms of sensuality, and no voice is lifted up imperiously to summon pastors to their duties. The clerical press casts aside all sense of decency and loyalty in its attacks on those who differ, and lacks controlling authority to bring it to its proper use. There is assassination and calumny, the civil laws are defied, bread is denied the enemies of the Church, and there is no one to interpose. . . .
>
> It is sad to reflect that prelates, priests, and other clergy are never found doing service among the poor; they are never in the hospital or lazar house, never in the orphan

asylum or hospice, in the dwellings of the afflicted or distressed, or engaged in works of beneficence, aiding primary instruction, or found in refuges or prisons. . . . As a rule, they are ever absent where human misery exists, unless paid as chaplains or a fee is given. On the other hand, you (the clergy) are always to be found in the houses of the rich, or wherever gluttony may be indulged in, wherever the choicest wines may be freely obtained.

No words we have uttered are severer in their condemnation of the Roman clergy in South America than those words written by Pope Leo XIII in order to call to book the clergy because of their failure in that country. The reasons why we should carry to these Latin people the gospel of our Lord and Master as it is found in the New Testament have been set forth by Dr. Robert Speer cogently and forcefully in a paper which appeared in *The Missionary Review of the Word* for March, 1911, entitled, "The Case for Missions in Latin America." From the reasons which he gives us justifying our work as Protestants I shall select three, and I shall give you them in his own words rather than in my own, for they state the case so clearly that they cannot be improved upon. He says:

Protestant missions are justified and demanded in South America by the character of the Roman Catholic priesthood. I fought as long as possible against accepting the opinion universally held throughout South America regarding the priests. Ever since reading as a boy *The Life of Charles Kingsley*, the celibacy of the priesthood had seemed to me a monstrous and wicked theory, but I had believed that the men who took that vow were true to it, and that while the Church lost by it irreparably, and infinitely more than she gained, she did gain, nevertheless, a pure and devoted, if narrow and impoverished, service. But the deadly evidence spread out all over South America, confronting one in every district to which he goes, evidence legally convincing, morally sickening, proves to him that, whatever may be the case in other lands, in South America the stream of the Church is polluted at its fountains. . . .

"Protestant missions in South America are justified because the Roman Catholic Church has not given the people Christianity. There are surely some who find peace and comfort, and some who see Christ through all that hides Him and misrepresents Him, but the testimony of the most temperate and open-minded of the men and women who were once themselves earnest Roman Catholics is that there are few whom they know in the Roman Catholic Church who know the facts of Christ's life, and fewer still who know Christ. The crucifixes, of which South America is full, inadequately represent the gospel. They show a dead man, not a living Saviour. We did not see in all the churches we visited a single symbol or suggestion of the resurrection or the ascension. There were hundreds of paintings of saints and of the Holy Family, and of Mary, but not one of the supreme event in Christianity. And even the dead Christ is the subordinate figure. The central place is Mary's. Often she is shown holding a small lacerated figure in her lap, and often she is the only person represented at all. In the great La Merced church in Lima, over the chancel is the motto: *Gloria a Maria*. In the oldest church in Barranquilla there is no figure of Christ at all in the altar equipment, but Mary without the infant in the center, two other figures on either side, and over all *Gloria a Maria*. In the wall of the ancient Jesuit Church in Cuzco, known as the Church of the Campania, are cut the words, 'Come unto Mary, all ye who are burdened and weary with your sins, and she will give you rest.' There are many, I am sure, who learn to love and reverence the name of Christ, but Christ as a living moral and spiritual power the South American religion does not proclaim.

. . . Protestant missions are justified in South America, because the Roman Catholic Church is at the same time so strong and so weak there. There priesthood has a powerful hold upon the superstition of the people. As we rode along one day in Brazil, with bare heads and rubber ponchos, an old woman came running solicitously from her hovel, mistaking us for priests, and crying, 'Oh, most powerful God, where is your hat?' To the people the priest stands in the place of God, and even where his own life is vile, the people distinguish between his function as priest in which he stands as God before the altar, and his life as man, in which he falls into the frailties of the flesh. Not only is the priesthood the most influential body in South America, but the Church has a hold upon politics and family life and society which is paralyzing. Its evil is not weak and harmless, but pervasive and deadly, and the Christian Church is called by the most mandatory sanctions to deal with the situation. But, on the other hand, the Roman Catholic Church does not have a fraction of the strength and power in South America which we had supposed it had, and the inefficiency of its work is pitiful. With enormous resources, with all the lines of power in its hands, it has steadily lost ground. The churches, save on festivals, are mostly ill-attended. The priests are derided and reviled. The leading newspaper in Chile, which bitterly attacked some statement which I made upon returning, about the character of the priests, a few weeks later printed a denunciation of the priests in Northern Chile far more sweeping than anything I had said. The comic papers gibe at them. This spectacle of a continent of men losing all respect for religion and leaving it to women, and to priests whose moral character they deride, is a grave and distressing spectacle. There is no sadder sight to be found in the whole world.

I maintain that if nothing more be said, that threefold indictment of the Roman Church in South America as failing to give the people Christianity, and yet as presenting something to them in the name of Christianity so as now to create in the minds of thinking men a revolt from Christianity, is a supreme and overwhelming reason why we should take to them the gospel of that vision of God which came to men in Christ. The author of *Ecce Homo*, when speaking of the Pharisees, said: "If a divine revelation be the greatest of blessings, then the imposture that counterfeits it must be the greatest of all evils." Or, in the words of the Lord: "If . . . the light that is in thee be darkness, how great is the darkness."

I solemnly indict the Church of Rome for misrepresentation of Christianity in Latin America. When I am charged with ignorance of history, my appeal is to history. When I am charged with not being familiar with the facts, my appeal is to the facts that are patent to all who look and see. No stronger appeal for evangelization is coming from any quarter of the world than from South America.

In the building of nations—if you will suffer me to use a figure the force of which will be perhaps more patent to many of you than to the preacher—the true method is that of reinforced concrete. What is concrete? In case I should manifest my ignorance, I quote from the dictionary, "a compact mass of gravel, coarse pebbles, or stone chippings cemented together by hydraulic or other mortar."* What is reinforced concrete? The phrase gripped me when I first heard it, and one day, sitting with my friend Mr. Charles Hay Walker in his study, I asked him what it was. He probably knows as much about reinforced concrete as most men, and he explained that reinforced concrete is that method of building in which metal and concrete are used. The metal prevents the concrete crumbling; the concrete prevents the metal buckling.

Nations must be built with reinforced concrete. The concrete of South America is its intellectual development, and all that means, of political emancipation and commercial advantage. But it must have the strong metal of religion. Where there is no vision of God, the concrete goes to pieces. Though you weld it with hydraulic mortar, the wash of the waves and the pressure of burdens will make it sag. Unless

* According to Webster's Dictionary, concrete is "artificial stone made by mixing cement and sand with gravel, broken stone, or other aggregate. The materials are mixed with sufficient water to cause the cement to set and bind the entire mass."

the Church of Christ that has seen the vision carries it to South America, then God alone knows the disaster that must sweep on those countries in the days to come.

There is only one appeal I can make to you as my eyes turn to that great continent, and I shall make it best in the words of one of the greatest missionary hymns ever written:

> Shall we, whose souls are lighted
> With wisdom from on high
> Shall we, to men benighted,
> The Lamp of life deny?
> Salvation! Oh, Salvation!
> The joyful sound proclaim,
> Till earth's remotest nation
> Has learned Messiah's name.

CHAPTER V

THE GREAT CONFESSION

And Simon Peter answered and said, Thou art the Christ, the Son of the living God. And Jesus answered and said unto him, Blessed art thou, Simon Bar-Jonah: for flesh and blood hath not revealed it unto thee, but my Father which is in heaven.

MATTHEW 16:16, 17.

THESE WORDS WERE SPOKEN AT A TIME OF CRISIS IN THE MINistry of our Lord and in the experience of Peter. Indeed, they constitute the pivotal words of that particular crisis. The confession of Peter completed the first stage of His work, and prepared for the second and final one. When, in the consciousness of one man, the victory of the Kingdom propaganda was won, the King set His face toward the passion whereby all men might pass into the Kingdom.

Our present theme is that of the confession of Peter, and there are four matters to which I propose to ask your attention. First, the man who made the confession, Simon Peter; second, the confession he made, "Thou art the Christ, the Son of the living God"; third, how Peter arrived at that conclusion, "Flesh and blood hath not revealed it unto thee, but My Father which is in heaven"; and, finally, what that confession meant to him subsequently.

First, then, the confessor. There is no man in these New Testament stories more fascinating than Peter. Every story about him interests us, and the more the portraiture of him is considered in its entirety, the more powerfully does it appeal.

The reason for this persistent fascination is to be found in his essential human greatness, and in his constant failure to realize that greatness. The appeal is twofold. We cannot read these stories of his life without feeling how near akin we are to him in certain essential, elemental qualities. We cannot read the story of his life without feeling how near akin we are to him in his blunders and failures.

His human greatness consisted in the fact that the elemental forces of human nature were all strikingly present in him. Other of these New Testament men were in certain senses greater than Peter: Paul in massiveness of intellect, John in mystic intelligence, James in practical ethical convictions; but in this man we find all the elemental forces. In mental power he was a great man, quick of thought, eager of inquiry, swift of conclusion. In emotional power he was equally great, a man of hot affection, burning anger, deep depression. In volitional power he was capable of making courageous ventures, heroic choices, dangerous experiments. All these elemental forces manifest themselves in him, and we are all in touch with him at some point.

We are brought into even closer kinship with him as we observe his failure. He was a man of mental power, yet characterized by strange blindness: to use a phrase of his own, "seeing only the things that are near," and unable to apprehend them in their true spiritual relationships; his was a mind quick, eager, swift, and yet never arriving at any final conclusion in his own unaided strength. He was a man of fine emotional power, yet contradicting the impulses of his love and wounding his lover. He was a man of remarkable volitional capacity, capable of courageous venture, heroic choice, dangerous experiments, and yet suddenly becoming craven in his fear and faltering by the way.

This is the man who at Cæsarea Philippi uttered the confession which brought our Lord to the culmination of the first stage of His mission. He was more than a Hebrew, he was a human. He was a type of all men in his elemental forces and experimental failures.

We now turn to the central matter, the confession which Peter made, "Thou art the Christ, the Son of the living God." There are very spacious values in these words. I believe that Simon said far more than he understood; in the thing he said there were values far beyond his comprehension, and the context proves it. I shall ask you, then, in considering this confession first to observe its structure, and from that observation to attempt to gather its value.

Evidently there are two parts to the confession. The unifying words are the first, "Thou art." After them the confession divides into two parts. First, "Thou art the Messiah"; second, "Thou art . . . the Son of the living God." The first was a confession on the part of Peter, of what he understood concerning the office of Jesus; the second was a confession on the part of Peter as to what he understood concerning the nature of Jesus.

"Thou art the Messiah." I use the Hebrew form of the word in order to interpret the thought of it. It becomes emphatic when we place it in contrast with other things that had just been said to Jesus. He had asked His disciples, "Who do men say that the Son of man is?"; and they had replied, "Some say John the Baptist; some, Elijah; and others, Jeremiah, or one of the prophets." Now we are immediately arrested by the fact that our Lord was not satisfied with these confessions, and that He proceeded to discover whether His own immediate disciples had formed the same conclusions—not to discover for Himself, but to discover to them—as He said, "Who say ye that I am?" Then came the answer, "Thou art the Messiah."

The multitudes had detected in the teaching of Jesus the

prophetic note, the supernatural note; they imagined that He was a prophet of the olden times returned. Peter confessed that He was the One to Whom all the prophets had given witness. John had only foretold His coming. Elijah had been a prophet of reform; but he was not able to establish the Kingdom. He passed, having failed, having only borne witness to righteousness and truth. Jeremiah had uttered his lamentations over the failure of his own ministry, and in the dungeon had sung the songs of hope that told of Another Who should accomplish that in which he had failed.

But the deeper note of the confession, and the more surprising one, was that in which Peter declared his conviction concerning the nature of the One Who had come to fulfil the prophetic outlook and aspiration: "the Son of the living God."

This confession reveals three conceptions in the mind of Peter: first, the Messiah; second, the Son; finally, "the living God." We shall appreciate the value of the confession a little more perfectly if we take these three conceptions in the other order, for in the confession Peter moved backwards, from that final fact of which he was then convinced, through that which lay behind it, giving it light and power and glory, to the fundamental truth of his religion. Let us begin where he ended. First, "The living God"; second, "the Son of the living God"; finally, "the Messiah." Thus the whole confession becomes far more glorious and wonderful.

Peter expressed in one brief phrase—which seems to be incidental, which passed his lips at the close of a confession—the central fact and truth of Hebraism, "the living God." That was the fundamental fact in the faith of Abraham, and in the law of Moses. The belief in one God was the very rock foundation of the national life. That this God was living was the message of all the prophets. With fine scorn, one of them had said of the idols which men worshiped, "There is no breath in them"! The God of Israel was "the living God," not a mere abstraction, not a mere force permeating the universe, having no personal consciousness, and therefore of no help to man in his personal life; but God, personal, alive, active—the living God. That was the fundamental religious conception of the Hebrew nation, and the ministry of Christ in the case of Peter had not destroyed it, but had emphasized it, set the seal of authority on it.

We now come to the central matter in the words, "the Son of the living God." Without staying to refer to the general teaching of the Gospel stories and the Epistles in detail, let me ask you to observe that the whole of the New Testament teaching concerning Jesus is that He was, in a lonely, unique, specific sense, the Son of God, not a son, but *the* Son; not one among a company of sons, but alone, different, separate from all others in the mystic relationship which He bore to God. This confession of Peter harmonizes with the whole teaching and attitude of Jesus toward this subject. He never spoke of Himself as on a level with other men in this respect, but maintained an attitude of separation whenever He approached the subject of His relationship to His Father. Even after resurrection He did not say, Our God and Father, but My God, and your God, My Father, and your Father. He did not identify Himself with men in His relationship to God. We have no account, for example, in any of the gospels that He prayed with His disciples. He prayed in their presence, but when He prayed He prayed on a different level. You will remember one remarkable word that seems contradictory, "As He was praying alone, the disciples were with Him." Have you ever observed that carefully? He was praying alone, away from them, while yet they were present. He never used the words to describe His own praying that He used to describe the praying of His disciples. When He told men to pray the word He used indicated an attitude which He never used of His own praying. When He spoke of His own praying He spoke of inquiring of a Father. When His mother came to him and said, "Thy father and I sought Thee sorrowing," using the word that had been current in Nazareth to describe his relationship to Joseph, He replied, "Wist ye not that I must be in My Father's house?" In the first recorded words that fell from His lips He assumed separate and lonely relationship to God.

At Cæsarea Philippi Peter looked into His face and said, "Thou art the Messiah, the Son of the living God." The confession spoke of the revelation of the Father through the Son, and indicated a conviction of the closest relationship between the Father and the Son. Let us flash on the confession of Peter another confession to be found in the writings of another disciple, whom Peter never understood until after Pentecost, and of whom he then became the close friend. John says, "In the beginning was the Word, and the Word was with God, and the Word was God. . . . And the Word became flesh, and dwelt among us (and we beheld His glory, glory as of the only begotten from the Father), full of grace and truth." That is the same thought of identity with the Father, revelation of the Father, co-operation with the Father. Thus in loneliness and separation, unique, special, specific, never repeated and never to be repeated, Jesus was "The Son of the living God."

So we come to the last conception, which was first in order of statement in the confession of Peter. This One was the Messiah, the Administrator in human history of the Kingdom of God, the One Who came for the fulfilment of all aspiration, hope, confidence, and, consequently, the One Whose authority over the affairs of men is ultimate and final.

Having thus considered the confessor, and his confession, let us inquire what was the value of the confession? Peter had arrived at a conclusion, in harmony with the declaration with which God commenced the propaganda of His Son. As our Lord was setting His face toward His public ministry the Divine Voice declared, "This is My beloved Son in Whom I am well pleased." That was the Divine thought of the King.

At Cæsarea Philippi Peter had come to the conviction that this was true; he had arrived at a conclusion in harmony with the Divine conception.

There were limits to the meaning of this confession in the case of Peter. Jesus was Messiah, King, Head of the Kingdom; but Peter had no true conception yet of the nature of the Kingdom. Jesus was the Son of God, and therefore was Administrator of the Kingdom of God; but Peter did not comprehend the method by which the King would enter into His Kingdom. Such was the scope, and such were the limits of the confession. Here was a man, human as we are, with all our elemental forces manifest in him, with all our failures also, looking into the face of Jesus of Nazareth and saying, "Thou art the Messiah, the Son of the living God."

How did he arrive at the conclusion? Here we are not left to speculation; we have the clear statement of our Lord. Jesus looked back into the eyes of Peter and said, "Blessed art thou, Simon Bar-Jonah: for flesh and blood hath not revealed it unto thee, but My Father which is in heaven." In that word of Jesus we have a threefold revelation concerning the method by which Peter had arrived at that conclusion. First, a negative word, "Flesh and blood hath not revealed it unto thee." Second, a positive word, "My Father which is in heaven" hath revealed it unto thee. Third, a mediatorial word, a word indicating the method by which God had done it, the word *revealed*.

First, the negative statement, "Flesh and blood hath not revealed it unto thee." Flesh and blood was a common phrase in Hebrew speech, which, in this connection, simply meant that the confession was not the result of human discovery, either his own or that of any other man. In the twentieth verse I read, "Then charged He the disciples that *they* should tell no man that He was the Christ." Why? Because flesh and blood cannot reveal it; no disciple can carry conviction to another man. Christian workers cannot convince men that

Jesus is the Son of God. Our business is to introduce men to Christ, that through Himself they may come to know Him by Divine revelation. The attempt of "flesh and blood" to reveal Him is the secret of all heresy concerning Him. Therefore He said to His disciples: You are not called to prove to men Who I am. They have their opinions; you know me by Divine revelation, and your business is to take Me to men, and to bring men to Me; let Me be the intermediate One between My Father and men; let the Father show them Who I am, that I may show them Who the Father is. That is the meaning of the charge to the disciples.

The positive word, "My Father which is in heaven," is a clear declaration that the conviction which resulted in the confession was the result of Divine revelation.

That brings us to the central word, *revealed*. It is derived from the word *apokalupto*, which means to disclose, to unveil. My Father hath unveiled this to thee, hath disclosed this to thee. How had God done it? I want to suggest to your most earnest consideration that I do not believe that our Lord meant that in some sudden illumination direct from God, as apart from Himself, the revelation had come. Not in the whisper of the morning, or by the thunder of the noonday, or through the voices of the night, had God told Peter the secret. How, then, am I to understand this word "revealed"?

I turn to another passage of Scripture, not that it has any direct connection with our theme, but that there is light in it which will help us. Take the opening sentence of the book that bears the name, Apocalypse, Revelation, and mark the construction of it carefully, "The revelation of Jesus Christ which God gave Him to show." The unveiling of Jesus Christ —that is the key to the Book of Revelation. However much we may differ in detailed interpretation of the book of Revelation, we shall agree that it contains three great movements: Christ unveiled in His personal glory to John, Christ unveiled in the mysteries of His grace, walking amid the candlesticks, unifying the Church; Christ unveiled in the process of His government by which He will ultimately set up the Kingdom. Now, how was He thus unveiled? God gave Him, Jesus, to show Himself; God, through Jesus, made Jesus known, as Jesus, through Himself, did make God known.

When Jesus at Cæsarea Philippi said, My Father hath revealed it unto thee, hath given thee this apocalyptic, inspiring confession, He claimed a victory for Himself. God had revealed to Peter the truth about Jesus through Himself, and so had ratified his fundamental convictions concerning God Himself. "Thou art the Messiah, the Son of the living God." How did he arrive at that conclusion? By listening to Jesus, by following Him, by the processes of His ministry, until, at last, everything culminated in the conviction which expressed itself in the confession, "Thou art the Christ, the Son of the living God."

I repeat, it was not the result of any whisper of the morning, thunder of noontide, or voice of the night, but the victory of the Word of God made flesh, and so revealing the truth about Himself and about God to man, that man through that revelation should come to conviction concerning Jesus, and confess Him as to office, Messiah, and as to nature, Son of the living God.

Let us glance over the whole process. How did it begin? It began in that wonder which John alone tells, of how one day Andrew found Simon and took him to Jesus, and Simon and Jesus stood face to face for the first time. Then Jesus said, "Thou art Simon the son of John: thou shalt be called Rock." In that moment the living God spoke to Simon through His Son, though Simon did not know it. There was music in the word; there was in it the revelation of a perfect understanding, as though the One had said, I know you, your name, your father, you are Simon, the son of John; and there was in it a prophecy, you shall be Rock. No one had ever said that of Simon before. It was the one thing no one ever expected him to become. What did he do? He surrendered, and went after the Speaker. Now, about two and a half years had passed away. Simon had listened to Jesus teaching, had heard the great ideals He had presented; he had watched His ability, had seen Him Master in every department of human life, material, mental, moral; he had seen all evil forces yielding to Jesus' word and banished from human life. He had watched Him, and had come into close personal touch with the supreme facts of the personality of Jesus. What were they? Let John tell us, "Full of grace and truth," that is, full of tenderness and thunder, full of love and light, full of compassion and passion for righteousness. Through the years Peter had followed and observed.

Now mark the crisis. The circumstances were those of apparent failure. The religious teachers were refusing Him, the political leaders were against Him; yet there came to the soul of this man the overwhelming sense that his Master was superior to all the forces against Him, and all the experiences of the years crystallized into a master conviction and he said, "Thou art the Christ, the Son of the living God." God had been speaking to Simon through the Son, and when Simon came, apparently by this human and utterly natural process to conviction, Jesus said,—let me say it reverently as in His holy presence—I have won a victory in one human soul. God through Me has spoken, so that this soul is illuminated concerning Me, and consequently is admitted to an understanding of the Father; My Father hath revealed it.

Finally, what did this mean to Peter subsequently? I observe in the first place that this great confession of Peter at Cæsarea Philippi constituted an irrevocable committal to Jesus. I know what is in your mind! You are saying, not irrevocable: Peter denied Jesus! I say again, an *irrevocable committal*. Through all the failing experience that apocalypse remained with him, and that confession held him. He was constantly recalled to it. Almost immediately Christ was rebuking him, and calling him the adversary, "Get thee behind Me, Satan, for thou art an offence unto Me." Then there were six days of silence, in which no disciple seems to have spoken to Jesus at all; they were so amazed because He had spoken of the Cross. Then followed the holy mount and the Lord in a new and mystic glory, and Peter said, It is good to be here, let us build tabernacles! By a voice from heaven he was recalled to Cæsarea Philippi, "This is My beloved Son, in Whom I am well pleased; *hear ye Him.*" Didst thou not say at Cæsarea Philippi, "Thou art the Messiah, the Son of the living God?" "This *is* My beloved Son . . . *hear ye Him.*" Thus he was recalled to his committal.

Presently in the judgment hall, when in answer to the flippant mocking of a serving maid, Peter denied his Master, the Lord looked at him, and that look recalled the committal, recalled the confession, and Peter went out broken-hearted to weep bitterly.

Then in the days that followed, days of darkness and despair—when he was saying within himself, The last words He heard me utter were words of denial, and my Lord is dead —suddenly, somewhere, no one knows where, somewhen, no one can tell exactly when, the same Son of God met him, and talked to him; and when long afterward he sat down to write a letter he wrote, "Blessed be the God and Father of our Lord Jesus Christ, Who according to His great mercy begat us again unto a living hope by the resurrection of Jesus Christ from the dead." When Jesus came to him and had a private interview with him, he was taken back to his confession that Jesus stood related to God as Son to Father, and the resurrection was the new birth of the old hope that had seemed to perish by the way of the Cross. I repeat, it was in irrevocable committal, and the power of the apocalypse and the consequent confession never departed from him.

Further, that confession resulted in his having to tread a new pathway of teaching and of testing. That confession was followed by the immediate glory of our Lord's confession to him, "I also say unto thee, that thou art Peter, and upon this rock I will build My church." That was the result of his confession.

Then followed the first explicit mention of the Cross. The shadow of the Cross had never fallen on the lives of these men before. Our Lord never told them about the Cross until after that great confession. Having made it, it was necessary that they should know not only the King, but the method by which He must come into His Kingdom.

And yet another result was the appalling discovery to Peter of himself. Jesus took the man who had made so high a confession as that, and showed him himself. You will all forsake Me, you will all deny Me, you will do it even after this crisis! Never, Lord; if all others do, I will not! It was indeed necessary that Peter should discover himself; even by the way of denial he must come to an understanding of his own weakness.

And still once more. There was a new finding of the Lord in resurrection glory. To that we have already referred.

The ultimate confirmation of the confession is found in Peter's letters. Let me read the opening doxology of his first letter, and the closing injunction of his last letter: "Blessed be the God and Father of our Lord Jesus Christ, Who according to His great mercy begat us again unto a living hope by the resurrection of Jesus Christ from the dead. . . . Grow in the grace and knowledge of our Lord and Saviour Jesus Christ."

Let me close with the word to which I have already drawn your attention. "Then charged He His disciples that they should tell no man that He was the Christ." That conviction can come only by Divine revelation, and that Divine revelation can come only from the Father through the Christ Himself. What, then, is our business? To bring men to Him, to lead men to consider Him for themselves, to present Him as He is, not affirming thus or so, or attempting to compel men to accept our view, but to let them see the Lord. In proportion as we do that in life and in ministry, in that proportion we are bringing men to the place where they will know Him by the Divine apocalypse.

If there be some man listening to me who asks how he is to arrive at that ultimate conclusion, I say to him, You must begin exactly where Simon began. Where did he begin? He met Jesus. You have done that already. Hear me, I am not talking in a country called heathen, but in this church. You have met Him. You say, I am not sure of the doctrines concerning Him. I reply, you have nothing to do with them yet. He has made appeal to your will, shamed your sin, troubled your conscience, revealed a new ideal of life, suggested to you the possibility of a nobler life. But I want to be quite sure about all the doctrines, you say! No, you do not; and you never will be until you know the Lord!

What did Simon do when he met Jesus? He listened to Jesus, he followed Jesus, and came at last to conviction and confession; and beyond the confession he passed through processes of discipline and of testing, of growth and development, until at last in true communion with his Lord he died for Jesus—as he had said he could in the days of feebleness—and glorified his Lord in that dying. So must we begin if we ourselves at last would make the great confession.

CHAPTER VI

THE PATHWAY OF THE PASSION

From that time began Jesus to show unto His disciples, how that He must go unto Jerusalem, and suffer many things of the elders and chief priests and scribes, and be killed, and the third day be raised up.
MATTHEW 16:21.

THE ULTIMATE THINGS IN THE EARTHLY MISSION OF OUR Lord were implicit in His doing and teaching from the commencement of His public ministry. They became explicit after the confession of Peter at Cæsarea Philippi. This is very clearly revealed in the synoptic gospels. Matthew and Mark distinctly say so, "From that time began Jesus to show unto His disciples . . ."; and Luke's narrative by its method corroborates Matthew and Mark. Until this moment He had said nothing concerning His Cross. In many a deed He wrought, and in many a word that passed His lips, there is evidence that He knew of His Cross from the beginning; but there was no definite statement, no clear word spoken.

In the words of our text we have a careful summary of the teaching of the dark days between Cæsarea Philippi and Calvary. The statement of Matthew here is characterized by simplicity, definiteness, and clarity; and enables us to approach our Master as did those first disciples, in order to consider what He Himself thought of the final things of His earthly mission.

As we reverently attempt to do this, let us remember that these men failed to apprehend His teaching until after Pentecost; and, recognizing that the promised Interpreter is with us, let us reverently and confidently depend on His guidance as we attempt to consider this revelation of the Master's conception of the meaning of the last things in His earthly mission.

Before considering the statement itself, let us observe the Speaker, the occasion, and the hearers. In proportion as we can get back into the very atmosphere of that hour at Cæsarea Philippi, and the days that followed, and are led to the Cross, we shall be able to understand the Master's statement better.

Let us first look at the Speaker, Jesus, and attempt to see Him as they, to whom He gave this teaching first, saw Him. What did they know about Him at that time? They knew much concerning His personal perfections, for I have no hesitation in saying that the supreme attraction to the early disciples was that of the Lord Himself. They knew Him as One characterized at once by majesty and meekness, as One —if I may use so simple and colloquial a form of speech— with Whom no one might take liberties: full of dignity, characterized in one sense by an aloofness even from His nearest disciples, so that they never came into very close fellowship with Him. Yet He was characterized by meekness in the broadest, largest sense of the great and wonderful word, being perfectly familiar with His disciples, and treating them as His own close personal friends. Thus they could tell Him any secret, even though they knew they could not discover His profoundest secrets, and could come to Him with all their sorrows, even though they must always have been haunted by the sense of sorrows in His heart which they could not fathom. Paradoxically, He attracted them at once by the appalling severity of His terms and the infinite compassion of His method.

They had also caught something of the glory of His great ideals. If I believe they were first attracted by the personal charm of Jesus, I also believe that they were held near to Him by these great ideals and spiritual conceptions, His reverent and yet apparent familiarity with eternity and with God, that touch of His spirit on all things material in answer to which the material things flamed with the light and glory of the spiritual and abiding realities. They were held, too, by His conceptions of God and His conceptions of man, and His ideals as to the material conditions of life, as He had revealed them in the great Manifesto, and in many incidental words—that strange and wonderful picture He had given them of the Kingdom in which the King is Father, in which men will have no further anxiety for the luxuries of life, but will have a new joy in the possession of the necessary simplicities. There, He taught them, the carking care about what men shall eat and what they shall wear will pass away forever, there the passion for righteousness will be supreme, and the realization of the law of love will come to its great and gracious fulfilment.

They knew Him also in the strange activities of His ministry, a ministry of pity and of power. Unable to understand Him, they had nevertheless seen Him Master in every sphere of life: in the material realm, in the moral realm, in the mental realm, so that with apparent ease he wrought wonders that amazed them and always in answer to the surging pity of His own heart.

Thus they followed Him until He led them to Cæsarea Philippi; and it was this One Who now began to tell them that He must go to Jerusalem and suffer, and be killed, and be raised again on the third day.

The occasion of the commencement of this teaching was that of the hour of triumphant foretelling following on the great confession of Peter. Peter had said to Him, "Thou art the Messiah, the Son of the living God," and in answer to that

Jesus had made His great confession to Peter and His disciples, "On this rock I will build My Church; and the gates of Hades shall not prevail against it. I will give unto thee the keys of the kingdom of heaven: and whatsoever thou shalt bind on earth shall be bound in heaven: and whatsoever thou shalt loose on earth shall be loosed in heaven." In that confession we detect the note of assured triumph: no doubt, no tremor, no conditions; certain, positive, complete: "I will build . . . and the gates of Hades shall not . . . I will give unto thee the keys."

"From that time Jesus began to show unto His disciples, how that He must go unto Jerusalem, and suffer many things of the elders and chief priest and scribes, and be killed, and the third day be raised up."

The confidants to whom He told this hitherto unrevealed secret loved Him. They were those—I dare not have said this if He had not said it a little further on, under the very shadow of the Cross—who had continued with Him in all His temptations. They were those who were appointed to share His toil and His travail. They were, as at last, in infinite love and appreciation, He termed them, His friends.

We turn now from these preliminary matters to the teaching itself. The method I propose to adopt is that of examination and application. Our principal business is that of examination. By way of application, I shall only suggest some possible lines of inquiry.

As I have said, Matthew summarizes all the teaching from Cæsarea Philippi to Calvary in these words: "He must go unto Jerusalem, and suffer many things of the elders and chief priests and scribes, and be killed, and the third day be raised up."

In that summary there are three matters which demand our attention. The first is that of the *compulsion:* "He must go unto Jerusalem." The second is that of the *course* marked out: "suffer . . . and be killed." The third is that of the *consummation*: "and the third day be raised up."

We begin with the compulsion, for that is the supreme note: "From that time began Jesus to show unto His disciples, how that He *must*." He did not from that time begin to show them that *He was going* to suffer and be killed, and be raised again. That is true; but to read the text so is to entirely miss the supreme note and emphasis, that which must occupy our attention, the declaration that He *must*. The idea of the word is quite simply that He was bound, that He was in bonds; the thought is that of compulsion.

We are immediately at the very heart of our meditation as we ask the question, Why *must* He go to Jerusalem? I desire, as quickly as may be, to deal with certain insufficient reasons which have been advanced as explaining this declaration of compulsion.

It has been said that the "Must" is simply a revelation of the fact that He was in the grip of circumstances, that we should interpret the "must" by the inevitability of the circumstances into which He had now come as the result of His own ministry. A careful reading of the story will show that this was not so. If He go to Jerusalem He must suffer, He must be killed, there will be no escape. But why go? Why need He go to Jerusalem? His loved ones attempted to dissuade Him most earnestly during the months that followed. Let it be remembered that escape was quite possible at that time. There was no material necessity for Him to walk back into the trap men were laying for Him. Then why could He not escape? It would have been quite easy for Him to leave the region. We have not found the meaning of the "must" when we think of the circumstances in the midst of which He found Himself.

Once again, it has been said that the "must" of Jesus was simply the declaration on His part of devotion to a great ideal, that He had preached the Kingdom of God, and men had refused the Kingdom, and that now He said to His disciples in effect: I have preached the Kingdom, I have enunciated its principles, I have revealed its laws, I have given illustrations of its benefits in the works I have wrought; men will not have it; I cannot depart from My ideal; consequently, I may as well go to Jerusalem, even though I die in the going.

According to that view, there was the suggestion of a touch of hopelessness in the words of Jesus, loyalty to the ideal, but hopelessness as to its ultimate victory. No, that is not it; that is Elijah under the juniper tree saying, Let me die and not live, because this people will not have my preaching; that is Jeremiah cursing the day he was born, because his ministry was an apparent failure; but that is not Jesus, as He set His face toward Jerusalem. That would have been to have abandoned His ideal. If all that He came to give the world was an ideal, a suggestive vision, a few principles of life, then I ask you to remember that such an ideal could best be realized, such a vision be interpreted, such principles be started in their mighty working career, not by death but by life. I quote again the preacher of the olden time, "A living dog is better than a dead lion." Moreover, that method would have contradicted His perpetual habit throughout His public ministry. Over and over again when hostility was stirred against Him He withdrew Himself, hid Himself. More than once He said, sometimes directly to His critics, sometimes by messengers, that He would continue His work in spite of all opposition until the hour should come which they could neither hasten or postpone, and to which He was moving with full knowledge of the issue. To declare that He simply meant that He must be true to an ideal and die for it, shuts out of view entirely the last part of the teaching, the fact of resurrection. We have not yet discovered the meaning of His "must."

Let us now attempt to find it. Here I say solemnly that speculation is not to be permitted. Mere opinion is untrustworthy. Unless the Lord explained Himself we are without explanation. Did He explain Himself? Is there anything that will help us to understand the real meaning of the "must"? Did He ever say anything like this before? If I tax your patience a little I am sure you will bear with me. I am going back chronologically, and I turn first to Luke's gospel.

"I must preach the good tidings of the Kingdom of God to the other cities also: for therefore was I sent" (Luke 4:43).

There seems to be very little connection between the two, but I have found my word again, and on this occasion Jesus gave the reason for the *"must"*—*"for therefore was I sent."* I go back in the same chapter of Luke and find the story of how at the commencement of His public ministry, He read concerning Himself from the ancient prophecy;

> The Spirit of the Lord is upon Me,
> Because He anointed Me to preach good tidings to the poor:
> He hath sent Me to proclaim release to the captives,
> And recovering of sight to the blind (Luke 4: 18, 19).

That is the first light I have on my text. "I *must* preach the good tidings of the Kingdom of God to the other cities also." Why? "For therefore was I sent."

I pass a little further back in the chronological order and I find the next incident in John. Jesus was talking to Nicodemus, in the stillness of the night, and once more in this connection the word seems to be incidental, and somewhat separated from our present consideration, but you will immediately see how near it is to the thought that occupies us: "As Moses lifted up the serpent in the wilderness, even so *must* the Son of Man be lifted up" (John 3:14).

But why the "must"? We are seeking the reason of it.

"God sent not the Son into the world to judge the world;

but that the world should be saved through Him" (John 3:17).

One other reference only, this to a very familiar passage. We have gone back now over more than eighteen years, and we hear the voice of the boy Jesus uttering the first words recorded of Him: "Wist ye not that I *must* be in My Father's house?"

I interpret the *"must"* at Cæsarea Philippi by the *"must"* as it recurred in the previous history of the Lord from the first uttering of it, and I discover that the compulsion which was laid on Him was that of the will of God, the fact that He was in the world for a purpose, for the accomplishment of a mission which God had marked out for Him.

From that glance back we look ahead for a moment. Turn to the second chapter of Acts, and listen to this very man Peter in the power of the Pentecostal effusion. What does he say about the Cross? "Him, being delivered up by the determinate counsel and foreknowledge of God, ye by the hand of lawless men did crucify and slay" (Acts 2:23). Just a little further on in the New Testament, in the letter to the Hebrews, the writer quotes from an ancient psalm in application to Jesus and declares this to have been the keynote of all His life of ministry: "Lo, I am come (in the roll of the book it is written of Me) to do Thy will, O God" (Hebrews 10:7). "We have been sanctified through the offering of the body of Jesus Christ once for all" (Hebrews 10:10).

He takes away ceremonial and ritualistic offerings that He may establish the final offering.

Gather up these passages in order that the light which comes from other portions of Scripture—that interpretation from the actual words of our Lord, that interpretation of the Holy Spirit on The Day of Pentecost and through the writer of the letter to the Hebrews—may help us to understand the meaning of the *"must"* of Jesus. Why *must?* Because He was cooperating with the will of God in order to achieve human redemption. That was the compulsion. Not the force of circumstances drove Him to Jerusalem. Not a heroic devotion to an ideal compelled Him to that last journey. The compelling power was the will of God and His devotion to that will. The compulsion was that of His volitional surrender to the purpose of that will in order to redeem the race. Because that was the compulsion, no friend could dissuade Him, no fear of coming pain could deter Him, no devil could deflect Him. He "must," because that was the will of God for the redemption of man.

Granted this compulsion, we are brought to the consideration of the course. If He will go to Jerusalem He will place Himself within the reach of the power of His enemies. Do you see Him going? Do not be afraid to let imagination help you. That One Whose radiant, gracious personality had wooed and won His disciples, that One Whose ideals had been so high and wonderful, that One Whose ministry had been full of pity and of power, resolutely setting His face toward Jerusalem, He is passing now into the very realm where His foes will be able to wreak their vengeance on Him. But He is not passing outside the will of God. He is walking right into danger, but into danger with God. That is the picture. Do not forget it as you watch the process.

The constituent elements in the life of Jerusalem were all represented in the Sanhedrin. That is, I think, why Matthew was careful to name all the forces that were represented. He must "suffer many things of the *elders* and *chief priests* and *scribes*." The elders were the civic rulers, the chief priests were the spiritual rulers, the scribes were the moral rulers.

What were their conditions? Let us begin with the chief priests. At that time, when Jesus was moving toward Jerusalem, the chief priests were Sadducean, and that meant a devitalized religion, as rationalistic religion always is. The scribes were externalists—how He had condemned them!—

and that meant degraded conceptions of morality. The elders were timeservers, place seekers and that meant degraded authority.

The Lord was now moving toward Jerusalem. Conflict was now inevitable. There could be no escape. Ideals were in direct opposition. There must be what James Russell Lowell described as

> One death-grapple in the darkness
> 'Twixt old systems and the Word.

As He passed into the region where these men ruled, Jesus went deliberately back to the place where He had denounced the priest, the scribe, and the ruler, denounced them because their rule had issued in the destruction of the city of God. Moved with compassion for the multitudes because they were as sheep not having a shepherd, angry with the rulers because of the suffering of the multitudes, He walked back into their sphere of influence. Now He must "suffer many things of the elders and chief priests and scribes."

I do not believe that Christ was referring in those words to any material pain that was coming to Him, or even to any anguish of Spirit that was in any sense self-centered. I think the suffering to which He went was sorrow of heart caused by the attitude these men were taking against Him, which attitude meant their own destruction. If you challenge me for a reason for that interpretation I take you to the letter to the Hebrews, and ask you to ponder most carefully the significant change in the Revised Version which I maintain is necessary to a right understanding of the sorrows of the Lord. The writer says, He "endured such gainsaying of sinners *against themselves!*" The Authorized Version reads "*against Himself,*" There was textual reason for that, but other renderings of the manuscripts read differently, "*against themselves.*" That was the nature of His sorrow, not that men were wounding Him, but that in their wounding of Him they were harming themselves, in their rejection of the ideals that He had presented they were making impossible the realization of their own lives. He must suffer at the hands of the elders and chief priests and scribes, and the sorrows of the Spirit of infinite love and compassion are created when men refuse the call of His love.

But there is another and final step in the course: "and be killed." The death of Jesus was sin in its final manifestation. It can do no other than crucify, for that is itself. That is sin in the heart and essence of it. Once more, it could do no more, for all is done. That is the crime of all crimes. That was the ultimate sin against love. That was the ultimate sin against life. It was the sin of all sins—they killed Him. In that killing, human sin said its last word, had its last day. It was the ultimate in evil; it was the murder of the Son of God.

Look again. Why did He die? He need not have died. He might have abandoned His great ideals; and He might have wiped the dust of the region that would not have His ideals from off His shoes. Or, like Socrates, He might have drunk the hemlock because men would not have Him. But that was not the meaning of His dying. We have seen that the compulsion was not that of circumstances. We have seen that our Lord died within the will of God, delivered up by the determinate counsel and foreknowledge of God. In His death He was not trying to persuade God to love men. He *was* God, loving men to the very end and to the very death. In the death of Jesus grace is seen in its ultimate mystery and manifestation. Here we stand in awe. That is the course of the "must": inevitable and unutterable sorrows and death, the death in which sin is compelled to its ultimate outworking, its last word, its final act.

Is that all? If there be nothing else, I have misinterpreted the story. If there be nothing else, Jesus was indeed as a son of man who died high and noble in his aspirations, but beaten, defeated. If there be nothing more, then sin has won, the last word of sin is the ultimate doom of goodness, the last deed of sin is victory over every aspiration that is high and noble. If there be nothing other than Jesus' death, then God have mercy on me, I am of all men the most miserable.

There is more! There is the consummation: "and the third day be raised up." The overwhelming importance of that word cannot be insisted on too often or too earnestly. I want you carefully to remember that this is not an accidental word, it is not an occasional word. It was persistent through all the teaching of the shadowed days. Take the New Testament and read carefully the Lord's references to the Cross from Cæsarea Philippi until it was an accomplished fact, and you will find He never referred to His Cross without also referring to His resurrection. Of course, if some man say to me, I question the truth of the records, I have only to say that such an attitude affects the whole story. It is not honest to make a selection of things that square with a view, and to reject a matter so persistent as this. There is no occasion when the Lord foretold the Cross that He did not also foretell the resurrection.

In view of that foretelling of the consummation what was His estimate of His own death? How difficult it is to answer that question! Let me try. When Jesus died death died; sin ended itself when it grappled with God; God in the unfathomable mystery of pain destroyed the works of the devil.

That is the final note in the *must* of Jesus. Geographically, Jerusalem; processionally, suffering and death; ultimately, the resurrection and life; spiritually, God willeth not the death of the sinner, but rather that he should turn from his wickedness and live. God made a way by which His banished ones may return to Him again.

In a few sentences let me suggest some lines of application. There is an immediate illustration in the protest of a disciple: Not that; that be far from Thee, that shall never be unto Thee! Not what? Peter was talking about the *course*, about suffering and death. The things he did not understand, which were not in his mind when he made the protest, were the first thing and the last thing: the *compulsion* and the *consummation*. The "must" he did not understand; the raising the third day he did not understand. How was he answered? By one of the severest sentences that ever passed the lips of our Lord, "Get thee behind Me, Satan." Why? "Thou mindest not the things of God, but the things of men." What are the things of men? The course, the suffering and death at the hands of lawless men! What are the things of God? The compulsion of redeeming love, the consummation of redeeming victory. Let that illustration be pondered and we have a line of application.

Is this ancient history? What of religion to-day? What of morality today? What of authority to-day? Are we in our national or civic life approximating to the ideals of Jesus? Is not much of our religion Sadducean, rationalistic? Is not much of our morality that of externalism? Is not very much of our authority that of office-seeking, place-seeking, selfishness, forgetfulness of all the shepherd qualities which are necessary to the exercise of true authority?

Are we not coming to an hour in which the Church of Christ has earnestly to ask herself whether indeed she really understands her Lord, whether she indeed is representing Him in the life of to-day?

I am not criticizing the Prime Minister, not for a moment, but when he had to make his appeal to two sides in the coal strike, which I am not now discussing, he pointed out to the owners that if this dispute went far they would suffer loss of property; he pointed out to the men that if this dispute went far they would suffer most from hunger. It was an appeal to selfishness on both sides, necessarily so, because we are so far from realization of the high principles and promises of Jesus. How are they to be established? The first thing is that the Church of God shall act under the compulsion which sent her Lord to Jerusalem, the *must* of the will of God, and the *must* of the will of God in order to redeem and remake individual men and the whole race.

Is that the master passion that drives us, consumes us, inspires us? If it is, the world will provide the Cross, believe me! And believe me, God will take care of the resurrection! Oh that it may be given to us to see the meaning of the "must," and in some measure to enter into fellowship with God's sufferings and make up that which is behindhand in His affliction.

CHAPTER VII

THE POWERS OF THE PRESENCE

Verily I say unto you, What things soever ye shall bind on earth shall be bound in heaven. And what things soever ye shall loose on earth shall be loosed in heaven. Again I say unto you, that if two of you shall agree on earth as touching anything that they shall ask, it shall be done for them of My Father which is in heaven. For where two or three are gathered together in My name, there am I in the midst of them.

MATTHEW 18:18-20.

THESE THREE VERSES CONSTITUTE AN INCIDENTAL STATEMENT by our Lord of essential truths concerning His Church. After the confession of Peter He revealed two secrets to His disciples, that of the Church and that of the Cross. Prior to the experience at Cæsarea Philippi He had never referred to His Church, neither had He spoken specifically of His Cross.

The Church, according to that first revelation, was to be at once His building, embodying the principles of the Kingdom; His army, at war with all opposing forces; and His witness, holding the keys of the Kingdom as the interpreter of His ethic to the world.

The Cross, according to that earliest explicit statement, was by the appointment of God, Jesus' way through suffering and death to resurrection, and, consequently, to the place of full and final authority.

Both these secrets were arresting and amazing, and their influence is discernible in all Jesus' subsequent dealings with His disciples. It was in the midst of instructions in this atmosphere, on the subject of forgiveness of sins, that is, human forgiveness of sins, that our Lord made the statements which constitute our text. I deliberately take them from the context, because they are complete within themselves. I do not propose to show the bearing of these statements on the subject which our Lord was dealing with at the moment, but to consider them themselves. Taken in the order of their utterance, you will observe that they consist, first, of two declarations of power vested in the Church, and, second, of a revelation of the secret and nature of that power.

The words are very familiar, and therefore it is all the more necessary that we observe them carefully. This is one of those familiar passages which we read through quickly, imagining that we know them; and we do know them, and yet, because of our easy reading of them, we may miss the things which are of supreme importance in them. In order to understand this teaching of our Lord, we must observe the interrelation between the statements. There are, first, two distinct statements concerning powers vested in the Church, and these culminate in, and are completed by, our Lord's revelation of the secret of these powers.

Each of the first two declarations is introduced by a phrase arresting attention. First, "Verily I say unto you"; and then, "What things soever ye shall bind on earth shall be bound in heaven, and what things soever ye shall loose on earth shall be loosed in heaven." Second, "Again I say unto you," and then "if two of you shall agree on earth as touching anything that they shall ask, it shall be done for them of My Father which is in heaven."

But to take those two statements apart from that which follows will be to misinterpret them. We must link them with that which follows, which is introduced by a word relating the final declaration to the first two: *"For* where two or three are gathered together in My name, there am I in the midst of them."

So that we have—and thus we may divide our meditation—first, a revelation of the twofold power of the Christian Church in the two declarations, and a revelation of the secret of that power in the affirmation concerning His perpetual presence within the Church, when the Church is fulfilling the conditions laid down. Even at the risk of wearying you, I emphasize the importance of noticing the *three* declarations, and how they are linked to each other. First He said, *"Verily I say unto you,"* arresting attention by that particular formula. Then, in order that He might note the fact that He was about to say something beyond that which He had already said, He again arrested attention by the words: *"Again I say unto you,"* and then He made the second declaration. Finally He introduced His last statement by the word *"For,"* showing that there is no meaning in either of the earlier declarations apart from the final one.

Let us first consider our Lord's teaching concerning the two powers vested in the Christian Church. These again must be seen in their interrelationship. As a matter of fact, in this wonderful passage our Lord passed from that which is manifest and external to that which, in the life of the Church, is secret and hidden; and, finally, to that which is the deepest and profoundest matter.

The manifest and external power is that the Church is to be the interpreter in the world of His ethic, that the business of the Church is to set up the moral standards for the ordering of human life, and to do that by revealing to men what God's will is concerning them. Now, in order to fulfil that, the Church must herself be familiar with the place where the secrets are discovered; and so He passed from that which is external and manifest to that which is secret, the power of prayer vested in the Church.

With regard to the first power, in order clearly to apprehend our Lord's meaning we must free our minds from false prejudices concerning the statement, "What things soever ye shall bind on earth shall be bound in heaven; and what things soever ye shall loose on earth shall be loosed in Heaven." As we read the verse to-day we are in danger of being in bondage to certain false ideas concerning its meaning. If only we could hear the words as they were heard by the men to whom they were first said, I think many of us would be startled, because the simple meaning of the words would be so self-evident, and would be so different from meanings which we have associated with them. Let me say broadly—not to discuss the subject at any length—that when our Lord uttered these words to His first disciples they would not convey to the disciples the slightest suggestion that He was conferring on them anything in the nature of sacerdotal power. Gradually the idea of binding and loosing has been transferred from things to persons, and all unconsciously we read the verse as though our Lord had said something quite different, as though He had said, "*Whomsoever* ye shall bind on earth shall be bound in heaven: and *whomsoever* ye shall loose on earth shall be loosed in heaven," as though He had conferred on the disciples some power by which they should hold men in bondage to their own sins, or set them loose from the responsibility accruing from their sins. There is a certain sense in which that is true. There is a teaching of our Lord that reveals the fact that He has conferred on His people in the exercise of their ministry the power to declare sins forgiven or retained; but that is not the subject in this statement. Here the consequences of sins are not in view. Rather, the thought is of the determination of what sin is. It is the setting up of a standard. As I have said, if only we could have heard these words uttered we would have understood as the disciples did. These were the common phrases of the hour: to bind, to loose. They were the phrases of the scribes, who were the moral interpreters of the age. The literature of the time abounds in illustrations. Great masters or rabbis were set over against each other in ethical discussion. This man binds such and such a matter, while this man looses it. The meaning of the phrase was that according to this man's interpretation, we may do thus and so, and, according to that man's interpretation, we may not do thus and so. Binding and loosing were words used in the common speech of the times, and we can understand our Lord's words only as we understand the meaning in that sense.

Briefly, then, what does the statement mean? That what the Church allows morally, ethically, is allowed, that what the Church forbids morally, ethically, is forbidden; that in human life the Church's responsibility to her Lord is to interpret to men the law of God, to set up the moral standards. Her business is to enunciate the law, to determine standards, and in hours of crisis to decide questions.

However, let me immediately draw attention to what that really means. What is this authority of which He was speaking? Was He telling these men that they might sit down in council, to discuss together whether or not men might do certain things? By no means. "What things soever ye shall bind on earth shall be bound in heaven," and why? Because these men would voice the will of heaven. What they bound on earth would be bound in heaven, and what they loosed on earth would be loosed in heaven, because originally these things were bound in heaven or loosed in heaven. The Church is not to discuss, not to attempt to formulate, but to express the law of heaven, the will of God, the ethic of eternity, in its application to the activities of time. The Church is to be the medium by which the will of God for man shall be known, shall be declared, shall be proclaimed, and that as to the standards of conduct and in the determination of questions as they may arise. But all the Church's decisions and determinations are of no value if they result merely from her discussions. They are valuable only as she is the voice of the good and perfect and acceptable will of God.

Therefore, the reading of this verse necessitates a warning. It is a most perilous verse if taken out of its connection. If to-day there should arise some new section of the Christian Church, which, basing its authority on this passage, should proceed to discuss the whole question of moral standards in order to give their opinion as to what men ought, or ought not to do in individual, social, and national life, forgetting that they have neither vision to see, nor right to affirm, nor power to enforce, save as this final thing is true in experience, "For where two or three are gathered together in My name, there am I in the midst," the result would indeed be disastrous.

Now, let us suggest an inquiry. How far has the Church of God this power to-day? No mere expression of my opinion would be of any value. I suggest, therefore, a simple test for your thoughtful consideration. Whenever in past history the Church of God has enunciated the ethic of heaven for the government of life in the world, one result has followed—or shall I be more accurate if I say, an alternative of result has followed?—men have obeyed, or they have opposed definitely and positively. Wherever the Church has lost the power to speak the actual will of God to the age, then though she has spoken her own thought, her own opinion, attempting to foist on humanity her own conceptions of what humanity ought or ought not to do, what has been the result? Absolute indifference. The Church addresses itself to the age as to the moralities of individual life, and the age is amused and goes its own way. The voice of the Church is heard speaking in the presence of great crises, but those who are in the conflict are not listening to what the Church has to say. Is that so? If so, it is because somehow the Church has lost her power to speak the veritable Word of God. I do not say that if the Church shall speak the Word of God, and enunciate the law of heaven to men, they will obey. I do say they will either obey or fight. Look back over the history of the Church. Every hour of ethical revival resulting from her ministry has been an hour of conflict and persecution, as well as an hour of reformation, remaking, and restarting of the true inspirations of human life. The terror of to-day is this, that we are not heard, that we are not noticed. Men care nothing about what we bind. They do not ask to know what we loose.

Let us pass now to the second of these declarations of our Lord. Here we are coming inside the Church. Let us prepare ourselves to hear these words of Jesus without any reservation; for if in the first case we have been in danger at least of reading into the words of Jesus values which they were never intended to contain, in the second case we have been strangely in danger of reading out of them values that lie within them. These words of our Lord are most remarkable words. "If two of you shall agree on earth as touching anything that they shall ask, it shall be done for them of My Father which is in heaven." How many of us believe that? In general terms, we of the Christian faith and the Christian name immediately say, Of course we all believe it. But do I believe it? I challenge my own soul. With all reverence let me put this statement of the Master in another form. This is what the Lord said, If the desires of two expressed to the Father symphonize, sound together, about *anything*, it shall be done, generated, caused to be.

The things Jesus said about prayer are stupendous. In

this word concerning the power of prayer vested in the Church two spheres are recognized: two of you *on earth*, My Father which is *in heaven*—the material and the spiritual, the things of which the senses may be conscious, the supreme spiritual fact that the senses may never discover. Notice again the contrast of persons, *"two of you," "My Father."* Notice, finally, the related activity: the two symphonizing in desire and in petition, the One causing the things to be for the two desiring. That is the picture. Whether that is scientific or not, I will postpone the discussion for a hundred years, because we shall know more about these things then. I am not at all eager to know whether this is true according to philosophy or science. It is true according to Jesus: two, their desires symphonizing, sounding together; One, the Father Who is in heaven, doing what the two desire. That is the power of prayer.

Here, again, a word of warning is needed. This is a most perilous verse if taken out of its connection, and we do not discover the real meaning of our Lord if we read it alone. We may build on it every form of heresy concerning prayer. We may imagine that this teaching is that if any two of us want something, and we agree together, we may get it straightway. That is not in the statement. We must read on: "because where two or three are gathered together in My name, there am I in the midst of them," His presence in the midst conditions the desiring, inspires the asking, and produces the answer.

Let us pause again for inquiry. How far has the Church this power to-day? What do we really know about symphony of desire expressed to our Father in the consciousness that the Lord Himself is in the midst? Sometimes I have made my protest against attempting to measure the strength of a church by the number attending the prayer meeting, and I know full well that a large number does not constitute a prayer meeting; but I know also that the number of absences reveals weakness on the part of those who are not there. If preaching is enough, then our Lord was mistaken. If multiplied organizations are what the Church needs, then He was entirely blind, for He gave no instructions as to the multiplication of organizations. He said if things are to be done, God must do them, and God will do them when you know how to ask Him. That is brutal and vulgar language as compared to the exquisite and beautiful language of the Lord, but that is what He meant.

If our moral influence is lost it is because we are not making use of our spiritual resources. If the world is indifferent to us when we talk of things that ought to be, and that ought not to be, it is because we are attempting to touch the restless, rushing world and arrest it, while we ourselves are suffering from the same fever of restlessness and rushing, and know nothing of the dynamic forces that are generated in the place of fellowship and prayer.

And so we pass lastly to our Lord's revelation of the secret of power in these two matters. If we are to have that ethical authority that binds and looses, commands attention and creates obedience or opposition; if we are to have that spiritual power that enables us in agreement of desire and expression to ask, and thus to produce, how is it all to be done? And we come to the final statement, in a few moments to reconsider it. "Where two or three are gathered together in My name, there am I in the midst of them." Mark the place, mark the conditions, but supremely observe the presence.

The place, and the glory of this statement of our Lord is in its dealing with place. I can indicate it for you exactly in two words: "*where . . . there.*" They signify exclusion and inclusion.

The exclusion of all special places. Walls are demolished. "See ye not all these things? Verily I say unto you, There shall not be left here one stone upon another, that shall not be thrown down." Veils are rent in twain, places are all superseded. Where? Not in Jerusalem, not in Mount Gerizim, not in St. Peter's at Rome, not in Westminster Abbey, not in Westminster Chapel. Oh yes, in all of them, but in none of them! The *where* of Jesus is universal, cosmopolitan, inclusive as well as exclusive.

As I sat and thought of this morning's matter my mind went back over my own life, and some very simple incidents came back to me. I went back to the days of youth on the Cotswold Hills and to rambles with one friend. We walked and talked, and we came to a stile, and there we halted. The fields were all around us, and no one else was near. There we two sat and talked of our Lord and of our Master, and then together, gathered in the Name, we prayed. There was a Third, "I am in the midst."

Then I remembered how, when I began to preach, I was conducting special services in Yorkshire, and some miners told me it was easy to preach, but that it was a different thing to cut coal. And so I went down with them and cut my stint all day long in a Yorkshire coal pit. Going along the workings, I suddenly came to a siding, and I heard a man say, Hallelujah! He was a Methodist. I paused a moment, and went in to that working, and two or three of us had a few minutes' talk, and we prayed there for the meeting to be held that night, and for someone whom they were anxious about. There down in the depths of the earth, three miners paused, for a moment, and a mission preacher prayed. *There* were the two or three gathered together, and the Lord was in the midst, and in the mine was the place of worship, and present were the priest, the altar, the sacrifice, the right of prayer, the power of prayer. There was generated the dynamic force that moves toward the coming of the Kingdom. Coming home from America on board a great liner with George Macgregor, one sunset evening, at the end of the boat, we talked of the things of the Master, and, our conversation merging into prayer, we knew the Presence, the real Presence.

Where? *There!* In the cottage, in the conventicle, in the citadel, in the church, in the cathedral. Not because these places have been officially set apart, but because they are consecrated by the two or the three gathered in the name.

But in these words of the Lord we have also the revelation of conditions. First as to number, two or three. There is definiteness and indefiniteness. Definite, two, the smallest gathering possible. You cannot have a gathering of one. You cannot be a church by yourself, my dear friend. A good many men would like to be. There must be two; this promise is not for the individual. Oh, thank God, there are gracious promises for the individual. I am not saying that I cannot pray alone. Our Lord was more insistent on private prayer than even on the fellowship of prayer. In the Old and the New Testaments the individual promises are many, "To this man will I look, even to him that is poor and of a contrite spirit, and that trembleth at My word." That is a great promise for the individual. But this refers to a gathering, an assembly, a fellowship, a *koinonia*. Two, there must be a definite meeting.

Then observe the indefiniteness of it. Two or three: units or tens, or hundreds, or thousands; it does not at all matter.

But what is the principle? In My Name! The more one ponders this word of the Lord, the more marvelous does it become in its mystic quantities, as well as in its clear and definite pronouncement. "In My name," quite literally, *into* My name. The phrase includes the thought of coming *unto* the name, and passing *into* the name, and consequently being *in* the name. It was in order that we might understand the phrase, "In My name," that we read those two passages, one in Matthew, and one in Philippians. They are the two great passages about the name "Jesus." I take those two passages, and I ask, What do they reveal to me? Jesus, according to the angelic prophecy, signifies His power to save His people from their sins. According to the apostle's teaching, God has given Him that name, "that in the name of Jesus every knee should bow, of things in heaven and things on earth and things under the earth, and that every tongue should confess." Then the two thoughts associated with the name are those of purity and authority. Purity not merely demanded, but communicated; He shall save from sins. Authority exercised: He is Lord of all.

What, then, is to be gathered into His name? To be gathered into His name is to receive His salvation, and to be made pure. To be gathered into His name is to submit to His authority, and to be ruled absolutely by Him. Now, give me two men, or a man and a woman, or two women, or two little children, who are gathered in His name, who have yielded themselves to Him, that He may make them pure, who have yielded themselves to Him that He may master them; where such are so gathered, He says, *there am I*. That is the Church.

Gathered, or led together, suggests the idea that some attracting power brings these people together. It is the attractive power of the Lord, interpreted to the mind of man through the ministry of the Spirit. So disciples are gathered together.

Thus we come to the great central truth: "There am I in the midst." Oh, if we could but see that picture, two or three gathered, and the Lord in the midst. Who was the Speaker? A little while before He had said, "Who do men say that *the Son of man* is?" The Son of man was the Speaker! And immediately He was answered, "Thou art the Christ, *the Son of the living God*"; and He answered, "Blessed art thou, Simon Bar-Jonah: for flesh and blood hath not revealed it unto thee, but My Father." The Speaker was the Son of God! Son of man, on the level of the two and the three; Son of God, identified with the Father. Son of man, on the earth; Son of God, in the bosom of the Father in heaven.

Now we see how that affects the other subjects. How does it affect this matter of prayer? If two of you shall agree on earth as touching anything it shall be done for them of My Father, for I am in the midst of the two or three gathered in My name. First He is in the midst of those gathered, creating their symphony of desire and of asking. Second, He is in the midst, co-operating with the doing of the Father in giving. If these things be true, then the matter of supreme importance is that we get to prayer.

How does that affect the declaration concerning ethical authority? What you shall bind on earth shall be bound in heaven, what you shall loose on earth shall be loosed in heaven, because I am in the midst, interpreting to you heaven's will, and so enunciating through you the true law for earthly conduct.

These, my brethren are high Church doctrines. These are the doctrines of our Lord Himself; and it is because we have so largely lost them, and have indulged in vaunting and boasting about a freedom that lacks the true spiritual note, that the world does not listen to us when we talk about binding and loosing.

Are we conscious of weakened powers in prevailing prayer? Then our first responsibility is that of gathering together in the name anew; and we must do so by the appropriation of His purity, by the way of His salvation, and by submitting to His authority, that in us the Kingdom may be established.

In proportion as He is King of my life and Lord of my salvation, in that proportion am I ready for the gathering together with other people of like loyalty to the Lord. Where there is such gathering together with the Lord in the midst we have the true place of prayer, and we hear the true voice of God.

If that first responsibility be fulfilled, then our consequent responsibilities are those of exercising the powers created, both in the practice of prayer and in the proclamation of the law, that through us our Lord may carry on His ministry and win His victories.

CHAPTER VIII

THE PATHWAY TO POWER

Then came to Him the mother of the sons of Zebedee with her sons, worshipping, and asking a certain thing of Him. And He said unto her, What wouldest thou? She saith unto Him, Command that these my two sons may sit, one on Thy right hand, and one on Thy left hand in Thy Kingdom. But Jesus answered and said, Ye know not what ye ask. Are ye able to drink the cup that I am about to drink? They say unto Him, We are able. He saith unto them, My cup indeed ye shall drink: but to sit on My right hand, and on My left hand, is not Mine to give but for whom it has been prepared of My Father.
MATTHEW 20:20-23.

THE FIRST WORD OF THE PARAGRAPH DIRECTS ATTENTION TO what has preceded it. "*Then* came to Him the mother of the sons of Zebedee with her sons, worshipping, and asking . . ." *When?*

The face of the King was set toward Jerusalem. Between the disciples and Himself the relationship was strained. Mark supplies these words in the narrative, "They were in the way, going up to Jerusalem; and Jesus was going before them: and they were amazed; and they that followed were afraid." That is a graphic description of the condition of affairs. Our Lord, with His face set toward Jerusalem, was going alone; the disciples, who had been His close companions during the years of public ministry, were following a little way behind

Him, amazed, as our word has it, dazed, as the actual word suggests; they were filled with a sense of coming calamity, and utterly unable to understand what He meant by His perpetual references to a cross, and His persistent setting of His face toward the city that was hostile to him.

During that period He took them apart especially, and repeated His statements as to what lay before Him with even more detail than before concerning His sufferings, in the most remarkable way foretelling the actual indignities to which He was about to be subjected: "They shall condemn Him to death, and shall deliver Him unto the Gentiles to mock, and to scourge, and to crucify." "*Then* came the mother of the sons of Zebedee with her sons, worshipping, and asking" that James and John might sit the one on the right hand and the other on the left when He came into His Kingdom.

Observe the simple facts of the story. Salome spoke for her sons. When the Lord began to deal with the request, He addressed the sons, not the mother. That is indicated by the fact that He employed the plural pronoun, "*Ye* know not what *ye* ask. Are *ye* able to drink the cup that I am about to drink?" And it was the sons who answered, "We are able.'

James and John He had surnamed Boanerges, sons of thunder; and it is important that we recognize the fact that when our Lord so surnamed these men, He was not describing them as they were, but as they should be. We have only the story of the surnaming in one connection; it is Mark who tells it, and he does so in close connection with another fact. In giving the names of the twelve whom He appointed to apostleship, he wrote, "Simon He surnamed Peter; . . . James the son of Zebedee, and John the brother of James, He surnamed Boanerges." In each case the surnaming was prophecy, an indication, not of what the men were as He found them, but of what they should become as the result of His dealing with them. That is quite clearly evident in the wonderful story of Simon, the elemental, restless man of great human forces but lacking the cohesive principle which welds them into rock. Jesus looked into his eyes when He first met Simon and said, "Thou art Simon . . . thou shalt be called Rock." He surnamed him according to what he should become. So also when He met these two brothers, or when He appointed them to the work of the apostleship, He surnamed them Boanerges. When He first looked into the eyes of Simon, He did not say, Thou art Rock, but Thou shalt become Rock. When He first looked into the eyes of James and John, He did not say of them, Behold two sons of thunder; but Behold two men who shall become sons of thunder. He surnamed them prophetically.

It is true that He surnamed them according to the capacities He saw in them, when those capacities should be fulfilled under His own ministry. He saw in Peter all the elements which, mastered by principle, should become rock. What Simon lacked when he first met the Lord was not any element of strength, but the master principle which should weld all the elements into strength. When He looked at James and John, James, of whom we know so little, and John, with the mystic, far-away look, John, who, looking at you, seemed to see not you but something infinitely beyond you; John the man whose eyes looked languorous with very weariness of things material, yet in whose eyes there lay the slumbering fires of infinite vision—these men, said Jesus, shall be Boanerges, sons of thunder. The word was Aramaic, and was intended to convey to Hebrew minds Hebrew conceptions. We must interpret the practical values by the poetic suggestions. If we take the word Boanerges to pieces we discover that the word for *sons* is the word which refers to the son as the builder of the family, as the one who continues its values and influences. Quite a different word from the word *bar* was this word *ben*, referring to the son as the one who received an inheritance of responsibility and transferred it. Thunder was always symbolic of power and authority. It is an interesting fact that in the Old Testament the word is almost exclusively employed to express something of the authority, power, and majesty of God.

Jesus looked at James and John and said, These shall become Boanerges, sons of thunder, offspring of the Divine majesty and authority, men who shall realize it and repeat it. These were the men who preferred the request.

Quite simply, that request was that when He comes into His Kingdom they might occupy positions of power in association with Him. Our Lord immediately challenged them, "Ye know not what ye ask. Are ye able to drink the cup that I am about to drink?" With equal readiness, and with remarkable immediateness they responded, "We are able." What, then? Mark it well: Jesus said, "My cup indeed ye shall drink: but to sit on My right hand, and on My left, is not mine to give except to those for whom it hath been prepared."

I need not tarry long to defend my change of the word "but" at that point; this Greek word *alla*, neuter plural of the word *allos* means contrariwise. You will find it in the New Testament translated by many words: and, but, even, howbeit, indeed, nay, nevertheless, no, notwithstanding, save, therefore, yea, yet. Twice you will find it in the Authorized Version translated "save"; once that translation is retained in the Revised Version. On the holy mount it is stated, "They saw no one, save Jesus only." Because this passage has been misunderstood, I use the word "except," which is equivalent to "save." Our Lord did not say it was not His to appoint to positions of power in the Kingdom. What He did say was that it was not His to appoint to positions of power any except those for whom the positions were prepared, and the positions are prepared for the men who are prepared for the positions.

THE PATHWAY TO POWER

The values of this story are persistent. General and hasty condemnation of James and John is very unwise. It is also futile, because in the moment of our highest spiritual aspiration and experience we share their ambition. However much we may condemn them, however much a superficial reading of the narrative may lead us to say they had no right to ask, however much we may be in sympathy with the other ten as they were moved with indignation against the two, in hours when spiritual life is rising to highest levels there is the desire for power and position, and we cry out that we also may sit on His right hand and on His left in His Kingdom, that there may be fulfilled in us also the prophecy that He whispered in our ear when in some holy hour of secret communion He declared that we should become sons of thunder. That was their request.

Let us endeavor to understand these men and our Lord's dealing with them. These, then, are the simple divisions of our meditation: first, the request of the sons of thunder; second, the answer of the Son of God.

The request of the sons of thunder was for places of power. It was, if you like to make use of the word, a selfish request; but it was a desire for self-realization in relation to their Lord. "Command that these my two sons may sit, one on thy right hand, and one on Thy left hand, in Thy Kingdom."

It is to be noted that when presently He dealt with the contrast between the rule and authority in His Kingdom and the rule and authority in the Gentile world, it was in answer to the indignation of the ten. He was not correcting James and John; He was correcting the ten who were angry with James and John. There was far more unadulterated selfishness in the ten in that hour than there was in James and John. I repeat, in some senses the request was selfish, but it was an expression of a desire for self-realization in relation to the Lord; it was in His Kingdom that they desired to occupy these places. As I have pondered the story I have come to the conviction that what they really meant was this: Oh, Master, Thou Who didst surname us Boanerges, fulfil the promise, make us Boanerges, true sons of thunder, men of authority, under Thee in Thy Kingdom, and over the affairs thereof.

Let us look at this a little more particularly, for in an understanding of it is the supreme value of our meditation. Observe, in the first place, that the request was founded on faith; in the second place, that it was conceived in ignorance, and ignorance is not sin save where it is persistent, wilful; in the third place, that it was expressed in magnificent heroism.

I say, in the first place the request was founded on faith. *Then*, when His face was toward Jerusalem, and He was persistently declaring to them that He was going to suffer and be killed, *then* they asked that they might sit on His right hand and on His left in His Kingdom. The request was founded on faith, the faith that He was King; on the conviction that was mightier than all their trembling, that He was coming, somehow, into His Kingdom. They were amazed, dazed, filled with fear; yet had they not seen Him, had they not tabernacled with Him, had they not listened to His words, had they not caught some glimpses of the high ideals of His heart? They were convinced that it was absolutely necessary, that, somehow, He would enter into His Kingdom. So, in spite of the threatening Cross, it may be that they were attempting to banish it from their minds, that out of some sort of compassion for Him they were trying to make Him forget it for the moment—it may have been for one, or both, of these reasons that they avowed confidence in the Kingdom and in Him as King. It was a request founded on faith.

It was also a request conceived in ignorance. They did not know Him. Verily, they had seen Him, they had listened to Him; but they did not know Him. They never knew Him until He was dead, buried, risen, and ascended! In one sudden rush of new life and light they knew Him in the Pentecostal baptism. They did not know Him when they made this request. They were ignorant of all the profoundest truths concerning Him. Neither did they know His Kingdom, they were still thinking within the realm of the material concerning the Kingdom. They were still thinking, in common with others of their nation, and in common with all the disciples, that He was about to set up an earthly kingdom with material benefits, with all the blessings of this life for humanity.

And they were not wholly wrong. That is another subject, yet I am bound to touch on it in passing. There are men to-day who seem to imagine that our Lord is not set on that kind of kingdom. But He is, and He will never be satisfied until the last wrong is righted, the last tear is wiped away, and humanity finds itself in a true brotherhood in relation to the Fatherhood of God. The King will never be satisfied while wrong persists, He will never rest until He reigns in this world, until

> The earth is the Lord's, and the fulness thereof;
> The world, and they that dwell therein;

and until the Kingdom is established in this world the King will never have finished His work.

But These men were only looking for the material; they had not discovered that truth which we are still slow to believe, that the material can be realized only through the spiritual. We shall never set up a true social order save as the men composing it are regenerate, renewed, remade within themselves. These men had not seen that the Lord's first work is spiritual, that He can proceed to His Kingdom only by the use of weapons, not carnal weapons, but spiritual. When they preferred their request their vision of Him was limited, their understanding of His Kingdom was imperfect. Moreover, their request was conceived in ignorance of what it involved,

They had not realized what it would mean to them if ever they were to realize this character of authority. They did not understand what their request excluded. If He should give them these places of authority they would lack exactly that kind of authority of which they had been so constantly thinking. It was a request conceived in ignorance, but ignorance is not sin.

Once again, it was a request expressed in heroism. I listen to the story once more and I hear our Lord as He said to these men, "Are ye able to drink the cup that I am about to drink?" And then I listen to their reply, "We are able." I know exactly what we have so often said; It was a foolish word! Yes, perhaps it was. Yet think again. What did it mean? "We are able." They meant to say, The purpose that inspires us makes us entirely reckless of possible consequences! It was exactly the spirit which actuated Peter when he said, Why cannot I follow Thee now? I will die for Thee! With our cool, calculating, cynical habits of mind, we have criticized Peter for his foolhardiness. What did our Lord say to him? You shall follow Me; that profound passion that is ready to risk death shall be fulfilled in spite of the fact that within a few hours you will deny Me! It was exactly the kind of passion our Lord was ever seeking, reckless disregard of cost in answer to a driving impulse of purpose. When we declare that Jesus called men to count the cost before they followed Him we are saying what is not warranted by any story in the New Testament. He never came to men and charged them to count the cost. He came to men telling them to follow at any cost, at all costs, without counting cost. I know there was one occasion when He said to men, What man of you if he is going to build a tower would not first count the cost; or what king going to war will not first count the cost? But the context shows that neither the man going to build nor the king going to war is the disciple, but the Lord. He was not teaching men that they must count the cost, but that *He* must count the cost, and therefore His terms must be severe. The severity of His terms was marked. If men will follow Him it must be regardless of cost. That man who sits down and quietly counts the cost of becoming a follower of Christ will never follow Christ. The only man who really follows Christ is the man who says, I am able, whatever the cup may be. It may be true in some sense that he is not able; but the venture of his faith, the heroism that dares, the passionate abandonment of himself to high enterprise, that is what the Lord is ever seeking. When a man says, I am able, in that spirit, even though he is not able, he will be able before the Lord has done with him. Let there be that heroic abandonment of everything, refusal to count the cost, that says, I am able; then the Lord will immediately look into the eyes of that man and say, You shall!

So we touch immediately on the response of the Son of God. Observe with great care, speaking generally of the response of Jesus to this word of James and John, that there was in it not a single touch of anger, not a single note of scorn. Let me emphasize that. I think if I had dealt with James and John (and that is the word, *dealt* with them—how fond we are of *dealing* with people) I would have shown them the unutterable folly of their request. I would have shown them their amazing stupidity. But there was no touch of anger, no suspicion of scorn, in the answer of the Lord. Let me very carefully illuminate this story by an earlier one. There was an occasion when Jesus answered in anger, when He answered, as it seems to me, with a touch of scorn. There was a moment when He said, "Get thee behind Me, Satan: thou art a stumbling block unto Me." That was when a man said in the presence of the Cross, Not that, not the Cross. But to these men who in answer to His question, "Are ye able to drink the cup that I am about to drink?" said, "We are able," there was no such rebuke. His anger was for the man who was not prepared to follow along the shadowed, mysterious way of the Cross. There is no anger toward these men. These men were very foolish! Yes, that is what you said about that girl who desired to leave her home and go to the foreign mission field where the climate was likely to kill her. It is exactly the same thing. When the soul faces heroically the drinking of the cup in comradeship with the suffering of the Son of God, even though that soul does not understand all it is doing, the high resolve, the noble purpose, the fine abandonment, hear from the King only an answer of great tenderness.

Then I pray you observe how the Son of God responded. He revealed their ignorance, He honored their heroism, and He indicated the line of their responsibility.

He revealed their ignorance by the declaration, "Ye know not what ye ask." That was not a rebuke, it was a statement. Then He helped them to understand what they were asking, and He did it by illustration. He brought them back to the beginning, "Are ye able to drink the cup?" He recalled them to His previous teaching, when He told them that He must go to Jerusalem and that there He must suffer and be killed and that He must be raised again, that He Himself was to become a son of thunder through suffering, death, and resurrection. So He revealed their ignorance to them.

Then they replied, "We are able," and He immediately honored their heroism. He admitted them to the fellowship of His sufferings—"My cup indeed ye shall drink." I am well aware that there are senses in which they never drank His cup, there are senses in which He drank the cup of unutterable, unfathomable sorrow alone; but it is equally true—and the New Testament is full of it, the epistles reveal it and teach it—that He did, and He does, admit those who follow Him to some share in His sufferings: "That I may know Him, and the power of His resurrection, and the fellowship of His sufferings," . . . "fill up on my part that which is lacking of the afflictions of Christ." These are the words of a man who came to understand his Lord and who was wonderfully admitted into fellowship in the travail that makes the Kingdom come. So our Lord said to these men, "My cup indeed ye shall drink." How verily they did! For one of them it was swift, sudden martyrdom by Herod's sword. For the other, the long, lonely exile in Patmos: "I, John your brother in affliction." Yea, verily, they drank of His cup.

But in that moment when He admitted them to fellowship with His suffering He admitted them also to the triumph of His glory. When in response to His challenge they said they were able to drink of the cup of His sufferings, the cup that was even then being pressed to His holy lips, in that moment He admitted them to resources of power, vision, virtue, victory. Then He admitted them to the forces that would make them sons of thunder, men of power, men of authority in the spiritual Kingdom.

He not only revealed their ignorance and honored their heroism, He indicated their responsibility. First by suggestion as He talked to them; and then by interpretation as He talked to the ten.

By suggestion; "My cup indeed ye shall drink: but to sit on My right hand, and on My left hand, is not Mine to give, but for whom it hath been prepared of My Father." Thus He suggested that the places are for those for whom they are prepared; and He confronted them with the cup, and left them uncertain about the positions of power; confronted them with the travail, and uttered no final word as to how they should be prepared for prominent places of power and position in His Kingdom, save only that He told them these were prepared by the Father.

The ten were indignant, and made their protest; and Jesus called them to Him, and interpreted the suggestion He had made to the two as He contrasted authority in the Gentile kingdom and authority in His own Kingdom. The perpetual law of power in the Kingdom is that of disrobing, stooping, bending, serving. The man who stoops the lowest rises the highest. That was Jesus' final word.

Of all this wonderful incident the ultimate is found in the words with which our Lord ended His instruction to the ten, those great, wonderful words that have in them so much of music, so much of the thunder of mystic power, that I hardly need do other than read them: "The Son of Man came not to be ministered unto, but to minister, and to give His life a ransom for many."

Lord, suffer us to sit, one on Thy right hand, and the other on Thy left hand in Thy Kingdom. Yes, the Son of Man is coming into a Kingdom; but He will enter into His Kingdom, not by compelling men to serve Him, but by stooping to serve men. How near to the Kingdom of God are we in the Church? How near are we in our theologies to an understanding of this strange, wonderful law of the Kingdom of God? Are we not yet thinking and preaching as though our Lord is demanding service from men? He says, No, "the Son of Man came not to be ministered unto, but to minister." Change the words, simple as they are, and use simpler ones. The Son of Man came, not to compel men to serve Him, but to serve them. This is His way to His Kingdom. Not by enlisting recruits, but by Himself enlisting to serve, is this Son of Man coming into His Kingdom. That is a strange and puzzling thing to human nature. That troubled John the Baptist and made him send the question, "Art Thou He that should come, or look we for another?" What art Thou doing? Gathering no army, consulting no committees, prosecuting no great propaganda! What art Thou doing? Walking about, serving people, binding up the broken-hearted, going to a village to help a suffering soul, spending long hours talking to one man! What was He doing? Serving. "The Son of Man came not to be ministered unto, but to minister, and to give His life a ransom for many." Let James and John, the ten, the twelve, the whole Church, hear this: His way into the Kingdom is the way of service, and service that shall crown itself in sacrifice; He is crowned by life, not preserved, but given as a ransom for many.

So with His followers. The disciples of supreme power are those of the lowliest service. I go back a little to look at James and John. Our Lord was on His way to Jerusalem, and going through a Samaritan village He fain would tarry there; but the Samaritans knew that His face was set toward Jerusalem, and they would have none of Him. Then James and John said, Let us call down fire from heaven to consume them! They were not sons of thunder then! They thought they were. So do we still when we curse those in opposition. But later James passed to hidden service, as one of the twelve on whom the Spirit fell, and at last to martyrdom. So he became a son of thunder. John went to Ephesus to write love letters tremulous with Divine affection, saturated with Divine compassion, musical with Divine tenderness; and on to Patmos, brother of all afflicted souls. So he became a son of thunder, a man of power, of authority. They learned the secret of service and of sacrifice through suffering.

The passion for power Jesus does not rebuke. It is a high and noble moment when we look Him in the face and say, Master, make us men of power in fellowship with Thee, let us sit at Thy right hand in the Kingdom, let us be close to Thee in the exercise of authority. It is a high and noble aspiration.

But the way of fulfilment is always the same. You must come with Me, says the Lord, drink this cup, and abandon all your rights; and girding yourselves with humility as with a slave's apron, pour out your lives in serving others. You will be misunderstood; they will smite you on the cheek! You will be misinterpreted; they will spit on you, scourge you, laugh at you, bruise you! But so you will rise to power. All this, the story is saying to me, to my shame. God help us together to catch the vision of the way to power, and help us to consent.

CHAPTER IX

THE GREAT COMMANDMENTS

One of them, a lawyer, asked Him a question, tempting Him, Master, which is the great commandment in the law? And He said unto him, Thou shalt love the Lord thy God with all thy heart, and with all thy soul, and with all thy mind. This is the great and first commandment. And a second like unto it is this, Thou shalt love thy neighbour as thyself. On these two commandments hangeth the whole law, and the prophets.
MATTHEW 22:35-40.

IT WAS A DAY OF QUESTIONS AND ANSWERS IN THE FINAL MINistry of Jesus. The last hours of His life were approaching. His enemies were closing about Him. The hour and power of darkness were at hand. Yet never did He stand out more clearly in matchless wisdom than in this dark hour. They had come to Him with the challenge of unbelief, questioning Him as to His authority, and He had replied to their inquiry in such wise as to silence them. They had come to Him in the spirit of political worldliness asking Him whether it was lawful to pay tribute to Cæsar or not. Compelling them to produce the current coin of the realm, the Roman denarius, He had uttered a word so full of philosophy that it abides until this time as the central teaching for all men who would relate the affairs of state to the affairs of the Kingdom of God. The rationalistic Sadducees had come with their pre-eminently foolish question concerning marriage and the resurrection, and He had so answered them as to rebuke them and silence them—or to be quite accurate and to translate the Greek word literally, the Saducees were *gagged*, and asked Him no more questions.

Then it was that the lawyer spoke to Him, asking Him the most subtle of all the questions, "Which is the great commandment?" The Greek word translated "which" in this question is qualitative rather than quantitative, so that what the lawyer really asked was, What is the nature of the great commandment?

On an earlier occasion, according to Luke, a lawyer had come to Jesus, asking Him, "What shall I do to inherit eternal life?" and the Master had replied, Thou knowest the commandments. "What is written in the law? How readest thou?" The lawyer had answered in these very terms, "Thou shalt love the Lord thy God with all thy heart, and with all thy soul, and with all thy strength, and with all thy mind; and thy neighbour as thyself." Jesus replied to him, "Thou hast answered right: this do, and thou shalt live." It may be that the question of the lawyer in the present text was the outcome of that earlier episode. The question was simply, What is the nature of the great commandment, as though there were no difference of opinion as to which was the great commandment. The wisdom of our Lord's reply is revealed in the fact that He quoted from the law, for these words are found in the law of Moses. In Deuteronomy we have the first, "Thou shalt love the Lord thy God with all thine heart, and with all thy soul, and with all thy might," and in Leviticus, the second, "Thou shalt love thy neighbour as thyself." Thus our Lord replied to the question by quoting the commandments, and the very two that a lawyer on a previous occasion had quoted as summarizing the whole law. To that quotation He added the declaration, "On these two commandments hangeth the whole law, and the prophets."

The Lord's answer was of the very nature of the question. The question was, What is the nature of the great commandment? Our Lord's reply was not, Thou shalt love the Lord thy God with *all* thy heart, and with *all* thy soul, and with *all* thy mind; but Thou shalt love the Lord thy God with thy *whole* heart, and with thy *whole* soul, and with thy *whole* mind. If you suggest that this is a distinction without a difference, I would point out that it is a difference between quantity and quality. *All the heart* is quantity; the *whole* heart is quality. Just as in the prophecy of Malachi it is not, Bring *all* the tithes into the storehouse; but Bring in the *whole* tithe. It is possible for a man to bring all the tithes, to be mechanically, mathematically accurate in his giving; and yet he does not bring the whole tithe unless he bring in the true spirit and for the true reason, thus introducing into the activity and attitude the spiritual element, which is the supreme. Our Lord does not merely ask for *all* of anything; He asks for *the whole.* The question was qualitative, What is the nature of the great commandment? The answer was qualitative: obedience must be qualitative. Speaking of the essential, spiritual man, the Lord declared that he must love with all the complex instrumentality of personality, with the whole heart, life, mind; heart, life, mind constitute instrumentality. Personality was addressed, and it was claimed that love must be with all the instrument, and that in the entirety of each part.

We turn from that examination of the question as to its true nature, and from that brief and hurried examination of the method of our Lord's answer, that we may consider this declaration of Christ for our own profit. We shall therefore consider, first, these great commandments themselves; second, these great commandments in relation to ourselves, ending with a final word on the Master's last declaration that on these two hang all the law and all the prophets.

The first commandment is that man is to love God. We immediately find ourselves face to face with a difficulty. Some people are quite honest enough to confess to the difficulty. Can a man love God? To some of you I apologize for the question; it sounds almost absurd! Yet, on the other hand, there are those who quite honestly say, I cannot love God. I think the difficulty is the result partly of misunderstanding of the meaning of love, and partly, and perhaps more immediately, the result of the fact that the men who say it do not know God. To know God is to love Him. One of the old writers has said, "Love consists in approbation of and inclination toward an object that appears to us as good." Whether that covers the whole ground I am not prepared now to discuss, but it does cover the ground of this particular question as to what loving God really is. Loving God consists in approbation of and inclination toward Him as we know Him to be good. Love of God must therefore be the outcome of knowledge of God. I can understand that the man who has no knowledge of God, no understanding of Him, no conception of God other than that which speaks of infinite intelligence and infinite power working together in the universe, will have no love for God—respect, reverence, awe, fear, yes, but not love. No man loves God who discovers Him only through nature. According to Paul, men are not left without witness concerning God, even though they have never had any direct revelation from God; for in the things that are created, said the apostle, man may discover the wisdom and divinity of God, man may discover, that is, the intelligence and the strength of Deity. As has often been pointed out, that truth has been reaffirmed within the last generation by the great physical scientists, who have admitted that there is to be discovered throughout nature a double-faced intelligence and power in mysterious and wonderful co-operation. But love is never born in the heart of man toward God by that discovery.

It is only when we turn from nature, not to neglect its message, not to undervalue the speech that day utters to day and night proclaims to night, but to listen for another voice and to hear what God says to man, not through the mediation of nature, but through the mediation of the Son of His love, that men come to such knowledge of God that love is created in their hearts.

Men are suffering to-day from mistaken notions of God. I am not speaking of the heathen. I am not even speaking of the great indifferent masses who are outside the churches. There are scores of people who are worshiping God reverently, and yet do not love Him. The reason is to be found in the fact that their conception of God is a false conception. They think of Him as a King, jealous with a jealousy that is entirely human and earthly, capricious in His dealings with the human heart, and stern and holy with the holiness that is the essence of cold morality, forevermore watching men only as the custodian of some eternal principle of righteousness, and waiting to punish the man who breaks the law. I for one could have no love for such a God. I do not believe any man can love such a God.

What, then, is God according to the Biblical revelation? The whole answer is contained in one of the shortest sentences in the Bible: "God is love." When we have read the sentence, there are two things we need to do: first, to observe that the whole Biblical revelation harmonizes with the declaration; and, second, to interpret the declaration by the whole Biblical revelation.

To see how the Biblical revelation harmonizes with the declaration, I begin at the beginning. I open the first page of the first book and I have declarations full of light, full of poetry. When I say they are full of light and poetry I do not mean they are untrue. The story of the first chapters of Genesis is the story of processes by which a temporal dwelling place was prepared for man. I think there is another unwritten history of this world behind that history of Genesis. Forgive me for repeating that which I have so often said here: we have no story of creation in Genesis except in one sentence, "In the beginning God created the heaven and the earth." All that follows is not the story of creation, but of restoration. I see the orderly process, ever on, and ever on; and in it I see Divine love working and, with infinite care, preparing for the crisis, the advent of man created after the Divine image in the Divine likeness, a being whose central majesty is the awe-inspiring majesty of will. It is a love story, the story of love preparing for the coming of man.

Everything between that and the final apocalypse of the new heaven and the new earth, the new Jerusalem and the establishment of the Divine order, is the story of love set on the accomplishment of purpose, patiently waiting and bearing. It begins in the inquiry, "Adam, where art thou?" I never read that without thinking of what I once heard Dr. Henry Weston, of Crozier, say: That, said he, is not the call of a policeman, it is the wail of a father's broken heart! The story runs through all the history: love bearing all things, enduring all things, hoping all things, a love that never faileth, the only love that fulfils the ideal of our own greatest poet, "Love is not love that alters when it alteration finds." So in my Bible I watch love moving toward its goal until the final anthem is sung, "Fallen, fallen is Babylon the great." "The kingdom of the world is become the Kingdom of our Lord, and of His Christ." Then sorrow and sighing shall flee away, and He shall wipe all tears from human eyes. The God of the Bible is the God of Love.

I must also interpret the declaration by Biblical revelation. As I do so, I find that this God is a God of such love that He will make no truce with anything that can in any wise harm those on whom His love is set. The love of God is not weak, sentimental, anæmic; it is mighty, courageous, full of blood. It is love that will make no truce with sin in the individual life, in society, in the race, but forever fights against it in order that humanity may be delivered from the things that spoil and blast. "God is love," and over against that I set another declaration, "Our God is a consuming fire." Is that contradiction? No, it is exposition. He is consuming fire for the destruction of all that destroys, for the blasting of all that blasts, for the blighting of everything that blights. He will restore the years that the cankerworm hath eaten. How? By the destruction of the cankerworm. Judgment is the strange act of God, rendered necessary by the malady with which He has to deal; but from the beginning to the end the love story is the story of love that never flinches or trembles in cutting out the cancer in order that health may be restored. "God is love" is the great message of the Bible from beginning to end.

All the light is focused on the Cross. "God commendeth His love to usward in that while we were yet sinners Christ died for us." These are old and familiar words, so old and so familiar that, alas, we recite them almost without emotion; they glibly pass our lips and produce so little sense of awe and amazement. But as we ponder them and believe them, love for God is born in the heart. "We love because He first loved us."

If this command to love Him were given to men who knew Him only in the fulness of His power, in the infinitude of His wisdom, then it might be possible that they would say, We bow in reverence and in fear, but we cannot love. But when we add to the testimony of nature the testimony of the Son Who is in the bosom of the Father, then the answer of the soul is inevitably and invariably that of the hymn,

> Love so amazing, so Divine,
> Demands my soul, my life, my all.

The love of God produces love to God.

How, then, are we to know that God is love? In one way the answer already has been given, yet let us face the difficulty a little more carefully, for there are men who stand in the presence of the Cross, who yet cannot see in it the revelation of God's love. Let us be patient with them, for we find our way into an understanding of the love of God revealed in the Cross, not by declaration, but by a new attitude of soul, which is a venture of faith. God speaks to us through the Son, in His teaching, in His Cross, and in His Resurrection. He calls us, commands us, to follow Him, to believe on Him—that is, not to be convinced of a truth about Him, but to trust Him as an act of faith, to go after Him. When we commence to do so we find the terms of discipleship are of the severest, "Whosoever doth not bear his own cross, and come after Me, cannot be My disciple. . . . Whosoever he be of you that renounceth not all that he hath, he cannot be My disciple." We make the venture, obey and command, and in obedience we discover the beneficence of the command. By obedience we come into an understanding of the infinite love of the law. Browning never reached a higher height in all his singing than when he said,

> I report, as a man may, of God's work—all's love, yet all's law.

Law is found to be the expression of love when it is obeyed. Obedience to the command of Christ produces results in the life that demonstrate the love that inspired the command. That is the argument for the man who cannot see that God is love, or that love is proven by the Cross of Christ. At the beginning, the command to love God may be the command to discover God by obeying Him. I cannot love Him unless I know Him. "The Son which is in the bosom of the Father, He hath revealed Him." I have looked, and yet I do not love. I am not persuaded, not sure, I hesitate in fear on the brink. There are great problems in this Christian fact that trouble me intellectually, and I am holding back. The very Cross appals me rather than fills me with a sense of love. How shall I find Him? How shall I know?

By obedience, by testing Him. That is the supreme challenge of Christianity. If any man will go after God by the way of the Cross, that man will inevitably come to know Him in such a way as to compel his love. If a man will prove Him by obedience, and not discover Him as love, then that man will have the right to say he cannot love Him. But that man is not yet born! Many men imagine they are perfectly honest in intellectual difficulty, and they are, up to a point; but the ultimate appeal to the man in intellectual difficulty is: test this doctrine by testing it! No man will begin to obey the law of God spoken in the Son of His love but that he will come at last to know that the God Who speaks is love, and that the sternest things He says are the tenderest, sweetest things of His love. Thy right hand, cut it off, thy right eye, pluck it out; because thy right hand causes thee to stumble, because thy right eye causes thee to sin. He that loseth his life! Ah, that is what I do not want to do. I want to keep my life. I want to realize myself. I crave for the fulfilment of all the forces of my being. If any man would come after Me he must lose his life. A stern word, surely not the language of love! Listen again! "Whosoever shall lose his life for My sake, shall find *it*," his life. That is a strange paradox but it is the experience of the saints and of all who put their trust in Him. He shall find it, his own life. If I consent to lose it by abandoning it to Him, as King, Lord, Master, I find it, and the life I yielded I possess.

> I lay in dust life's glory dead,
> And from the ground there blossoms red
> Life that shall endless be.

We can know God only by obeying Him, making the venture, taking the first command that He lays on us and obeying it; by so doing we shall discover that the reason of the challenge is love and the way of obedience the way of realization. "Thou shalt love the Lord thy God." He can be loved only as He is known. He can be known only as He is obeyed.

The second commandment, Jesus said is like the first, and it is the outcome of the first. "Thou shalt love thy neighbour as thyself." What will inspire such love to my neighbor? Only the love of God. When love of God is removed from self to God then that love will seek the objects of God's love. When I see that my neighbor is as dear to the heart of God as I am, then, if God's love to me has won my love to Him, my love inevitably goes out to my neighbor. An illustration of that principle is found on a human level in that old sweet story of David. When David came into his kingdom he inquired, "Is there yet any that is left of the house of Saul, that I may show him kindness for Jonathan's sake?" Can you find me anyone Jonathan loved? If you find me anyone that Jonathan loved, I must love him. They found Mephibosheth, who was lame in both feet, and David took him to the royal palace, set him at the royal table, gave him the royal bounty, and loved him, all for the sake of Jonathan. I said it was an illustration on a low level; but it is a true level. When a man has seen God and his heart has gone out in love to God, he will turn and say, Are there any of the off-spring of God that I may love for the sake of God? That man will begin to love his neighbor as himself when his love for himself has been transferred to God and has come back in the mystery of the finding of himself in right relationship to God. Then a passion is born in his heart to go out and seek those who are missing the vision, the virtue, and the victory, and bring them back again to the Father's house and to true relationship with Him.

This love of neighbor is no sickly sentimental thing. For that reason I read from Leviticus. Christianity is supposed to be an advance on Hebraism; it is an advance on Hebraism; yet sometimes, when I pause to test the action of Christian people by the laws laid down for the Hebrews, I wonder! Did you notice how very practical that passage in Leviticus was? Thou shalt not glean the corners of thy field, but leave them for the poor. Thou shalt not gather the fruit that falls from thy vineyards and trees, but leave it for the needy. How about your gardens? How about your trees? It is quite impossible, you tell me; one cannot obey that kind of thing in this age. Then God have mercy on the age! Twitchell of Hartford, Connecticut, told me how, when war broke out between Spain and America, he preached on the advantages of war. Charles Dudley Warner sat and listened to him, and when he had done, said to him, "I would like to have moved a resolution, that in view of your sermon Christianity should be postponed to a more convenient season!" He was right if Christ and God are right. Loving your neighbor is not singing hymns about your neighbor, not holding religious sentiments toward your neighbor, not merely hoping that some day your neighbor will go through the pearly gates into heaven. Loving your neighbor is to pour out the life in sacrificial attempt to heal his wounds, rest his weariness, and lift him to the level on which God would have him dwell. Thou shalt love thy neighbor as thyself.

Glance again at these great commandments, and consider them relatively. I want to observe, first, that this inexorable standard of law cannot be lowered without the destruction of the life for which the law was made. If God abandon His requirements then all will be failure. No human life comes to perfection in any other way than by the perfect love of God. No human life ever comes to perfection of possibility that is loveless toward the neighbor. It is an inexorable law. God will brook no division of the man, either in heart or soul or mind; because that part of the heart or soul or mind that fails in love is atrophied, it will perish. The lover of God will love men; and he must, or he breaks the law of God and denies the love of God.

Yet hear again the great commandments and mark how reasonable they are. "With all *thy* heart, and with all *thy* soul, and with *all* thy mind"; not with thy neighbor's heart or soul or mind. If indeed it be true that your heart is a small thing, that your life is a weak thing, that your mind is a feeble thing, yet God is asking for that small heart, weak life, feeble mind. Only, I pray you, remember this, your heart is not so small as you have imagined, your life is not so weak as men have thought, your mind is not so feeble as you yourself have dreamed. If you will but love with all that you are, you will find enlargement of heart and life and mind in the power of love. Do not sigh through the days because you do not love God as someone else does. He does not ask you to love Him as someone else does. He asks you to love with all your heart. Just as I am, weak, poor, unworthy, I come in answer to the love of God, and begin to love, and that is all He asks.

Again, "Thou shalt love thy neighbour as thyself." There is room there for a whole sermon, "*as thyself*." How do I love myself? Remember that this must be conditioned by the first commandment. We are thinking of that love of self which is true and proper. My love of self in love of God becomes a passionate desire that I may be what God would have me be. That is the true love of self. "Thou shalt love thy neighbour as thyself," passionately desiring that he may be what God would have him be. Love of self does not make me blind to my shortcomings. Love of my neighbor does not make me blind to his shortcomings. True love of self makes me the enemy of the things that spoil me. True love of my neighbor makes me the enemy of the things that spoil him.

Mark this, the whole heart, mind, soul for God; for thy neighbor "as thyself" seeking that the whole heart, soul, and mind of thy neighbor shall harmonize in perfect response to the love of God, and so shall be fulfilled all the meaning and mystery of thy neighbor's being.

May I not affirm that if we know God the command is easy. God is lovable, because God is love.

> O God, of good the unfathomed sea!
> Who would not give his heart to Thee?
> Who would not love Thee with his might?
> O Jesus, Lover of mankind,
> Who would not his whole soul and mind,
> With all his strength, to Thee unite?

So sang a man who loved his God. It is the question of his astonishment that anyone can do other than love the Lord. That is the question of every man who in obedience to the law of God has discovered the love of God, and in whose heart and soul there springs responsive a new love to God.

Remember the final statement of the Lord. On these two depend all the law and the prophets. Take the word simply as it referred to the ancient economy: the whole expectation of the Mosaic economy is fulfilled by the man who loves God; the prophets, their denunciation of sin, their call to righteousness, are obeyed in answer to the impulse of the love of God. The new fear of God, which is the beginning of wisdom, is love of God. The old fear of God, which was the beginning of unutterable folly, was slavish fear, fear born of ignorance of Him, fear that made men hurry away, banish His name, refuse to meet Him. The new fear is not fear that He will hurt me, it is fear lest I should hurt Him, fear lest I cause sorrow to His heart, fear lest my sin wound Him again. That is the fear that is the beginning of wisdom, and that is the fear of love.

So God claims and calls for love, and He enforces His claim and argues His call by His own great love. You say to me to-night, I do not love God. Then act as though it were true that He loves you; obey Him, follow Him, and you will discover in the pathway of obedience that He is love. "Seek first His Kingdom," kiss the scepter of the King, and you will find that on the throne is the Father of infinite compassion.

CHAPTER X

THE EVANGEL OF GRACE

The gospel of the grace of God.

ACTS 20:24.

THE TEXT IS NOT A COMPLETE SENTENCE; IT IS ONLY A PHRASE, but what a phrase it is! The mere reading of it lifts the soul to the highest levels of thought; the horizons are set further back, and the sense of the spirit is that of space, beauty, and strength.

The three outstanding words suggest the supreme things of man's hope and confidence: Gospel, Grace, God. The seven words leave the three shining in a connected glory: "the Gospel of the Grace of God." The music is in an ascending scale. "The gospel," and the word is suggestive of hope and expectation, "of the grace," and immediately we are in the presence of the mystic melodies that merge into the ultimate harmonies: "of God," and once again the music ascends into the sublimity of unuttered silence. "The gospel of the grace of God."

"The gospel," good news as to the things that are possible to sinning men, to the sons of sorrow, to souls burdened with the silences of the unexplained things. Grace, the attitude and activity making these things possible to the sons of men. God, the source whence all the gracious gospel proceeds.

"The gospel of the grace of God"—not a sentence, but a phrase. Yet what a phrase, a phrase which is in itself a theme, a phrase which I reverently affirm might be written on the cover of the Divine Library as its title, "The gospel of the grace of God": a message, the supreme burden of all Christian preaching and teaching, from the days of our Lord Himself, through the period of apostolic exposition, and on through the centuries of prophetic utterance, evangelistic appeal, and perpetual application, and a burden to all such as have entered experimentally into the things suggested by the phrase.

The phrase was used by Paul at Miletus in his farewell to the elders of the church at Ephesus. He was on his way to Jerusalem. At the time his experience of the communion of the Holy Ghost was that of the Spirit's witness that bonds and affliction awaited him. The sky was dark with gathering clouds of trouble, yet he did not count his life dear to him, but he did count it of supreme importance that he should fulfil his ministry of testifying to the gospel of the grace of God. He had received that ministry in personal experience, and by the direct, immediate command of his Lord. This is his own account of how it was received: "The Lord said, I am Jesus Whom thou persecutest. But arise, and stand upon thy feet: for to this end have I appeared unto thee, to appoint thee a minister and a witness both of the things wherein thou hast seen me, and of the things wherein I will appear unto thee; delivering thee from the people, and from the Gentiles, unto whom I send thee, to open their eyes, that they may turn from darkness to light, and from the power of Satan unto God, that they may receive remission of sins and an inheritance among them that are sanctified by faith in Me." Thus, according to his own account, in those solemn hours of first communion with the risen and glorified Lord he had been called to testify to "the gospel of the grace of God." His first preparation for this work was his own experience of that gospel as it was revealed to him, not by an apostle, but in the Person of the Lord Himself. Now, after a period of well nigh a generation of faithful service, he was looking back over the way, and he crystallized the burden of his wonderful apostolic ministry into this phrase, "the gospel of the grace of God."

What is that gospel? The text does not declare it; the text refers to it. I cannot take this text and deal with it statement by statement; for while it is flashing with the splendor of the central words of Christianity, it makes no statement, but it assumes the burden of the apostle's ministry, the message of all Christian prophets, the great love story of the evangelists, "the gospel of the grace of God."

I have already touched on the significance of the words by way of introduction. I refer to them briefly again. The gospel is good news. There is not a note of anger in this message. There is no syllable of judgment within this gospel. It may be necessary sometimes to strike severer notes, and to tell foolish, wayward men what must be the inevitable result of refusing to listen to the message of the gospel; but no condemnation is in the gospel itself, it is the way of escape from condemnation. There is no judgment here, it is the message of the infinite compassion and mercy of our God.

It is good news of grace. Grace defies definition as surely as love defies definition, and as certainly as God defies definition. Grace is love in itself and in all its abounding activities, and love is God in Himself and in all His wondrous attributes. Who, then, can define grace? In its application to human need our fathers defined grace perfectly when they declared that grace is free, unmerited favor. But grace existed before favor was needed. Grace was in the heart of God before it was necessary that it should be operative in the interests of men. There is no definition of grace save by the way of the activity of grace. I know what grace is when I observe what grace accomplishes. I understand the real meaning of the grace of God only when I am brought to an apprehension of what grace does. So, leaving the word in its mystic glory, in that mystery which is revelation, and that revelation which ever enfolds itself again in infinite mystery, we proceed to inquire what grace has done for its own self-revelation.

I propose to say three things concerning this inclusive gospel. First, the gospel of the grace of God is a declaration concerning the attitude of God toward sinning men. Second, the gospel of the grace of God is a revelation of the activity of God on behalf of sinning men. Finally, the gospel of the grace of God is a proclamation of the fact that man, sinning man, may be accepted by God.

But let it be remembered that the gospel of the grace of God is centered in the Son of God, "The beginning of the gospel of Jesus Christ, the Son of God," so opens one of the evangelists' stories. If it be the gospel of the grace of God it is the gospel of the Son of God. This good news to humanity has come through the Son of God. There is no gospel to be found anywhere for sinning men apart from the Son of God. There is no gospel in nature; law is there; beauty, glory, strength, are there. As I observe nature I discover God in His might and in His wisdom. I so discover God in nature that I am quite able to sing with the psalmist in profound astonishment,

> When I consider Thy heavens, the work of Thy fingers,
> The moon and the stars which Thou hast ordained;
> What is man, that Thou are mindful of him?

The glory of God revealed in nature is such that I am amazed as I think within my own limited experience of myself that God can have any thought for me, or visit me; but when, turning my eyes from the wonders of the Divine revelation in nature, and looking within, I know my sin, not merely the inherited poison, but the actual rebellion, that I myself have chosen evil when I have known good, I turn back to nature and I ask for good news, I find that nature has no good news for the one who breaks law! To break law is to be broken by law. To sin against the rhythmic operations of nature is to be ground to powder by the magnificent forces of nature. There is no gospel in nature. Poets may tell you that nature weeps. Nature has no tears of pity for the breaker of law. We speak of the gentle kisses of the sun. The sun on the man who breaks law is scorching, flaming, destructive. There is no gospel in nature.

There is no gospel in human religion. Human religion may be perfectly sincere. Human religion may have certain values. These things I am not now discussing. But there is no gospel in human religion. The sincerest souls of men that have groped after some form of religion have confessed that they found no gospel. The ultimate note is always one of hopelessness. After many reincarnations the soul at last may reach forgetfulness, nothingness, loss of individuality! That is not a gospel. It may be the last speculation of despair; but there is no gospel in it. There is no gospel in human religion.

If we would have a gospel we must come to the Son of God, for it is only in and through Him that we hear its music, know its promise, or are brought to understanding of all its gracious facts and forces.

This gospel of the grace of God, which is the gospel of the Son of God, is the declaration of the attitude of God toward men. In this regard Christ is Revealer. Christ did not come into this world of ours in order to create a new attitude on the part of God toward man. He did not come to change the mind of God. He did not come to persuade God to be gracious. He did not come to propitiate God, and turn Him back again to the sons of men. He did not come to reconcile God to man. There is never a note in all the New Testament that declares He did. I care nothing for the casuistries in which you tell me that if I am reconciled to God it is the same thing. It is not the same thing. It is a fundamentally false conception of the mission of our Lord and of the terms of the gospel to declare that Jesus Christ came into human history to change the mind of God. He came to reveal to man the mind of God, to reveal the abiding attitude of God toward men. In Him God was unveiled, not changed. Through Him God spoke no new message, but the perpetual message of His heart. The gospel of the grace of God is first of all a declaration on the part of our Lord of the attitude of God toward men.

Is it possible to summarize that declaration in brief phrases? I shall attempt to summarize by saying that in the declaration there are three things. The gospel declares God's love for the sinner. The gospel declares God's hostility to the sin of the sinner. The gospel declares God's determinate counsel and purpose to make possible the canceling of sin, in order to gain the peace and the purity of the sinner.

In the first place, the gospel declares that God's attitude toward the sinning man is that of love. That is fundamental. All this gospel is contained in that one verse, the simplest and profoundest in all the New Testament, the most familiar to this congregation, and the least explored as to all its rich and varied values, "God *so* loved the world, that He gave His only begotten Son." The gospel reveals the fact that during these probationary days no man can put himself outside the love of God by whatever he may do. It is an old and familiar story; doubtless you have heard it from me: a Sunday-school teacher was asked by a boy in his class, Teacher, does God love naughty boys? The teacher said, No, certainly not. What blasphemy, unintentioned and quite thoughtless, but absolutely untrue! My dear Sunday-school teacher, that boy who worried you most today, God loves him, and loves him in his naughtiness. The gospel of the grace of God is, first, a declaration in the history of the world that God loves men however they have sinned, however far they have wandered, however deep the stain may be, however polluted is the heart. God loves men. Oh that we knew how to preach it, that we knew how to say it, that we knew how to proclaim it to men fast bound in sin and nature's night, this great and gracious fact, the first value of the gospel, its fundamental message: God loves the sinner in his sin.

If that be fundamental the resultant truth is that the gospel teaches us God's hostility to sin. That is not to contradict the first statement but to give true exposition to it. Because he loves man God cannot compromise with the poison that destroys. The intensity of the Divine hostility to sin is the Divine love for the sinner. The white heat of God's anger against every form of iniquity is the abiding fire of His infinite love for man. So that no man can be at peace with God and with sin at the same moment. The gospel declares that; that is its burden, its message. It was the message of the life of our Lord, the message of His perpetual teaching; it was the last and awful message of the Cross, that if a man be at peace with sin God is at war with him for very love of him. No man can be at peace with his sin and with God at the same moment. I do not say that no man can sin and be at peace with God. A man may be at peace with God, and yet blunder by the way, fall into sin, but the moment he has sinned the sin he is at war with himself and with his sin. That is evidence that he is at peace with God. The gospel reveals fundamentally the fact that God loves the sinner, and necessarily the resultant fact that God is at war with sin.

But that is not all the gospel declares concerning God. If the gospel did not reveal to us these attitudes, love toward the sinner, and hostility to sin, there is no message of hope in it. The attitude of God revealed in the gospel is an attitude essentially of purpose and of power in order that the sin against which His wrath is kindled may be removed, so that the sinner for whom His love burns may be delivered.

God cannot rest in the presence of sin without making possible its removal. That is the heart of the gospel, the reason of it; that is the grace of God. God hates sin, and therefore all the resources of His might and of His wisdom must provide a way of salvation, and the *must* depends, not on any human standard of right and wrong, not on any claim that man can have on God; the must depends on God's nature, His being, His heart; He must, because of what He is in Himself, make a way by which His banished ones may return, He must accomplish the possibility of human redemption. Grace in God is compassion, and compassion is sorrow, and compassion is passion in action.

The gospel of the grace of God is, first of all, a declaration of these attitudes toward men in their sin. It may be that unfallen angels need no gospel. It may be that in some sweet morning by and by, when we have done with the trammels of the flesh and have entered into that larger life, we shall discover other worlds peopled by wondrous beings of whom we have never heard, and of whom we have never dreamed, who never, never sinned, and therefore never needed a gospel. But the phrase of my evening message is a phrase for this world, sin-stricken, sin-smitten, a phrase for men who are conscious of evil in their own lives, of crimes committed, of sin permitted; and it unveils before the wondering and astonished sinner's sight the heart of God toward himself. Toward men who are out of time with the rhythm of the universe, who by their own pollution have introduced discord into its order. God is full of love, and hates only that in men which spoils them; and the moving of His compassion makes it necessary for Him—necessary, in order to be true to the profoundest, deepest things in His own nature—to make possible the putting away of sins that the sinner may be restored to the fulfilment of life.

Our second declaration grows immediately from our first. The gospel not only reveals the attitude of God, it declares His activity on behalf of sinning men. If compassion is passion in action, the gospel declares what that action is. Here, again, Christ is at the center. As He is the Revealer of the Divine attitude, He is the Redeemer in the Divine activity.

He came to accomplish in time and in human history the determinate counsel of God in eternity. He came from the Father, into the world, and returned to the Father. He came from the Father in order to carry out in human history and in time and in human observation for the purpose of the capture of the human will the things which are in the very nature of God, and which in the presence of sin, are eternal verities and not merely the accidentals of time.

Man awakened to a sense of his spiritual life is always awakened to the consciousness of sin. Man awakened to the consciousness of sin through being awakened to a sense of his spiritual life, looks back, looks in, and looks on. He looks back and there is with him the burden of the past; he remembers the sins of the years, and asks what can he do with them. He looks within and is conscious of the importance of the present, the inability not to do again the thing he did yesterday. The sin of yesterday, how it burns; like a phantom of the night it haunts the soul; in the gay hour of brightness and frivolity the sin of yesterday passes before the vision, and the sun is eclipsed and the whole world is plunged in darkness. But the agony of all agonies is that the man, conscious of that sin of yesterday as guilt, is yet more conscious that it is in him as power mastering him. He vows in the silence of the night that he will never sin the sin again and ere twenty-four hours have passed over his head he has sinned it, and knows he will sin it again, and yet again.

The guilt of the thing done yesterday, God have mercy on my soul, how terrible a thing is that! It is that sense of sin that the greatest master of English poetry expressed in the tragic and awful language of Lady Macbeth, "Out, out damned spot." You do not need to go to a theater to see that acted, it is acted in your own soul. Yes, but keener than that, more terrible is this, that I shall put another stain there, and I cannot help it! That is the tragedy of sin.

With that sense of the past on the soul, and the sense of

present incompetence weighing on the spirit, the eyes are lifted to the great future with its terrors; they are inevitable, they are the results of these things of yesterday and today, the guilt of past sin, the power of present sin; all the future is lurid with the gray of gathered thunder clouds. That is the tragedy of a soul conscious of sin! If the gospel is worth anything it must deal with all that.

"The gospel of the grace of God" first proclaims pardon for the sinner, the forgiveness of sins. You tell me it is a moral impossibility, and over against your moral impossibility I place the mystery of the Cross. If you can explain the Cross in the terms of time, if you reduce the Cross to the level of a Roman gibbet on a green hill in Palestine and a dying man, of course it can never deal with moral guilt to the satisfaction of a human soul, to say nothing of the satisfaction of an eternal, holy God. But when the Cross is seen as a mystery, a mere unveiling in time of that which is eternal in principle, an unveiling in the awfulness of a vulgar tragedy in blood of the breaking, crushed heart of the God Who suffers because men sin, then I begin to feel that the spot will come out, I begin to know what can be expressed only in the imperfect language of material symbolism, but which is in itself the essential mystery of redemption, "The blood of Jesus Christ cleanseth us from all sin." The gospel reveals the Divine passion, pain, agony, sorrow, whereby the past is canceled, made not to be, put away, forgiven.

But that is not enough, I must be superlative; this is a superlative theme. I will speak for myself. Hear me as a witness rather than as an advocate. It is not enough that the thing I did yesterday is forgiven. Unless the power that compelled me to do it is broken within me, it is not enough. If the message for the past is the mystery of the Cross, the message for the present is the might of the resurrection. The one lonely, supreme event in human history is that He rose from among the dead, and that by way of that resurrection He revealed to men the fact, not only that His life was perfect, and that by His passion it is possible for Him to forgive sin, but that His life, perfect within itself, bruised in the mystery of the great atoning work, is liberated that it may be bestowed upon sinning men, that they may share His purity in power, and that by living relationship with the risen Lord they may obey His sweet and mighty word, "Go and sin no more." The gospel proclaims not merely pardon for the past, it proclaims power for the present. If not, it is not a sufficient gospel. But it is sufficient. The witnesses are here. It is not the habit to call witnesses in this building; I sometimes wish it were, but they are here, men and women, young men and young women, who know that the power of Christ is equal to snapping chains, putting out fires, and setting their feet in the high way of holiness that leads to life.

The witness of the power is the demonstration of the pardon. If I preached simply the great mystery of the Cross whereby men are pardoned, and then I saw men who professed to believe it continue in their sin, I would doubt my gospel. But when the process from pardon is that of power over sin, then I am convinced of the actuality of the pardon our Lord pronounces.

Finally, has the gospel anything to say to me about tomorrow? For I call the testimony of the saints, wherein I bear my part, that whereas we know the joy of sin forgiven and whereas in part we know the power that triumphs over sin, we also have to say, as this same apostle said when he wrote to his Philippian children, I am not yet perfected, I have not yet apprehended that for which I was apprehended in Christ. Is there to be ultimate deliverance? Is there to be a day of full realization? Will all the powers of my personality one day harmonize with the good and perfect and acceptable will of God? Let my question be answered from the same letter.

He has already said, "Not that I have already obtained, or am already made perfect. . . . I count not myself yet to have apprehended." But he did not sit down and sigh. What did he do? "One thing I do, forgetting the things which are behind, and stretching forward to the things which are before, I press on towards the goal." What goal? Read to the end of the great paragraph. He speaks of a day in which the Lord shall "fashion anew the body of our humiliation, that it may be conformed to the body of His glory." That is the last and final perfecting of the life. All my life, mysterious, complex, made more wonderful than ever by the revelation of His gospel will harmonize with Himself, and I shall see God and be satisfied, and shall stand unashamed in the light of the heavenly spaces: "He shall present me faultless before the throne of His glory."

The last word may be spoken very briefly. "The gospel of the grace of God" not only reveals the attitude and proclaims the activity of God, it declares the acceptance of men by God; Jesus Christ is the Revealer and the Redeemer, therefore He is the Reconciler. He came to bring God to man's consciousness, and to bring man to God's fellowship. If God may be brought to the actual consciousness of man, then man will be brought to fellowship with God.

This phase of our gospel again is threefold. It declares, first of all, our reception by God in and through Jesus Christ, in Christ Jesus made nigh, accepted in the Beloved. Such are the rich and gracious phrases of the New Testament revelation.

It declares also our regeneration, re-creation. In Christ Jesus we are made one with the Father, "partakers of the Divine nature." He Who condescended in infinite mystery to tabernacle in flesh as the result of the operation of that incarnation consents to tabernacle in flesh to-day, "Know ye not that your body is the temple of the Holy Ghost?"

Consequently, acceptance with God means renewal in

Christ Jesus; we are heirs of God, and therefore all His resources are at our disposal, and so we "grow up into Him in all things."

We may be acquainted with the terminology of the gospel, with the terms of the gospel, yet we may be lost. It is not enough to hear the evangel. It is not enough to apprehend some of its spacious meaning. If you will go back in that address of Paul to the elders of the church at Ephesus you will find the conditions on which men may enter on all the virtues and values of the great gospel. "Repentance toward God and faith toward our Lord Jesus Christ," repentance, change of mind which is active, determined. The gospel is the message that calls men to that. "Faith toward our Lord Jesus Christ," the attitude and activity of risk, venture. The gospel is the argument for that.

What of my yesterday? Jesus promises me pardon, forgiveness. What of my present incompetence? He declares that He has power sufficient to enable me to go and sin no more. What of to-morrow? He illumines to-morrow with the promise of His own advent and of my resurrection and of ultimate fulfilment of all God's purpose in my creation.

Shall I venture on Him? Shall I make trial of His word? And the answer yes is the activity of faith. When a man hearing the gospel shall answer its call to repent, and its argument for faith, then, presently, "the gospel of the grace of God" shall be to that man not theory merely, but the joy of his life, the strength of his endeavor, the peace and assurance of his soul.

CHAPTER XI

TONGUES LIKE AS OF FIRE

The Symbol of the Church

And there appeared unto them tongues parting asunder, like as of fire; and it sat upon each one of them.
ACTS 2:3.

THE DAY OF PENTECOST HAD COME. THE WEEK OF WEEKS had run its course. Nine and forty days had passed since Passover. Devout men from every nation under heaven were at Jerusalem for this Feast of Weeks, and in an upper room a few men, insignificant, and yet chosen in the economy of God as witnesses for the initiation of a new world movement, took part in the fulfilment of that of which Pentecost, the Hebrew Feast, had been but a shadow. The Teacher and Master of these men had been crucified at Passover, and by His crucifixion all their hopes had been destroyed, all their aspirations disappointed, their very faith in His ability to do what they had hoped He would do shaken to the foundation, indeed had collapsed. Their faith in Him personally had never faltered, their love of Him had never failed; but by that Cross it had been demonstrated to them in such a way that they found no appeal from the demonstration that He could not set up His Kingdom, and so they had been scattered.

Then the supreme and arresting wonder of the Resurrection had been the means of gathering them together again. By that Resurrection their Lord and Master was declared to them to be far more than they had ever dreamed. He was the Son of God in a profounder sense even than Peter had understood when at Cæsarea Philippi he had confessed His Messiahship. By that Resurrection they were, to use the language of Peter himself in one of his later letters, begotten again unto a living hope. Hope had failed, faith had faltered, love had lived; but now in the resurrection glory hope was renewed, faith in His ability to accomplish His purpose was renewed, and love became nobler, purer, finer.

For many days He had tarried, always near at hand, though mystically and strangely. Sometimes absent from them; and then swiftly and without notice, present among them, right there, where they thought He was not. At other times walking with them by the way, sitting with them at the board; and then suddenly absent from them, not there, where they were quite sure He was. Such were the strange comings and goings of the forty days, appearances and disappearances, appearances in order to strengthen faith and to reassure them that He was alive, disappearance in order to train them to do without the bodily manifestation and the bodily presence.

Then He vanished out of their sight, and for ten days they had been waiting in the upper room. Jerusalem filled with the crowds, devout men from every nation gathering there: Parthians, Medes, Elamites, all with different accents, from varied localities, gathered for the Feast of Pentecost, for the Feast of Weeks. But the central fact of this particular feast was not wrought out in the temple courts, but in the upper room. It was a moment and an event of untold importance in the history of humanity. We are not gathered here simply to recall to our minds something that happened, or that men imagined happened, two millenniums ago. That which began then is going on still. New forces then began to come into action in human history which within a generation touched the whole known world; they moved the Roman world to its center, influenced the Greek world throughout all its great cities, and scattered the Hebrew world, and, spreading through all these, made revolutions everywhere.

In that hour, in the upper room in Jerusalem, the results of the life and death and resurrection of Jesus were beginning to be applied to the experience of individual souls. The light that broke upon these men in the upper room in that hour was a light in which they saw their Lord as they had never seen Him. The sound of the mighty rushing wind that filled the house where they were assembled was in some mystic sense a tone in which all the voices of the past became articulate with a new message; they heard the voices of other days merging into the ultimate harmony of the speech of the Son. In that upper room all the values, the virtues, and the victories of the life and death and resurrection of the Lord were made to them more than theories, they were rendered experiences. They were in that hour brought into new and vital relationship with Him such as they had never known in the days of His flesh, nor could have known. In that hour was fulfilled the word which Christ Himself had spoken in the upper room, and which had filled them with trouble at the time, "It is expedient for you that I go away: for if I go not away, the Comforter will not come unto you; but if I go I will send Him unto you. . . . When He, the Spirit of truth, is come, He shall guide you into all the truth. . . . He shall glorify Me: for He shall take of Mine, and shall declare it unto you." That promise was being fulfilled. The new economy of the Spirit of God in human history was beginning. The Church of God, the Christian Church of God, was born in that hour.

In this story there is no sentence or phrase which is not suggestive and worthy of the closest study. From it I select the one visible sign which was granted to these men in that hour of the new and special coming of the Holy Spirit: "Tongues parting asunder, like as of fire."

It is to be observed that the initial hours in this new economy were hours in which it was necessary that there should be certain signs drawing attention to the new facts and symbolizing those new facts. Thus there were the sound of the rushing, mighty wind, the sign of the disparting fire into the shape of tongues, and the accompaniment of the strange and wonderful gift of tongues, all which things were merely initial. All these things were sensual, that is, they appealed to the senses. They were introductory, initial, presently to be done away when the larger spiritual truth should be realized. That I think we need to remember. Just as, during the forty days prior to ascension there were signs appealing to the senses given to the disciples, the appearance and disappearances of Christ, all intended to train the disciples to do without these things; so in the first movements of the new era of the Spirit's operation there were signs granted, all intended to cease when they should no longer be needed. I believe that in the history of the Christian Church there have been eras when God has restored men by signs. He may be going to do it now, I do not know. But, remember, whenever it is so, it is in itself a sign of failure preceding it. Spiritual life on its highest level asks no sign, and needs none. Signs are only for the drawing of men spiritually dull into apprehension of spiritual things. God did, in the economy of infinite patience and unsurpassing grace, employ these signs at the beginning. From these earliest of signs, then, I take that of the visible token given to these men in the upper room.

Let us consider, first, the tongues which these men saw as being the true symbol of the Christian Church. Second, let us consider the material of the symbol, fire, in its valuable and important suggestiveness. Finally, let us consider the teaching of the fact that this is the symbol of the Church.

First, then, I ask you to observe that this was the moment when the Christian Church came into being. I would draw a most careful distinction between the Church and the Hebrew people. I know there are senses in which we may speak of them as constituting in a bygone economy the Church in the wilderness, the assembly, the ecclesia in the wilderness. But here was the birth of the Christian Church. In this moment the units were baptized by the Holy Ghost into unity. From this moment you have no longer a group of individual men brought near geographically, kept near sentimentally; but you have rather a number of units made near and one vitally by the baptism of the Holy Ghost. That is the Christian Church. The Christian Church is not a fortuitous concurrence of individuals admiring an ideal, or who decide, as among themselves, that they will obey an ethic. The Christian Church is a holy company of men and women who have been baptized by the Holy Ghost into living relationship with the Lord Jesus Christ. That baptism of the Spirit took place in the upper room, and these men became the Church. Coincidentally with that baptism they saw tongues parting asunder, as of fire; and by that token God gave unto them, and unto us for all time, the true symbol of the Christian Church. I sometimes feel that we have suffered almost incalculable loss in that we have forgotten this fact, and that the Church of God has made the gravest mistakes by selecting symbols other than the Divine one as representing herself and suggesting her nature and her mission. The Cross is not the symbol of the Christian Church; yet for generations we have made it our symbol, putting it upon our buildings, incorporating it into our art, wearing it as a sign. There are those who wear it as an ornament and at the same time live in ungodliness, that is blasphemy! I am not now thinking of these, but of devout souls who wear it as a sign. I think I am right in saying that the men's movement in the Episcopal Church wear as their sign a Maltese cross. There is a sense in which I like to see them, for I like anything that confesses definite Christianity—that is why I love the Salvation Army uniform—but the Cross is not the true symbol of the Christian Church. In the history of the Christian Church Satan never gained a more signal victory than in the hour in which he made men forget that the tongue is the true symbol of the Church.

Why is it that I thus affirm that the cross is not the symbol of the Church? Because the cross is not the final thing; absolutely necessary, no one will misunderstand me; but not final. The Cross was the instrument in time whereby sin did ultimately manifest itself, and God's central point wherein He did reveal the fact that grace is mightier than sin, and can triumph in love. "It is Christ that died, *yea rather, is risen again.*" If you would have a truer symbol, something nearer to the actuality of the case, you must have a symbol, somehow, of an empty grave with the stone rolled away; but even that is not final. The symbol which suggests at once the nature and office of the Church is the tongue of fire.

Think with me of how simple and remarkable a thing this is. Consider the symbolism of the tongue as apart from the fire. It is a theme I can only suggest, I have not the time, nor would it be the place generally, to discuss the power of the tongue. In the broadest outlook, I pray you remember that man is peculiar in his power in this fact, that he is endowed with language, and that through the medium of thought expressed in language, all things begin to be, of good and of evil, in human history. All the history of human advancement is the history of the use of the tongue. Behind it there is thought, but thought has ever been expressed powerfully and prevailingly by the tongue. Among men there are many different circumstances and surroundings, manners, and maxims and methods, laws and languages, but the fact of the ability to speak and to express by means of the tongue is universal.

Think for a moment of the power of speech. Think what a power the tongue has been in dealing with vast masses of people. Think of the more wonderful power of the tongue in dealing with individuals. Let me take an illustration from English political life. There is a man who is largely out of sight in English political life now, Joseph Chamberlain. I never heard him speak in public, that is my loss. Those who did, know how he was able to influence multitudes. But I have sat with him in quiet committee work, and there he was one of the strongest men in persuasive speech I have ever known. I have known him sit down with a committee of twelve men gathered around him, ten of whom came entirely opposed to his view. Before the hour was over twelve men voted for him. It was the power of speech, the power of a strong man, a strong thinker, having strong convictions, and able so to state his case as to communicate his convictions. You can have a strong man and strong thinking and strong conviction without persuading other men; but the power of speech is that of so presenting conviction and viewpoint as to capture other men. It is but an illustration. I take it from that sphere because I want to indicate the fact that this is one of the greatest powers of humanity, and because we have so largely lost sight of it in the Christian Church. The power of the tongue in the propagation of the evangel of Jesus Christ has been supreme. The history of preaching is in itself enough to make any man proud that God has called him to be a preacher. There is nothing mightier in the history of the world than the history of preaching. Let the mind travel back over the Christian era; mark the great hours, the new movements, the advancements, and you will always find the preacher there!

Think of the power of personal speech, expressing thought, repeating thought, arguing thought, until the central citadel is captured, bent toward the King, and made receptive of the evangel. There is no power like it. This whole company of men and women baptized into living union with the Lord Jesus Christ felt in the thrill of that new baptism the desire to speak, and the symbol of their new office was that of the tongues parting asunder, as of fire, and it sat upon each of them! The use of the tongue in the work of Jesus Christ is supreme, the Church's mission in the world is to make Him known, and she is to do it by the tongue, and that in a threefold exercise: the tongue of praise that sets His glory forth, the tongue of prayer that speaks to Him and through Him to the Father concerning all human need, the tongue of prophecy that declares to men the will of God. In that moment when the Spirit came there was created in history a new institute of praise, of prayer, and of prophecy. The Church of God became the central institute for the praising of His name, that in which all the praise of creation and of the world should become articulate. The Church of God became a new institute of prayer, that in which priests, intercessors, should find the right of way into the very sanctuary of the Most High to speak of the burdens of humanity, and plead the cause of the suffering and oppressed. The Church of God became a new institute of prophecy, an institute made up of men and women who should come from the secret place of the most high, where they had listened to the ways and the will of God, and passing out among men should proclaim that way and will, and declare the fact of His redemptive mercy.

But whether they praise or pray or prophesy, observe that the instrument is the tongue. In that symbol was focused the thought of the purpose of the existence of the Church on earth. The Church is to witness, to speak, in praise and prayer and prophecy, the great things into the experience of which she herself has come. That is the business of the Church, not the business of an order within the Church, but the business of the entire Church. Every individual member of the Church of Jesus Christ baptized into relationship with Him, sharing His life, feeling the thrill of His Spirit, desires to talk about it, unless that desire be quenched, refused, hindered until it perish. In that hour in which you first consciously yielded to the Lord, or felt the mastery of His Lordship, you desired to speak of the experience. I put it in the two ways because I think they cover two kinds of experience. There is a man here somewhere who could take me to the very spot where he gave himself to Christ, he could take me down to a pew in some chapel in the country and say, right there, on such a date, at such an hour, I gave myself to Christ. Another man here has no such experience, but there was some hour somewhere, somewhen, perhaps in the midst of ordinary life, when the consciousness of the relationship to Jesus Christ swept over his soul. Be the experience the first or the second, the first outcome of it was a desire to tell someone, generally the nearest and dearest; the father to tell his boy, the brother to tell sister, friend to tell friend, the desire to talk of these things. The tongue fired by the baptism of the Holy Spirit is God's method for proclaiming to the world the evangel of His Son, and it is the perpetual unchanging symbol of the Christian Church, the symbolic expression of the oft repeated word of our Lord, that we are witnesses.

Of course, as we have often seen, but which it is not our subject now to dwell upon, yet which ought to be mentioned, behind the witness of the lip there must be the witness of the life. But there must also be the witness of the tongue. Have you ever spoken to anyone about your Lord and Master? I should like to dwell upon it at some length. You will be very much surprised, if you begin to speak for your Lord, at how many men are eager to hear you that you thought cared nothing about Him. Talk to multitudes if God calls you; but if not, then to individuals: the power of the tongue in individual speech is ultimately more wonderful than the power of the tongue in dealing with vast audiences.

But now let us notice that the symbol is that of a tongue *like as of fire*. Let us read our Bibles accurately. Someone wrote to me recently that these were tongues of actual fire, and that men still received them, and knew it because they had experienced burning sensations in their bodies! As though men could ever apprehend a spiritual force carnally! It is the carnality of this modern movement that is its condemnation. "*Like as of fire.*"

One's mind travels back through the Bible and remembers how perpetually and fittingly fire is the symbol of God. This was so in the burning bush, the bush that was burned with fire but not consumed. Out of the mystic flaming glory of the burning bush there came the voice, "Put off thy shoes from off thy feet, for the place whereon thou standest is holy ground." When, presently, the devout, persistent inquirer asked what was the name of the God of the bush, the answer came, "I am that I am." The symbol of Himself by which He chose to arrest the attention of the shepherd in the wilderness was that of fire filling the bush, but not consuming it. The inclusive declaration of the New Testament is full of value: "Our God is a consuming fire." But if I would have the true interpretation of the fundamental suggestiveness of the symbol I go back once more to the passage I read from Isaiah, which can never be read, it seems to me, without producing in the soul a sense of majesty and awe. The young prophet was in the early part of his ministry, the throne of Judah was vacant for the first time in the life of the prophet: "In the year that king Uzziah died I saw the Lord sitting upon a throne, high and lifted up." What was the consciousness that came to the prophet's soul in the presence of the unveiled glory of God? "Woe is me! for I am undone; because I am a man of unclean lips and I dwell in the midst of a people of unclean lips." Then there flew one of the seraphim, and bringing the live coal from off the altar touched the lips of the man and said "Lo, this hath touched thy lips; and thine iniquity is taken away, and thy sin purged." After that came the challenge of God, "Whom shall I send, and who will go for Us?" and that man, his lips cleansed by fire, said, "Here am I; send me."

The symbolism of all that is not that the fire is mere inspiration or energy; it is a cleansing agent, it was to cleanse the lips of the man that the seraphim touched them with the live coal. Tongues of fire, the fire is that which cleanses the tongue. Let me read you something by way of contrast from the epistle of James:

"The tongue also is a little member, and boasteth great things. Behold, how much wood is kindled by how small a fire! And the tongue is a fire; the world of iniquity among our members is the tongue, which defileth the whole body, and setteth on fire the wheel of nature, and is set on fire by hell."

What a strange contrast! What an intended contrast! The tongue is an instrument, needing inspiration, always finding inspiration in fire to make it prevailing; and the fire is always either a polluting or a purifying force, which depends entirely upon whether the origin of the fire is the heaven of God or the hell that is underneath.

How powerful the tongue becomes when set on fire by hell. What mischief it can work in families! What mischief it can work in communities! What reputations it can blast and damn forever! What disaster it can work among the nations! A whispering tongue set on fire by hell can put two nations at war with each other.

Over against all that stands this symbol of the tongue of fire, holy fire, fire of the Divine Being, fire that cleanses, purifies, energizes, inspires with an influence high and holy and noble. What victories it can win! What breaches it can heal! What comfort it can bring! How it can knit man and man, and create the fellowship of believing souls! The tongue of fire—it must be of fire, and it must be of this fire.

That leads us to our last thought, the teaching of the symbol concerning the interrelationship between the tongue and the fire. The tongue is distinctly human, the fire is wholly Divine. The tongue of fire is the human instrument, surcharged, inspired by the Divine nature. It suggests the union of God and man for the specific purpose of witnessing, declaring, beseeching; as though God did beseech you by us, we pray you in Christ's stead, be ye reconciled to God. That can be said without producing any effect. It needs the tongue of fire to say it. The human word, the Divine power; the human speech and the Divine power, cleansing, revealing, persuading.

The phrase employed concerning the apportionment of the gift is suggestive. Tongues, plural, "like as of fire; and it," singular, "sat upon each of them." One fire parting asunder into tongues: "It sat upon each one of them," that is not merely a statement that upon each head there was a tongue of fire, but a statement that upon each head a tongue of that which was one fire.

Upon whom did the symbol rest? Upon men and women. And if you pass on, you have a quotation from Joel which Peter claimed to have been fulfilled in this experience: "Your sons and your daughters shall prophesy. . . . Yea, and on My servants and on My handmaidens in those days will I pour forth of My Spirit." What a revolutionary thing the coming of the Spirit of God is!

"Your young men shall see visions, and your old men shall dream dreams." Visions have to do with things that are still to come; dreams have to do with things that have happened. The old men in the power of the Holy Ghost shall speak of the past so as to enable us to understand it. The young men in the illumination of the Spirit shall speak of the future so as to enable us to act to-day. Tongues of fire.

What, then, are the great truths of this symbolism? That the Church is God's instrument of declaration and of witness. That every individual member of that Church is responsible in a measure for the proclamation of the power of the Holy Spirit. That human weakness is utter and absolute. That until there be the touch of fire there can be no proclamation that will prevail, but that there is no lack of equipment if we are in very deed children of God. Pentecost is not past; it is present. The day of spiritual power was not yesterday; it is to-day. While we have, and while we ask, no visible sign such as this, yet in this very hour of our worship we may have the presence and power of the selfsame Holy Spirit. In proportion as we realize what it is to be a member of Christ and of His Church, and are submitted to this indwelling Spirit, the Paraclete, the Advocate, the Comforter, in that proportion we shall be prepared to declare, announce, witness, and by the human tongue cleansed by the fire of God, inspired by the fire of God, He will win His victories and establish His Kingdom.

CHAPTER XII

MEN LOOKING FOR THEIR LORD

Let your loins be girded about, and your lamps burning; and be ye yourselves like unto men looking for their Lord.
LUKE 12:35, 36.

EVERY MAN HAS SOME CONCEPTION OF LIFE AS A WHOLE, A conception which affects all his attitudes and activities, even though at times unconsciously to himself. This is illustrated by the different figures of which we make use when speaking of life as a whole. We liken it to a race, to a voyage, to a pilgrimage, to a quest, to a warfare; and in every case a complete conception is presented to the mind by the figure of speech. Under the figure of a race we think not merely of the track along which men run, but of the goal which they desire to reach. Under the figure of a voyage we think not merely of the seas which men cross, but of the harbor which they fain would make. Under the figure of a pilgrimage we think not merely of the pathway which winds through the valleys and over the mountains, but of that city, the habitation which men fain would reach. Under the figure of a quest we think not merely of the diligent painstaking search, but of that glad hour when what is sought for is found. Under the figure of a warfare we think not merely of the clash of conflict, but of the crowning joy of the ultimate victory.

In every case, moreover, the ultimate is the inspiration of the immediate. Men run in order to win. Men are careful concerning the navigation of their passage in order that they may reach the harbor. Men are earnest in their prosecution of the pilgrimage, that they may finally come to the city of their desire. The diligence of the quest is inspired by the passionate desire to find what is sought. All the earnestness of the conflict is born of the passion for victory.

Every man, I repeat, has some conception of life. He may not express it figuratively; indeed he may never have formulated it for himself; perhaps he has never talked about it, never thought of it, on the surface of his thinking; and yet underneath that surface thinking he has some conception of what his life means to him. To some men life would seem to be a day of business, the goal of which is the amassing of wealth. To others life would seem to be one constant opportunity for pleasure, the intervals being filled with strenuous work in order to secure that pleasure. Whatever his conception of life may be, it determines the conduct of a man and affects all his relationships in this world. Conduct based on conception creates character, and a man will conform in character to what he makes his conception of life.

In this word of Jesus He reveals the true conception of life in the case of those who have yielded themselves to Him. It is the Christian conception, that is, the conception of the follower of the Christ, of whatever man has seen His beauty and heard His call, and responding to both, has passed under His direction, and shares in all the values of His redeeming work. According to our Lord's teaching, that man becomes in all the activities of his life, in all his relationships with his fellow men, in all the conduct of the passing days, a man looking for his Lord.

This conception is altogether too largely lost sight of by Christian men to-day. When Dr. Denney wrote his volume on the Thessalonian epistles he said some things that are very worthy of consideration. He declared that the bloom of beauty on apostolic Christianity was created by the upward look, by the fact that those early Christians did most certainly live, looking for the Lord. He went further and declared that where that expectant attitude is lost, the upward look abandoned, while there may remain very much of Christian strength, that bloom is lost. I believe all that to be most true and most important. Therefore I have turned this evening to this subject, and I shall ask you to meditate with me the conception of life which our Lord suggests; the attitudes of life which will result from such a conception, and the character which response to the conception will invariably produce.

First, then, what is this conception of life? Life becomes, according to this view, a period the duration of which, long or short no man knows, a period ending not with death but with the coming of the Lord Himself. According to this view, in that moment when a man yields himself to the Lord Jesus Christ, the boundaries of his life are changed for him. The boundaries of life to the man not yielded to the Christ are his birth and his death; that man looks back through the years to the day of his birth, the day of beginning; and he looks on speculatively, wonderingly, tremblingly toward the day of death; life is bounded for him by the day of birth and the day of death. To the Christian man the boundaries are altered. The boundary of his life begins with his first meeting with Jesus. In the hour when the Lord comes to him, in the hour of the Lord's first advent to his personal experience, life begins. The other boundary is the moment when the Lord shall come to him again, gathering him to be with Himself. All that is expressed by Paul in that one brief and wonderful word, "To me to live is Christ." Those are the words of a man who had lost count of all except that in his life which was Christ-conditioned. He said, in effect, after three and thirty years of personal comradeship with the Lord, Life began for me when Jesus apprehended me, "to me to live is Christ," He is the origin of my life. Before that first meeting with Christ I had other experiences, other ambitions, other values; but things that were gain I count loss, I blot them out, I cancel them; they are of no value. Life began for me, said the apostle in effect, when above the brightness of the sun, the Lord shone upon me and possessed my life. What is the other boundary of life for this man? According to his own writing in that same autobiographical chapter, it is the hour in which He shall fashion anew the body of our humiliation, that it may be conformed to the body of His glory. To all Christian men life's boundaries have thus been changed. Said the same apostle to the Thessalonian Christians, "Ye turned to God from idols"—such was the beginning—"to serve the living and true God"—such was the process—"and to wait for His Son from heaven"—such is the consummation. The coming of Jesus to the soul is the beginning of the Christian life, and it is to be consummated by His coming again.

This means that the goal of the life of the individual Christian is always out of sight. Finality is never reached, ambition is never fully realized in these passing days. It means that all other hopes are subservient to this one glorious hope of the coming of the Lord Himself, of looking into His face, of being changed into His likeness. That is to be the hour of supreme, perfect satisfaction in the experience of the Christian man. The man thus looking and waiting for the Lord is willing that every other hope should not be realized if but the interference shall be that of the glad hour of the Advent of the Master. The man waiting for his Lord recognized the larger hope in all the smaller; and the smaller hopes are forevermore conditioned by the larger. Every man here is living in the expectation of some event toward which he is moving in the ordinary course of things in his own life; looking for the day of graduation, looking for the day when he shall commence the stern work of life, looking for the day when after the process of effort he shall have arrived at a place of power. Such hopes are the very inspirations of conduct. But the Christian man, while having all such hopes, has as the supreme, the ultimate, the profoundest hope, the coming of the Lord; and all these lesser hopes are conditioned by that supreme hope. The truly Christian man will have no desire in his heart to postpone the coming of the Lord that he may reach some other goal; he will be perfectly ready, willing, glad, to know that every other goal toward which he properly runs is lost, canceled, because the Lord Himself will greet him.

This conception of life means that all fear is checked, corrected, hushed to rest. The man who lives waiting for the coming of the Lord will know nothing of panic in the midst of catastrophe, will know nothing of despair in the hour of apparent defeat. The glory of that certain Advent of the King will transfigure all the sackcloth, illuminate every hour of bereavement, irradiate with glory every dark cloud that sweeps across the life. The man who lives forever waiting for the Lord, looking for Him, is the man in whom fear never gains the mastery. Fear will assail the soul, for so are we fashioned; fear will threaten the courage, for so are we made; but when fear arises, then the upward look and the eager expectation will check the fear and cancel it so that the soul is again filled with new courage.

Yet I pray you observe that the ideal is this: if the goal is out of sight and finality can never be reached for this man until he see his Master, nevertheless, the goal reached, the hope realized, the fear forever ended, these things are always close at hand. In the midst of the most strenuous running the goal is expected immediately. In the hour when fears threaten the soul, hope is victorious because at once the Lord may appear.

The Christian life is not a race the end of which is seen,

nor a course of probationary preparation the length of which is known. The end of the Christian life to the Christian soul, according to the Lord's conception, is always the next step.

"Men looking for their Lord." This is a return to first principles, the life dependent on the unseen. In the terms of the abiding values of the incarnation, that is the true view of life, that it is forevermore linked to the unseen and waits the disturbance of God. The life that is never disturbed is the life that is always prepared to be disturbed. The life that is always disturbed is the life that is seeking never to be disturbed. When a man's life is poised toward eternity and God; when a man understands that God has a plan for his life and is leading, guiding him, and may at any moment change the direction, thwart the purpose, recall the order, issue new commands, then that man finds profound peace and content, and with loins girt about, and lamps trimmed and burning he is ready for the commanding word, undisturbed because forever waiting to be disturbed. So in the terms and value of the incarnation that master principle of life is made real and personal to the Christian soul. As the God Whom no man hath seen at any time came into observation by the way of incarnation, so ere He passed from the earthly scene He left this word with the sons of men: Expect Me again. I shall return, I shall come again in My glory. Live as though expecting Me.

In the forty days between the resurrection and the ascension our Lord trained His disciples to this conception. Have you ever tried imaginatively to enter into the experience of those men during those forty days? They never knew where they would see Him next. Suddenly appearing in their midst, no door opened, no bolt shot, no preparation made; but He was there with them. His presence, parousia, nearness, they were made conscious of! With equal suddenness He disappeared. The appearances and disappearances of the forty days were but to train these people to the consciousness of

His constant presence, and to the fact that at any moment He might appear. That is the teaching of the New Testament about the coming of our Lord. Nothing in human pomp or pageantry can express the true idea of this great truth of the New Testament as to our Lord's second Advent. Even in the hymns to-night we were away from Scripture truth. When we speak of the sound of chariot wheels, we are affected by the coming of kings and queens of earthly lands. When King George V is to appear, we wait for him, and there are signs and tokens, outward signs, of his approach. It will not be so when our King shall come. He will come with a voice and a shout, and the voice and the shout will synchronize with the manifestation; and ere we know it, as swiftly and suddenly as He appeared in the upper room, we shall be face to face with the King, we shall see Him, and the vision will be the final movement in our transformation, for we shall be like Him.

This, then, is the true conception of life according to Christ: He came to me in the hour when I yielded to Him, He is coming to me again; when, I know not; and life, between the initial coming when I became His and that final coming when He will become mine in a profounder sense than ever before, is a waiting, looking, watching for Him.

That leads us to the consideration of the attitude of those who hold this conception: "Ye yourselves like unto men that wait for their Lord." That is the old version. The Revised Version reads: "Ye yourselves like unto men looking for their Lord." In this case I think we suffer loss by the change. *Looking for*—yes, if we quite understand what we mean. But it does not mean star-gazing! In the word translated "looking for" there is really no thought of the activity of the eye. The real thought is that of men who are eagerly expecting to receive, to receive a guest, men who are expecting to give hospitality. Not men who have abandoned duty in order to look for portents and signs, and presently for the Lord;

but men who in fulfilment of duty are forevermore prepared for the King Himself, and in that sense looking for the coming of the Lord.

The attitude, moreover, is that of men waiting for the Master, for the King, for the Supreme One! Not looking for a servant, although, infinite mystery of His great and wonderful grace, He does say to them that if, when He comes, they are waiting, He will gird Himself and serve them. Not men who are waiting finally to give hospitality to a friend, although they are to give hospitality to Him, and He comes for the reception of that hospitality, for He cometh and knocketh and asks admission. The attitude is that of waiting for the Lord Himself. The thought is that of supremacy, of control, and leads us back to the initial words which reveal the true attitude of waiting: doing His business, "let your loins be girded about"; seeking His interests, "let your lamps be burning."

For an understanding of our Lord's meaning we may go to the scene of His glorious ascension. When He had ascended on high and passed out of sight, the Galileans stood gazing up into heaven, and were immediately, if not rebuked, at least corrected: "Ye men of Galilee, why stand ye looking into heaven? This Jesus, which was received up from you into heaven, shall so come in like manner as ye beheld Him going into heaven." Then at once the upward gaze ceased, and they turned back to obedience and waiting; and presently, when baptism of the Spirit came to them, they went out into service, with loins girded about, the girding of the loins the sign of bond-service to the King; with light burning, the flashing light the revelation of their care for His interests. So are men to wait for the Lord: with loins girded, and lamps burning, going about the King's business.

We wait for His coming as we fulfil our appointed tasks, as girt about, His bondslaves, we carry the light of His own life, and serve Him and our fellow men for His sake. Such is the true attitude of waiting for the Lord.

So finally let us inquire what is the character that is produced by those who adopt this attitude as the result of this conception of life.

First, the character toward the Master Himself will be partly of separation and partly of submission. It seems to me it needs no argument, and hardly requires illustration. If I really am expecting that He may come, then my relation to Him will ever be that of separation to His will and of submission to His law. Make what personal application of it suits your individual case. Suffer the personal application which I venture to make. If a man shall always preach, expecting that he may be interrupted in his preaching by the parousia, the presence of his Lord, what a difference it will make to his preaching. If a man shall always transact his business through the six days of the week expecting that at any moment in the midst of any transaction, the Lord Himself may be there, to call him away from things material to the eternal habitations, how it will safeguard his transactions.

It will not make him less diligent in his business, but it will make him infinitely more diligent in seeing to it that his business conforms to the will of his God.

The effect of this doctrine on a man's character in regard to his fellow men will be that of the constancy of his cheerfulness, and love. Cheerfulness! I freely confess that to me herein is a problem! I have long been strangely puzzled by the fact that some men who profess to hold this doctrine, and to be waiting for the Lord, are the most cheerless men I know. I cannot understand it. Surely it is the result of some wrong conception of the doctrine itself. Is He coming? Then there should ever be light on the brow, and the eye should never lack luster. Let me speak the things of actual experience. How often my brow is shadowed and my eye lacks luster. It is because I forget. When next you see me in that mood know this, I have forgotten that the Lord is at hand! When we remember, the result is perpetual sunniness, rejoicing forevermore, an eager, glad look of expectation in all our attitude toward our fellow men. That cheerfulness, moreover, will proceed out of a great love; for if I expect to meet Him, I know how He loves all men, and to quote the language of John, I should surely be ashamed before Him at His coming, if coming He found me lacking in love toward my fellow men.

How does this expectation affect Christian service? It has been declared that to hold this doctrine of the New Testament and preach it, to believe that the apostles were not mistaken and that Jesus was not mistaken, is to cut the nerve of Christian service. I declare that to expect that the Lord may at any moment appear to me, coming to me Himself, is to give immediateness and thoroughness to every piece of work that I take up in His name. Immediateness. He may come and the thing He has commanded me to do may not be done. Therefore let me do it forthwith, straightway, lest the opportunity be gone at His coming, and I be found to have neglected the thing that He commanded, and gave me time to do.

Again, to expect Him, is to give the quality of thoroughness to all our work. I should like when He comes that whatever I am doing, whether preaching or playing. I may be doing thoroughly, for there is nothing this Lord of life hates more than halfheartedness: "Because thou art lukewarm, and neither hot nor cold, I will spue thee out of My mouth."

Take one larger outlook. If in very deed this be our conception, and we are waiting for the King, that waiting and that expectation will create patience in the soul, patience with God, patience with the Church, patience with the world.

Patience with God. Did the suggestion sound somewhat

irreverent? Then bear with me, if perchance I speak only for a few in this audience. There are some for whom I know I may speak. There are hours in which we feel impatient with God; at least—shall I amend the declaration?—there are hours in which we are tempted to be impatient with God. I am not referring to the hour of personal sorrow and suffering; I am not referring to the hour in which we ourselves are buffeted, bruised, defeated, but to those larger hours, those more tragic hours, when the world's agony surges on our souls, when we stand face to face with wrong; then we cry out with old Carlyle, God is doing nothing. If we have never had such an hour it is because we have never yet put our lives very near to the world's agony and the world's need.

If I take this word of Jesus and believe it, and interpret it, not as men too often have interpreted it, but according to the whole scheme of His teaching; and I see that His coming means, not a catastrophe in which the world will be destroyed, but that it will be the advent of yet another day of opportunity for the world, the beginning of another movement in time; that it will be a crisis as real and definite, and no more mysterious than the crisis of His first advent; and that proceeding from it, His Kingdom will be set up—if I have caught that view I shall count that the long-suffering of God is due to His patience, to the fact that the processes of to-day are necessary to the perfection of the crisis of His coming, and a preparation for the larger process that lies beyond.

Patience is not laziness! Patience does not say, Therefore, because He is coming, I have no responsibility and have nothing to do. Patient waiting for Christ and patience with the world in the light of the glory of the coming of the Christ mean loins girt about, lamps burning, service rendered, haste upon the King's business, restful haste, peaceful speed, dignified diligence, recognition of the fact that in all the details of my service to-day I am in co-operation with the great processes by which God is preparing for that Advent, and which are necessary for the larger movements that lie beyond this age.

So to wait for Him is to have the life forevermore full of song and of peace:

> My life flows on in endless song;
>   Above earth's lamentation
> I hear the sweet, and glorious hymn,
>   That hails a new creation;
> Through all the tumult and the strife
>   I hear the music ringing.
> It finds an echo in my soul—
>   How can I keep from singing?

Finally, it is a very solemn and searching consideration that our Christian life may always be tested, gauged, valued, by this fact of the Lord's return. His word is, "Behold I come quickly." The true answer of the Christian heart is always, "Even so, come Lord Jesus." Anything that prevents that answer is out of place in our lives. Anything that makes it difficult for us to say, "Come quickly, Lord Jesus," is an element of weakness. That ambition which makes me seriously hope, even though I hardly dare confess it, that He will not come yet is a false ambition. That enterprise, however high and holy it may seem, which makes me desire to postpone the Advent until it be accomplished is a false enterprise. That hope, that new joy, to which I am looking forward, has in it something of wrong, producing in my heart something of disloyalty if it make me desire to postpone His coming. So we are to test all ambitions, all enterprises, all hopes, by this ambition, this enterprise, this hope of the Lord's return.

I have most carefully avoided any reference to human almanacs and calendars, to mechanical and mathematical calculations. Their effect has been to bring this doctrine into disrepute, and thousands of men desiring to be truly loyal to Jesus Christ are afraid of it because someone once said He would come on such a day at such a time, and He did not come! Men have been trying to find out the day and the hour which the Lord said no man knoweth, not even the Son, but only the Father. The moment we introduce into this great doctrine the element of the mathematician, the element of the almanac and calendar, times and seasons, we postpone the sense of the coming of the Lord. If it should be that any man in this house has ascertained for absolute certainty that Jesus the Lord is coming again, let us say, for the sake of illustration, on the 25th of December, in the name of God let him not tell me, because that knowledge would put Him all those months away and I expect Him now. The moment men begin to try to fix a date they controvert the teaching of the New Testament and contravene the purpose of the glorious truth. The Church has been commanded to wait for His Advent.

There are many apocryphal stories of our late beloved Queen Victoria, but there is one story that is certainly true coming on the authority of the man to whom the word was spoken. Talking with him one day on this very doctrine, she said, "There is nothing I should love more than to live long enough to lay my crown at His feet when He comes." That is the true attitude. It was not in His will that she should do so. It may be that I also shall come to the valley all shrouded in mist, but even there the consummation will not be the mere consciousness of death, but the dawning glory of His presence breaking through the mist, the vision of the face of the One Whom not having seen I have loved.

So we are to live, not as men fearing death or thinking of it, but as men looking for the Lord. May the Lord direct our hearts into patient waiting for His coming.

CHAPTER XIII

THE SON OF MAN—DELIVERED UP

The Son of Man is delivered up to be crucified.
MATTHEW 26:2.

THE FIRST THIRTY VERSES OF THIS CHAPTER ARE CHARACterized by contrast, by conflict, and yet by a strange and arresting co-operation. We are in the vestibule of the Holy Place of the sacrifice of the ages. The air is heavy with the electric sense of approaching storm; yet it seems so still, and clear, that we hear and see acutely, and things commonly veiled are startlingly revealed as we read these wonderful words. Let us attempt, then, reverently to listen and to watch. Our theme is the story of the whole paragraph, the keynote is the text. In these words of our Lord, spoken to His disciples, we have His introductory declaration to everything that was now to follow in the mission of the King. Let us first examine the words, and then the whole scene in their light.

It is well that we should remind ourselves in the first place of the occasion on which our Lord uttered these particular words. Matthew is careful to tell us, "It came to pass, when Jesus had finished all these words." The declaration followed immediately on the Olivet prophecy which is recorded for us in chapters twenty-four and twenty-five of this particular Gospel.

In order that we may come the more readily and the

more accurately into the atmosphere necessary for the understanding of these words of Jesus, it may be well to recall that prophecy and its setting.

The loneliness of Jesus at this time was very pronounced. The Olivet prophecies were uttered to His disciples in answer to an inquiry, which inquiry resulted from things He had been saying to the rulers of the people in those last days in which He had definitely and finally rejected the Hebrew nation, for the time being, from the position which they had occupied in the economy of God. When Jesus uttered the prophecy on Olivet He had been rejected by His own nation, and He had rejected them. Solemn words had passed His lips: "The Kingdom of God shall be taken from you, and given to a nation bringing forth the fruits thereof." A sad and awful wail had passed those selfsame lips: "Behold, your house is left unto you desolate." He was strangely alone. A group of men were gathered round about Him, His own disciples, those whom, having loved, He loved unto the end, and that in spite of their failure to understand Him. But they were unenlightened, were entirely unable to apprehend the profoundest passion of His heart, or the things that He was saying to them. There He sat on Olivet's slope, outside the city of His love, surrounded by a few men utterly unable to come near to Him in the deepest and profoundest things of His spiritual life.

And yet I pray you observe His dignity, His authority, the glory of His outlook, the assurance of His words, the unfaltering courage and confidence of every sentence that He uttered. He was looking on, far beyond the immediate surroundings, His glance encompassing the centuries that lay ahead, and the millenniums. He had been thinking of the ages yet to come in the economy of God for this world; and as He uttered His prophecy we are amazed at the clarity of His vision; but more amazed at His assumption of authority, and His absolute certainty of victory. He speaks of things immediate, and then of things nigh at hand, of the destruction of Jerusalem and strange experiences through which friends and foes alike would pass in the coming days, until, at last, in a passage which, if I may reverently say such a thing of the Lord, was characterized by singular majesty and beauty of diction, He drew a picture of all nations being gathered before Him, and He alone the Arbitrator of their destinies, finding His verdicts, passing His sentences.

Such was the Olivet prophecy. "And it came to pass, when Jesus had finished all these words, He said, Ye know that after two days is the feast of passover, and the Son of Man is delivered up to be crucified." With set intention, as I verily believe, Matthew thus emphasized the occasion on which these particular words passed the lips of our Lord. As we have seen in recent studies in this Gospel of Matthew—perhaps almost monotonously to some people—a great change passed over the method of Jesus' ministry at Cæsarea Philippi. From the moment in which the great confession was made, He commenced to speak of the Cross; returning to the subject again and yet again, it ran through His teaching, saturating and ever permeating all His thinking.

On Olivet's slopes having uttered His prophecy, suddenly, startlingly, He recalled them to the thing He had been speaking of through all those months, but with a new emphasis, declaring no longer that it is necessary that these things should be, but that the hour had come. "The Son of Man is delivered up to be crucified."

Now let us try to understand what our Lord really meant when He said this. In the Authorized Version the text reads: "Ye know that after two days the passover cometh, and the Son of Man is betrayed to be crucified." Let me immediately clear the ground by saying that I consider that to be not merely a mistranslation, but a very misguiding mistranslation.

I shall ask you to observe a word and a tense in this statement of Jesus. The word is now rendered, "*delivered up*." Taken in its simplicity, as the men would undoubtedly take it who heard Him utter it, the word simply means to be given into the hands of a person. It does not in itself suggest either faithfulness or faithlessness. It may describe an act of treachery, but it may describe an act of trust. To deliver up, to deliver over, to surrender, to yield to a certain person, or to a certain set of circumstances, whether in the keeping of faith, or by its violation, whether traitorously, or trustfully, does not appear in the word itself. Therefore we must interpret the word according to its setting, according to the whole movement in the midst of which we find it.

In the next place, let us observe a tense. "The Son of Man *is* delivered up." Here there is no question. Grammarians will all be in agreement with me when I say that this is the simple statement. There is no difference of opinion, no quarrel about manuscripts. Here we have undoubtedly the accurate word. "The Son of Man is delivered up." Now, as a matter of fact, at the moment when Jesus said this He was perfectly free; as a matter of fact, at the moment—I speak entirely within the limitations of the moment and the human—He could have escaped. He was not arrested. It would have been perfectly easy for Him to do what His disciples had urged Him to do again and yet again; in the quiet silence of the night He might have left Jerusalem. It is perfectly true, as we shall see, that men everywhere were plotting for His arrest, that one of His own number was in the intrigue, but at the moment He was not arrested, He was free.

The difficulty has been recognized by expositors, and I find that one has suggested that He used the present tense for the future, and another that He used the full relative present, as though He had said, "The Son of Man is being delivered up." But you will immediately see that all this is gratuitous.

He said, "The Son of Man is delivered up," and I abide by the thing He said, that which was simply and actually true at the moment when He said it. As yet not apprehended, as yet not within the final meshes that were being woven around Him by His enemies, He saw all the future clearly, and He spoke with quiet, calm assurance. Speaking first within the terms of a calendar with which they were familiar, He said, "Ye know that after two days the passover cometh," and then, "The Son of Man *is* delivered up." That was not the full relative present in the sense of meaning "is being delivered up." That was not the careless affirmation of a speaker who described the future in the terms of the present. That was the statement of One Who spoke in that eternal present which was the tense of His deepest nature and His profoundest life. That was the statement of One Who had already said to His enemies, "Before Abraham was, I am," thus putting into contrast the past tense of the founder of the nation, with the ever-present tense of His own consciousness, and claiming that His own abiding consciousness antedated the past experience of the founder.

And He made use of exactly the same tense when, after the Olivet prophecies, He said to the group of disciples who were with Him, in the shadow of the impending Cross, "The Son of Man *is* delivered up to be crucified."

And yet it is perfectly evident that our Lord was now drawing their attention to the fact that the actual crucifixion was imminent. That was the accommodation of the eternal present of His own consciousness to the tenses of their consciousness. He spoke to them because the eternal was merging into the temporal; that which was abidingly true in His own consciousness, from the standpoint to which we shall come in a moment, was now about to become patiently, observantly, historically true. In that declaration He indicated to them the fact that the deliverance which was the initiation of their own national history, and of which the passover was but a shadow, was about to be fulfilled. The eternal fact in the Being of God, adumbrated in the passover for the sake of the people that He would make, was now to be wrought out into actual visibility and accomplishment in the history of the world.

This was no mere passing intuition, foretelling something that was about to happen. It was a profound declaration that the thing which is in the divine economy was now to become visible in human history, "The Son of Man is delivered up."

During His life He had spoken of the final hour on more than one occasion in the tenses of human consciousness. And more than once those who understood Him best, especially John, drew attention to the fact that our Lord said to men, "Mine hour is not yet come." John, writing of Him, said, "No man took Him; because His hour was not yet come." At the wedding feast Jesus said to His mother, "Mine hour is not yet come." It is a most superficial exposition which declares He could not work the miracle, for He did work it immediately. There was profound meaning in His answer even when she—dear, sweet soul, highly favored of God, and forever to be held in regard by the sons of men, the Virgin Mother—was desirous of precipitating some manifestation of His power in order to further the accomplishment of His Mission, He said, "Mine hour is not yet come."

From that first utterance and throughout the ministry of Jesus the same declaration is found, but He was ever speaking in the terms of human experience. To Herod He sent this message: "Go, and say to that fox, Behold, I cast out devils and perform cures to-day and to-morrow, and the third day I am perfected." That was His Word to the man who would fain have ended His ministry for very fear of Him, or for fear of his own sin. In it Jesus declared that the perfecting hour, the ultimate hour, the strangely mysterious hour on the dial of time, in which eternity would express itself in the terms of redemption, was not yet come. It was postponed until, His public ministry ended, the Olivet prophecy uttered, He quietly said to His disciples, "After two days the passover cometh, and the Son of Man is delivered up to be crucified." In the terms of human thought, He was on the eve of being delivered up; in the economy of God, He *is* delivered up.

It was language which revealed the voluntary nature of the sacrifice of the Son of God. It was language expressive of the great volition; it was language that defied all the attempts that His enemies were making to arrest Him! In effect, He Who sat in the heavens, laughed, and had in derision the men who were set against His anointed! And the laughter and derision of God were born of the fact that through the processes of their opposition He was marching to their salvation, and to their ultimate redemption!

There came a day when a man who saw Him, and gave himself to Him, and became His great Apostle to the Gentiles, with his own hand wrote, or to his amanuensis dictated, these words, "Who loved me, and *gave* Himself up for Me." The word there rendered "gave" is the same Greek word as the word here translated "delivered up." He loved me, and delivered up Himself for me. He was delivered, not by Judas, not by the priests, not by the rulers, not by the Roman procurator, but by the infinite, overwhelming, all-compelling passion of the heart of God.

Thus the little incidents of time and space, and of human calendars and almanacs are lost, and in the vestibule of the Holy Place of the sacrifice of the ages we hear the Master say, "The Son of Man is delivered up to be crucified."

Reverently we now turn back to the whole paragraph, that we may survey the scene or scenes in the light of that declaration. Let us spend one moment in noticing a matter of chronological order in this chapter. In the first five verses we have a story, which is continued at verse seventeen. Verses six to sixteen constitute an interpolation, something that the evangelist wrote here, not in chronological order but for the purpose of explaining something else that he was about to write. This great declaration of Jesus was made two days before the passover. John in his Gospel, giving an account of this selfsame event in the house of Simon, says it was six days before passover. Consequently, the things recorded from verse six to sixteen happened four days before Jesus made the declaration we have considered.

Now I take up my Testament and look at two little words. In verse six, "*When* Jesus was in Bethany," and I run on to verse fourteen, and "*Then* one of the twelve, who was called Judas Iscariot." Then it is seen that the two incidents are joined together. First, Mary, with her alabaster cruse of ointment, and then Judas, with his intrigue and his plotting. With that chronological order in view I go back to my first five verses and once again I notice two little words. In verse one, "*When* Jesus had finished all these words"; and in verse three, "*Then* were gathered together the chief priests." Thus once more I am face to face with two things happening simultaneously. Jesus was talking to His disciples, and He said, "After two days the passover cometh, and the Son of Man is delivered up to be crucified." While He was saying that, at the very hour, Caiaphas and the priests and the rulers were planning to arrest Him, and they said, "Not at the feast, lest there be an uproar among the people." In chronological order, the last thing is the feast, the final passover in the old economy, the first passover in the new, the transference by act of Jesus of the ancient passover to the new feast.

Such are the scenes. It will readily be seen that I cannot, and it is not necessary for my present purpose that I should, deal with any one of these in detail. But for a few moments let us by the help of God's Holy Spirit move back into the midst of them. The feast in Bethany, the aroma of the ointment that filled the room, the criticism of Judas, the speculation of the disciples! Then the Olivet discourse in the interval between other matters! Then our Lord uttering these great words, while somewhere priests were plotting to arrest Him! I say let us try to get into the atmosphere of it all!

If we watch, I think that the first matter to impress us—let me put it from the standpoint of personal experience—the first matter that has impressed my soul in the reading of this paragraph is that of the wonderfully strange co-operation that is manifest. God in Himself and through His Son is seen moving toward the Cross, the Son declaring that He is delivered up to be crucified; according to a Pentecostal interpretation, the Son delivered up by the determinate counsel and foreknowledge of God. On the other hand, Satan in himself and through his children, through those to whom Jesus had but recently said, "Ye are of your father the devil," who "was a murderer from the beginning," and "a liar, and the father thereof,"—Satan, through his children, moving toward the Cross, determined that it should be erected, plotting for it. Then, back in those earlier days, Mary at Bethany preparing Him for His burial, with the keen intuition of the heart of a woman seeing the shadows on His face more clearly than others saw, desiring to do something that would tell Him she saw and understood, breaking all the bounds of prudence as she poured the spikenard on feet and head, preparing Him, as He said, for His burial. And Judas, going to the priest, saying, What will you give me? plotting for His death.

Now, is not all this in itself strange and arresting? Heaven, and earth, and hell, all at work against each other, toward one end and purpose. The strangest of all conflicts, and yet the most marvelous of all co-operations. God, in the Person of His Son, moving toward the Cross, arranging for it; Satan, expressing himself through his emissaries, moving toward the Cross, arranging for it; Mary, sweet and tender lover of the Lord, anointing Him for burial; Judas, base, a master traitor, sacrificing his Lord for thirty pieces of silver. God and Satan, Mary and Judas, co-operating toward the Cross. It is the wonder of all wonders, one of the most amazing pictures in the New Testament!

Then, when I have observed this strange and wonderful co-operation, I look again, and the conflict is as self-evident as is the co-operation. Beneath all the things which are, after all, on the surface I discover a conflict, a conflict of intention, a conflict of method, and when I come to the human level, a conflict of attitude. On the higher level I see spiritual forces in antagonism. God Himself, Who is a Spirit, and the spirits of evil in conflict of intention.

What is the Divine intention? As God in His Son moves toward the Cross, my inquiry may be answered by the simplest of all statements, but verily there is none better. The divine intention is at all costs to save men. What was the intention of Satan as he moved toward the Cross? It was the intention at all costs to destroy the Saviour. Thus we see two opposing purposes of the universe concerning humanity, moving to the same goal, but with an entirely different intention. God set upon saving men at all costs, Satan set upon the destruction of the Saviour.

When I come into the realm of that which is more visible and more patent, I have again a striking revelation of conflict of method. Jesus said, "After two days the passover cometh, and the Son of Man is delivered up to be crucified." The priests and the elders said *Not* at the feast, lest there be an uproar among the people. Notice the conflict of method, in what it reveals of the underlying principles and purposes. Begin with the priests. Not at the feast. Why not? It was the language of temporizing policy: We mean to kill Him, but we must be careful. Not at the feast; there will be an uproar!

There you have a revelation of the whole genius of that which is common in government and authority, the whole genius of that which renders a people distressed, scattered, undone; the whole genius of that against which Jesus Himself had flung Himself with almost relentless fury in His teaching. "Woe unto you, scribes and Pharisees, hypocrites." That is the genius of all false government, a policy which temporizes, is affected only by temporal concerns, and temporal interests.

Over against that is the language of Jesus, the voice of God. At the passover. And why at the passover? Because in all His appointments of feasts and fasts, of ceremonies and rituals, in the ancient economy, there had been profound and eternal significance; and now, with the finest delicacy of fulfilment, God kisses His symbol into actuality, and the actual, ultimate, final passover in human history shall be accomplished at the hour of the passover among the people to which it had symbolized things yet to be. On the one hand, the mastery of eternal principle; on the other, subservience to temporal policy.

And once more, and now we are on another level, we are among our own kith and kin; we are simply looking at humanity, no longer at the conflict as between God and Satan, no longer at the conflict as between Jesus, the Shepherd King of true and final authority, and the false rulers of the people; no longer at the conflict as between principle and government, but at a conflict of attitudes between human beings in the presence of the one great Lord and Master and Saviour of humanity. Mary and Judas; lavish expenditure and selfish economy! But you say these things are too small in the light of such vast things! What is an alabaster cruse of ointment in the presence of all these infinite things? What is the opinion of the man who holds the bag about what ought to have been done with the nard in the presence of the infinite things? The small things of all human lives are the sacramental symbols of the great. Nothing is small.

> No lily-muffled hum of a summer bee,
> But finds some coupling with the spinning stars.

Right in the midst of the vast things of eternity, breaking out through the speech of the Son of God, behold the two human attitudes which stand forevermore in contrast. Lavish expenditure for very love, improvident pouring out in a tribute of adoration of the most costly things! That is Mary. On the other hand, selfish calculating economy! That is Judas. These things are revealed in the vestibule approaching the Holy Place where the sacrifice of the ages is to be offered.

But there is one more contrast. I leave the first paragraph, and the second which chronologically is first, and I come to the passover itself and to the feast. And I ask you in all quietness and solemnity, and I shall use as few words as I know how, to look at the contrast. Behold Judas at the passover and Jesus at the passover.

Incarnate evil sitting as a guest, receiving the hospitality of Jesus, while all the time in possession of the blood money of the Son of God, maintaining hypocrisy to the end by asking, "Is it I, rabbi?" That defies exposition.

Incarnate love, sitting with the betrayer, suddenly breaking out into thanksgiving, in prospect of the suffering which should make possible the saving even of Judas, if Judas will but trust Him. That is the ultimate contrast of the scene.

Let our final thought center on the conflict. God, determined on the Cross in order to save men; Satan, determined on the Cross in order to destroy the Saviour! My question seems almost irreverent—I pause, and yet I must put it. Who won? If Christ rose not, then I am of all men most pitiable. If Christ rose not, God failed, and Satan won. I greet you! He rose, and I cannot end this meditation in the vestibule save as

I recognize that there flashes back upon it all the light of the resurrection morning. And by that sign and token I know that God won!

Ah! how those words follow me. Some of my nearest friends will be tired of hearing me repeat them, but I cannot help it:

> One death-grapple in the darkness 'twixt old systems and the Word!

In that conflict it was the Word Who was victorious, and not the old systems. There sin and grace came to grips, and not grace was destroyed, but sin. The victory was with the Son of God.

All this is more than history. "The Son of Man is delivered up," not at this moment, on this day of our calendar, delivered up by sin to death, in order that sin may live; but delivered up by God to death, in order that sin may die, and men may live.

The final question is not whether we are with the priests desiring to slay Him, or with God detemined that He shall die. That is not the question at all. That is settled. We have agreed with the priests and sinned; we have consented to His dying by our sin.

The question now is what shall we as sinners do in the presence of the death which He accomplished, and the word "accomplished" can be used only of it, because beyond the death was the resurrection? What shall I do with this death? Shall I trust it, or shall I spurn it? Upon my answer to that question will depend—because I have heard the evangel, because I have stood under the shadow of His Cross—my relation to God through the ages that are to come.

Then be it mine to say, So help me God, so help me God,

> I take, Oh, Cross, thy shadow
> For my abiding place;
> . . . .

Content to let the world go by,
To know no gain or loss—
My sinful self my only shame,
My glory all the Cross.

CHAPTER XIV

GETHSEMANE: THE GARDEN OF SPICES

Then cometh Jesus with them unto the place called Gethsemane.

MATTHEW 26:36.

IN THE HEBREW ECONOMY, ON THE DAY OF ATONEMENT the High Priest entered the Holiest of all three times. First, he passed within the veil, carrying fire in the golden censer and incense in his hands. There he cast the incense on the fire, and the cloud of it overshadowed the Mercy Seat, and prepared for his ministration, which was about to follow. He entered the second time within the veil, bearing with him the blood of his own sin offering, which he sprinkled on his own behalf. Finally, he entered with the blood of a sin offering for all the people.

When in the fulness of time, and in fulfilment of the ancient and divinely appointed ritual, our High Priest came to the great Day of Atonement, He entered the Holiest of all twice in the exercise of His holy office; once bearing with Him the incense and the fire, once with the sin offering for all the people. He had no second entrance such as Aaron had, because He had no sin offering for Himself. He was "holy, guileless, undefiled, separated from sinners," and so it was on their behalf that He needed to appear.

Venturing thus to borrow the symbolism of the ancient ritual, and to see it being fulfilled in the activities of those final days in the mission of our Lord, it ever seems to me that in Gethsemane's Garden we see Him passing alone within the veil, bearing the fire and the incense, and on Calvary's Cross we see Him entering with the sin offering for all the people.

It was while He hung on the Cross that all ritualism ended and symbolism was forevermore made unnecessary, the last symbol being the destruction of symbol as the veil of the temple was rent in twain from the top to the bottom.

Last Sunday evening we saw Him delivered up by God's determinate counsel, by Satan's malicious hate, by Mary's tender anointing, by Judas' base treachery. It was a revelation of conflicting co-operation moving towards the sacrifice of the ages. This evening, as God in His gracious goodness and by the solemnizing power of His Holy Spirit shall help us, we go a step further. From that outer court of turmoil we pass through the Holy Place to the awful stillness of the Holiest of all. It behooves us here and at once to confess that these things are too high for us, that they are the secret things which belong unto the Lord, and that no attempted exposition of the letter of this chapter can be a final exposition of all the spiritual activity, of which the letter is but the external symbol. Nevertheless, if the secret things belong unto the Lord, the revealed things are for us, and through them, though we may not wholly apprehend the hidden mysteries, we are brought into touch with them; and so with all reverence of spirit we draw near to Gethsemane and desire to behold, to consider, the High Priest of our confession.

In that ancient ceremony the fire taken from the altar was the symbol of dedication, while the incense of sweet spices beaten very small was the symbol of the graces of character which make one acceptable to God. In that going in of the priest both fire and incense were necessary. The incense must be cast on the fire and consumed, suggesting the fact that the most perfect of humanity must be abandoned to the will of God and find its ultimate use in outpouring itself in order to accomplish the purpose of the Most High. And it ever seems to me when I read the story of Gethsemane that this is exactly what took place in the Garden in the case of our Lord and Master. Here He reached the ultimate hour of His personal dedication.

To change the figure, the infinite music of His life was ever true to the chord of the dominant struck by the psalmist long ere He came: "Lo, I am come; in the roll of the book it is written of Me: I delight to do Thy will, O My God." His first recorded words were these, "Wist ye not that I must be about My Father's business?" And then on through all the period of His life, in the natural and beautiful days of childhood, in the growing strength and glory of youth, in the stern years of manhood, in all the difficult pathway of His public teaching, everything was true to that first call. Had we met Him anywhere and asked Him for the deepest reason of the journey He took, or the deed He wrought, or the word He spoke He would ever have answered in the selfsame words, "My meat is to do the will of Him that sent Me." In the process of that life of dedication, He came again and again to the place of trial and testing, and yet with undeviating loyalty and magnificent determination His life was dedicated from first to last to the will of God.

But now in the Garden came the supreme and final test. Here there was presented to Him again that which He had seen from the beginning, the coming of the Cross; and the question arises—not for Him, but for us—will the life so wondrously devoted be complete in devotion in this strange and awful hour?

Ere He passed within the veil to represent sinning men, the High Priest entered Himself in His own right, no longer by an act of symbolism, but by the actuality of a personal experience, carrying the fire and carrying the incense, and on that consuming fire He cast the incense of His own sacrificial and beautiful and perfect life; and the cloud of it overshadow-

GETHSEMANE: THE GARDEN OF SPICES 185

ing the Mercy Seat was the prelude of His coming again with blood in behalf of sinning souls.

All this is but figure of speech, all this is but the language of symbolism, but it is only through these things that we can approach such sacred matters. Let us therefore immediately reckon as with ourselves that all the other figures and occurrences on this page of the Gospel are important only as they are connected with the central matter; and let us reverently attempt to observe the graces of our Lord as they were revealed in Gethsemane, the consuming fire, as it was most evidently present; and then that activity, so appalling, so awe-inspiring, by which the graces and beauties of the Christ were brought into contact with the consuming fire, and the dedication of His personal life to the will of His God was brought to consummation and to glory.

First, let us observe the graces of the Lord as they are revealed in the story. And immediately we recognize that it is almost impossible to analyze a fragrance. If only I knew how to read that chapter as it should be read comment would be almost unnecessary. But I am always conscious of failure when I try to read such a story, because in my reading you think about Peter and about Judas, and they ought to be almost out of sight for the ineffable and supernal glory of the one central figure of the Christ. And yet they are needed for a revelation of His grace. And if for a little while we may find our way far from our immediate surroundings into that Garden, and somewhere hide ourselves away that we may watch, then we shall see amid the common-places and brutalities of the last hour the glories of Jesus—and I advisedly now use that human name—the graces and the beauties of His character stand out clearly. Then let me speak to you of the things that impress me, prefacing anything I may say by saying this to you. You have seen glories that my eyes have never seen. I can speak only of the things that *I* see.

As I read the story I am first of all impressed with the

majesty of Jesus. I have not carelessly chosen the word "majesty." I earnestly desire that now it may be delivered from all our false and materialistic ideas concerning it. It is derived from the comparative of *magnum*, "great," and it suggests something beyond mere greatness; it includes within itself the thought of dignity, but not of patronage; of aloofness with which no liberty can be taken in certain senses, but which is always near at hand in the hour of need—Majesty! It suggests what the Psalmist meant when long ago he said, "The Lord reigneth; He is apparelled with majesty"; or what he meant when on another occasion he sang, "The voice of the Lord is full of majesty."

The majesty of Jesus is revealed, first of all, in His knowledge of all the program that lay ahead. He had been in the Upper Room, they had eaten together the ancient Passover, He had instituted the new feast, symbol of the new Covenant; they had joined in singing the great Hallel, and then they had left the Upper Room and walked down across the Kedron toward the shadows of Gethsemane. On the way He told them in language chosen from their own ancient Scriptures exactly what was about to happen, "All ye shall be offended in Me this night: for it is written, I will smite the shepherd, and the sheep of the flock shall be scattered abroad." He had a perfect knowledge of the way along which He was going, He had an absolute confidence of the issue of that through which He was about to pass, notwithstanding the fact that He was also conscious of all the awfulness of the cup, for He said to those men as He told them of their coming scattering because of the smiting of the shepherd, "After I am raised up, I will go before you into Galilee."

I see His majesty finally in His demeanor in the presence of His enemies, for the story as Matthew tells it is not complete. We need all the other stories to see all the details, and to what I have read to-night we must especially add that one wonderful touch which comes to us from the pen of John the Seer: our Lord looking at the men who had come into the Garden to arrest Him, and His words, "Whom seek ye?" They said, "Jesus of Nazareth." And He replied, "I am"! And in a moment they fell backward. It was the flaming glory of the infinite majesty of God, not shining in some spectacular flame, but suddenly focused in the splendor and the dignity of His humanity.

Then I look again, and perhaps more closely, and I am impressed by the revelation of His *meekness*. And again the word is not lightly used nor lightly chosen. I have little care at the moment for the meaning of our particular word "meek." Rather I am thinking of the word He actually used of Himself when in the midst of His public ministry He said, "I am meek and lowly," that wonderful word which has never been perfectly translated, the word that suggests strength harnessed for service, the meekness that is gentleness. And what is gentleness? It was George Matheson who once said that

> "we use false figures when we speak of gentleness. We speak of the gentleness of the brook. The brook has no gentleness, it knows no gentleness. It rushes on its way, and exerts all its force over all the pebbles down the mountain side. If you would know what gentleness is, behold the mighty ocean lulled to rest, the ripples of which kiss the golden sand and bathe the feet of the little child. What it might do! How it might spread rack and ruin. But its strength is held in check for service."

That is meekness. "Thy gentleness," said an ancient singer, "hath made me great." No, behold, I pray you, the meekness of the Man. It is revealed first in His sifting of His disciples. Judas was excluded; then, halting at the very portal of the Garden, Jesus left eight of them behind, and permitted only three to go a little farther with Him because they were better able to make the effort, until at last, knowing that He was about to enter where they could not follow, He left them, charging them to watch with Him, Himself going alone to face the unutterable sorrow. There is a wonderful revelation here of strength. There are hours of unutterable anguish that come to our hearts which we cannot bear without the presence of a friend; and even though we know the sight of our anguish would break the heart of our friend, we must have that friend. At least I am such. But here was One so full of meekness that He would leave them.

Then observe Him dealing with their failure. Mark the patience of His method with them, no angry word from beginning to end. Even when He did rebuke them for sleeping He said, "The spirit indeed is willing." What recognition of their intention, even when He rebuked their fault!

I am impressed still further with the *sympathy* of Jesus as it is revealed in this story, and again the word is selected, and so far as I am able, with care. What is sympathy? Bearing with another, feeling with another, entering into the experience of the other, and sharing it. That was perhaps most wonderfully manifest at the last. I think it is often missed by readers of the story. I am quite sure it has been missed by commentators and expositors over and over again. "Then cometh He to the disciples, and saith unto them, Sleep on now, and take your rest: behold, the hour is at hand, and the Son of Man is betrayed into the hands of sinners." Some expositors have declared that when He said "Sleep on now, and take your rest," He spoke satirically to them because they were asleep. What misunderstanding of the Lord! No, you need more than the colon of the Revised Version to read this story correctly. You need a period, indicating a pause, a halt. Not satirically, but definitely and of infinite patience, and out of the fulness of His sympathy He said to them, as starting from their slumber at His return they looked at Him, "Sleep on now and take your rest." How long a time passed I cannot tell, but it was some period ere He woke them with the words, "Behold, the hour is at hand. Arise, let us be going." Jesus waited for them while they slept, watching over them. He knew all that was waiting for them on the coming day, all that through which they soon must pass of base denial, of flight, of terror; and so He, the supreme Saviour, watched the men who could not watch, sat by them in infinite sympathy as they slept. That sympathy was revealed again in something not recorded by Matthew, how when, in blundering zeal Peter wounded Malchus, with quick sensitiveness our Lord felt all the anguish of the pain, and with a touch, the last act of His divine surgery, healed the ear of Malchus.

And yet all these are but characteristics. There is yet something profounder, deeper, in which all these find their place, His compassion; not His pity merely, not merely the sympathy on which we have been touching, but that profounder, deeper fact, unfathomable as God, His *compassion*. It is found everywhere, for compassion was the secret of His being in the Garden at all. As we attempted to show in our meditation on His own great word, "The Son of Man is delivered up," no arresting hand of man apprehended Him. Observe how with kindly and gracious irony He spoke to the men at the close of the scene, "Are ye come out as against a robber with swords and staves to seize me? I sat daily in the temple teaching, and ye took me not," which means, Ye could not take Me, could not arrest Me, till Mine hour was come. And now do you imagine that with swords and staves you will accomplish it? Nay! "All this is come to pass, that the Scriptures might be fulfilled"! The reason of His being there was not that they had trapped Him, but that His compassion had compelled Him.

And so finally, and it is a thing that must be added—yet there are senses in which it seems almost irreverent to add it, so patent is it—I am impressed with His awful *purity* and sinlessness. That was the strength of everything else. It was the reason of His majesty, it was the strength of all His meekness, it created the keenness of His sympathy, and it was the inspiration of His compassion. And I will now repeat what I have said before.

Incense! I go back to the ancient economy, for I am also a child, and I must have my pictures and my helps when I stand in the presence of such things as these. I find in the ancient economy that the incense was compounded of sweet spices. What they were none can tell us finally. They are written for us on the pages of our Bible: onycha, stacte, galbanum, frankincense, and salt. It was a wonderful compound. What was this onycha? We do not know, and may at once confess it. All the clue we have is that of the Hebrew word which comes from a root that signifies the lion, the symbol of kingliness and dignity. I would lay no undue emphasis on that, but it is the only clue we have. Stacte was a highly fragrant gum, most certainly a type and symbol among these Eastern people of gentleness, of grace, of beauty. Galbanum was a product produced from a plant by bruising it, and was typical always of sympathy. Frankincense was the type of the priestly office. Salt was the element of purity. Whatever these men of the ancient time saw in their incense, looking back at it through the light of the glory of our Lord and Saviour Jesus Christ, we see suggestiveness in that incense of sweet spices compounded together, and permeated by the salt that purified. And let us ever remember that in that ancient economy men were forbidden to use this compound for personal gratification. It was sanctified, it was holy to the Lord.

I behold in that Garden One Whose garments smell of myrrh and cassia and aloes out of king's palaces, One Whose character is full of all gracious fragrance. It is Himself Who is the glory of the scene, the supreme beauty, the altogether lovely One, the well-beloved of the Father, always well pleasing to Him.

And now we turn to the symbolism of the fire. It was the symbol of the purpose of God, of the will of God; and the purpose of God and the will of God are the outcome of the nature of God. How shall I tell the story of the nature of God invisible and infinite? I will tell it thus. "God is love"! "Our God is a consuming fire"! These are not two facts but one, two statements of one essential truth. Mingling in the fire are the qualities of holiness and righteousness, and merging in the fire are the qualities of compassion and of mercy. Holiness and righteousness and mercy and compassion, all proceed out of the infinite mystery of His nature. Now these essential facts of the Deity of God reveal to us the secret of everything in this Man of His right hand; they discover the reason of the determinate counsel and foreknowledge of God, in answer to which He trod the sorrowful pathway to the Cross, and finally reached the Cross itself.

Mark His references to the fact. The first is discovered in His quotation of the ancient prophecy, "I will smite the shepherd and the sheep shall be scattered." The actual words occur in that final burden of Zechariah's prophecy: "Awake, O sword, against my shepherd, and against the man that is my fellow, saith the Lord of Hosts; smite the shepherd, and the sheep shall be scattered; and I will turn mine hand upon the little ones." Whatever we may think that meant, Jesus quoted it and applied it to Himself, and gave the fact of that writing as the reason impelling Him on that onward pathway. So also, when at last He awoke the sleeping disciples, mark the word He uttered, "The hour is come." At your leisure take your Gospels, and see how that figure of speech ran through His conversation, and observe how constantly on the pathway to the Cross He said, "Mine hour is not yet come." At last He said, "The hour is come."

He recognized He was in co-operation with God in the fulfilment of eternal purpose. The majesty of the will of God was on His soul. In that last word of the story, when He said if He besought His Father He would send Him twelve legions of angels, I pray you think of the angels He refused, and then inquire why did He not ask for them. The answer is found in

His own words, "How then should the Scriptures be fulfilled?" The recognition of the fact that He was in co-operation with God, not working against Him—God was not working against His Son, and His Son was not working against God—was always with Him. The zeal of God's house consumed Him. The fire was the will of God.

And so we reach, for a few brief moments tarrying in the inner place, that paragraph of inward anguish thrilling with power, on which, it seems to me that the cloud of the incense ever rests, so that the final word can never be said concerning it. You will notice in the story that three times over He cast His incense on the fire. He took all of Himself, and abandoned it in devotion to the will of His God. Mark the prelude to His first activity. He said to His disciples, "My soul," My life, "is exceeding sorrowful, even unto death." My life, My soul, all that I am. The things that we have been trying to look at! All the graces of Christ to which I have made reference were for joy and not for sorrow; they were the things that make for joy, they were the things of joy unspeakable, and full of glory. Yet He said, This life of Mine, into which no sorrow ought to come by reason of what it is in itself, is exceeding sorrowful, for all the things that are things of joy are contradicted. My authority is set at nought, my majesty is mocked, my meekness is refused, my sympathy is answered with scourging and with spitting; all the frankincense of my profound compassion is being trodden underfoot, and my purity is hurt and offended by the awful pollutions through the midst of which I pass. And He was called to that experience, called to endure it.

And now behold Him within the veil in the presence of God, alone with God; the sense of the coming sorrow surging through and through Him: "Father, if it be possible, let this cup pass from Me." This is but a revelation of the keen sense of the impending sorrows. But now behold: the priest casts the incense on the fire! "Nevertheless, not as I will, but as

Thou wilt"; if this be Thy will, I consent to the bruising of My life, that the things which should make for all joy should experience all sorrow. So the incense was cast on the fire.

Passing back, He found the sleeping disciples. And I pray you mark the infinite beauty of His recognition of their willingness to keep awake. "The spirit indeed is willing." Then He passed again into the Presence. And now the wording is slightly changed, and I see not merely the sense of the coming sorrows, but the sense of their inevitability. If it be not possible that this cup shall pass—then the incense of all His perfect life was flung upon the fire—"not as I will, but as Thou wilt."

Again glancing toward the disciples sleeping there, in infinite pity He allowed them to sleep on without disturbing them, and once more returning into the Presence He said the same words.

We do not read this story aright if we tarry over the words that indicate the appalling sense of coming sorrow. They did but serve as prelude to the final, utter, absolute devotion of Himself to the will of God.

As our High Priest is seen standing in the Holy Place and casting the fragrant incense of His life on the consuming fire, behold a cloud covers the Mercy Seat!

So I glance back once more at the book of Leviticus, and I read, "I will appear in the cloud upon the Mercy Seat which is upon the ark; that ye die not." A few verses further on I read that this incense was to be brought and burned on the fire in order that the cloud of the incense might cover the Mercy Seat on the testimony that the offering priest might not die.

Whatever that may have meant for Aaron in those early days, and for subsequent High Priests, I turn to the letter to the Hebrews, and I read, "Who in the days of His flesh, having offered up prayers and supplication with strong crying and tears unto Him Who was able to save Him from death, and having been heard for His godly fear." He was heard, He was answered, He was saved from death. "My soul is exceeding sorrowful even unto death." He stood for a moment so overwhelmed by sorrows in His humanity that it seemed as if they must kill Him. He had said, "No man taketh my life from me. I lay it down, and I will take it again." In order to have a second entrance to the Holy Place with atoning blood there must be a dying in act, not by the ordinary pathway of humanity, but by the authority, and for the purpose of a great compassion. Thus in the hour of His praying our Lord was delivered from death that threatened Him, which was the mere death of crushing sorrow. So He offered the incense, devoted Himself to the ultimate in the economy of the purpose of God, and was heard in that He cried. He did not die in the Garden, but moved from there to the Cross itself.

By that triumph, says the writer of the letter, He became the author of eternal salvation. And presently passing in again to the Holy Place, He prevailed, and men are made nigh.

I pray you, believe me, this is not the final word, these are only some of the things of the glory of that Garden scene. May He, in His compassion, Who was patient with sleeping disciples, and full of majesty and of meekness in that unutterable hour, cleanse the words and thoughts of our attempted exposition, and may He bring us nearer and nearer yet to the heart of His sorrow.

CHAPTER XV

THE DARKNESS OF GOLGOTHA

From the sixth hour there was darkness over all the land until the ninth hour.
MATTHEW 27:45.

THAT IS A VERSE WHICH WE ARE IN DANGER OF READING hurriedly. We treat it too often as though it were merely the record of something incidental.

As a matter of fact, it is the central verse in the story of the Cross. Indeed, the Cross itself is not mentioned, no word is spoken of it or of the Christ; they are alike hidden, and yet the period was one of three hours' duration, the very central hours of the experience of the Saviour of men. Christ and the Cross are alike hidden within that verse, and that fact is most suggestive because in those hours transactions were accomplished which through all eternity defy the apprehension and explanation of finite minds.

It is not to be passed over lightly that all the Synoptists record the fact of that darkness. Three hours of darkness and of silence! All the ribald clamor was over, the material opposition utterly exhausted, the turmoil ended. Man had done his last and his worst. Beyond that period of the three hours' silence even human actions were expressive of pity. Nothing has impressed my own heart, or amazed me more in reading this story anew, and attempting to meditate upon it in view of this service, than what I shall venture to describe as the wonderful psychological conditions of those hours beyond the hours of silence. It is as though that appalling silence and that overwhelming darkness had changed the entire attitude of man to the Saviour. The very vinegar they offered Him to drink was offered Him in pity. What they said about Elijah was expressive of their desire to sympathize. The centurion's testimony was that of a man whose heart was strangely moved toward the august and dignified Saviour. When presently they found Him dead, and therefore did not break His bones, the spear thrust was one of kindness, lest perchance He might still suffer, in spite of the fact that He appeared to be dead. Multitudes dispersed from the scene at Golgotha smiting their breasts, overwhelmed with a sense of awe, and strangely moved by some new pity. And there is no picture in all the New Testament more full of pathos and of power than that of the women standing silent and amazed through all those hours of His suffering, and still standing there beyond them.

Then also the cries which passed the lips of Jesus beyond the darkness were all of them significant of accomplishment. "My God! My God, why didst Thou forsake Me?"—for that was the tense; a slight change from the tense of the actual Psalm, a question asked by One Who was emerging from the experience to which He referred. And then as John is most careful to record for us, "Knowing that all things were now finished, He said, I thirst." Beyond that came the words of the great proclamation, "It is finished." And at last the words of the final committal, full of dignity, were spoken: "Father, into Thy hands I commend My spirit." Everything was changed beyond the hours of silence and of darkness.

Much has been written about these hours of darkness, much which is not warranted by any careful spiritual attention to the story itself. You will call to mind how, at great length many years ago, it was argued that the darkness was that of the sun's eclipse. But that is entirely impossible, for Passover was always held at full moon, when there could be no eclipse of the sun. The darkness has been described as nature's sympathy with the suffering of the Lord, but that is a pagan conception of nature, a conception of nature as having some consciousness apart from God and out of harmony with His work. It has been said that the darkness was brought about by an act of God, and was expressive of His sympathy with His Son. I immediately admit that that is an appealing idea, and has some element of truth in it, in that we may discover the overruling of His government; but to declare that that darkness was caused by God because of His sympathy with His Son is to deny the cry of Jesus which immediately followed the darkness and referred to it. The darkness was to Him a period when He experienced whatever He may have meant by the words, "Thou didst forsake Me."

If I have succeeded in these words spoken in reverent spirit, in suggesting to you the difficulty of those central three hours, then our hearts are prepared for going forward.

I submit to you thoughtfully that no interpretation of that darkness is to be trusted save that of the Lord Who experienced it. Has He flung any light on the darkness which will enable us to apprehend the meaning of the darkness? Did any word escape His lips that will help us to explain those silent hours? I think the answer is to be found in these narratives, and to that teaching of the Lord we appeal in order that we may consider the meaning of the darkness, and the passing of the darkness, and thereafter attempt reverently to look back at the transaction in the darkness.

First, then, as to the *meaning of the darkness*. What was this darkness? How was it caused? What did it really mean? That this question is of importance is proved by that to which I have already drawn your attention, the fact that Matthew, Mark, and Luke alike record it, and that with care, as having taken place at this very time. The reference is made by each one of them in detail. It was something to be noted, something to be remembered, something which made its impression alike on the evangelist who saw the King, and the evangelist who saw the Servant, and the evangelist who saw the Perfect Man. We cannot pass it over as though it were merely incidental, and consequently we shall attempt to discover its meaning in the light of what our Lord Himself said ere He passed into the darkness.

Luke records for us a fact not mentioned by either of the other evangelists, that in Gethsemane Jesus said to the man who came to arrest Him, "This is your hour, and the power of darkness." That was a most suggestive word, spoken as I have reminded you, in Gethsemane ere He passed from the garden to and through those trial scenes which we have not read this evening, but with which you are familiar. Last Sunday evening we attempted in reverence to behold the High Priest casting the incense on the fire in those hallowed experiences of Gethsemane. When that was over, just as He was leaving the garden Jesus spoke to the men about Him, "This is your hour, and the power of darkness." This is your hour! More than once during these Sunday evenings in which we have been meditating in the neighborhood of the Cross it has been necessary to refer to that phrase or conception, and I go back to it again, not to tarry at length with it, but to ask you most carefully to ponder it. At the commencement of our Lord's public ministry He referred to an hour which was not yet, to an hour which was postponed, and during the course of His ministry you will find that the evangelists more than once allude to the same hour, and to that hour, whatever it might have been, as to a postponed hour. Men attempted to arrest Him, but they could not because His hour was not yet come. Men desired to encompass His death, and wrought with all their strength, all their wit so to do; but they were unable, because His hour had not yet come. And not always by the use of that particular phrase, but over and over again our Lord was looking forward toward some consummating, culminating hour which no man could hurry, and which no man could postpone, but which He did perpetually postpone until in the economy of God its set time should have come.

"We must work the works of Him that sent Me while it is day. The night cometh when no man can work," was one of the profoundest sayings of Jesus in illuminating His own immediate ministry, having larger values, I will readily admit, but often we miss the profoundest value because we fail to observe the first intention. There was an immediate application of that word, which the Revised Version helps us to appreciate by a change of number in the personal pronoun. "We" —He was speaking of Himself and His disciples—"We must work the works of Him that sent Me while it is day; the night cometh," a time of darkness and desolation, "when no man can work," when you must stand aside from co-operation and fellowship with Me. That was the consummating hour to which He looked, the night of darkness which at last would come, in which no man could work, but God alone must work.

Now, in the light of that all too rapid examination of a very definite movement manifest in the ministry of our Lord, we come to Gethsemane. They were about to lay hands on Him, and to lead Him away to Caiaphas and to Pilate and to Herod, and again to Pilate and to death. Then He said, "This is your hour, and the power of darkness." The night, the hour postponed had arrived, and this was its character. From the sixth hour until the ninth hour there was darkness over all the land. We have no picture of the Son of God during those hours, no record of a word passing His lips. It was the period of the infinite silence, the period of the overwhelming darkness.

What, then, is this that Jesus said concerning the darkness? It was the hour of evil, it was the hour under the dominion of the powers of darkness. In those three hours we see the Saviour in the midst of all that which resulted from the action of evil. Not without remarkable suggestiveness did the great apostle speak in a letter written long afterwards of Satan as "prince of the power of the air"; and not without suggestiveness did he speak of him as presiding over the age as ruler of the darkness. Not without significance did John, the beloved apostle, when opening his Gospel and writing concerning Jesus say that in Him was life, and the life was the light of men; that the light shineth in darkness, and the darkness apprehended it not, comprehended it not. Neither the word "apprehended," nor the word "comprehended" means "understood" in this connection. The declaration is not that the darkness did not understand the light, but that the darkness did not extinguish the light. The apostle's declaration at the commencement of the Gospel is that the light was always shining, and however deep and dense the darkness, it never succeeded in entirely extinguishing the light. The darkness apprehended it not, did not put it out. In that very negative declaration of the apostle you are brought face to face with the positive purpose of evil, with the purpose of Satan. What was Satan's supreme desire? To extinguish the light. "There," said John of Jesus, "was the true light . . . which lighteth every man, coming into the world." Satan's purpose was to extinguish that light.

From the very beginning of the shining of that light, focused in history by the Incarnation, the one supreme purpose of the enemy was to apprehend it, to comprehend it, to extinguish it, to put it out. And in these three hours of darkness we are face to face with the time when all the force of evil was brought to bear on the soul of the Son of God, and all the unutterable intent and purpose of evil wrapped Him about in a darkness that is beyond our comprehension.

In that moment there was material darkness. It was the material symbol of the empire of sin. If the questioning of the heart shall become so material as to inquire—and I grant you it almost necessarily must—whether Satan did in some way actually produce the material darkness, I shall have to reply I cannot tell, but I believe he did. I believe that by some action of those spiritual antagonisms, the world of principalities and powers, of which the early Christians were far more conscious than we are, and therefore more ready to fight with, under the captaincy and leadership of the prince of the power of the air, there was wrought out in material experience a symbol of the spiritual intention of hell.

I suggest for some quiet hour the study and examination of Biblical symbolisms, and especially the use of this figure in Biblical literature, the figure of darkness. For the purpose of illustration I confine myself entirely to this Gospel of Matthew. Listen to these phrases, and immediately you will see how darkness is indeed a symbol of spiritual evil. "The people which sat in darkness." "If thine eye be evil, thy whole body shall be full of darkness. If therefore the light that is in thee be darkness, how great is the darkness!" "The sons of the kingdom shall be cast forth into the outer darkness." "Cast ye out the unprofitable servant into the outer darkness."

Wherever the word occurs in this Gospel of Matthew, indeed wherever it occurs in the New Testament, or its equivalent in the Old, it is the symbol of spiritual evil in its issue and in its ultimate. Darkness is the twin sister of death. Death and darkness express the ultimate in evil. And in this hour, when the Lord Himself was passing to death, there was darkness; and that material darkness which impressed the evangelists and the multitudes, and changed their attitude of mind toward Him, was but the outward and visible sign of the more mysterious and unfathomable spiritual darkness into the midst of which He had passed. Through the channel of His earthly life all spiritual things were having material manifestation. The Incarnation itself was but the working out into human observation of the truth concerning God. And now, in the hour of the dying of the Son of God, in that infinite, awful mystery, spiritual evil had its material manifestation in the darkness that settled over all the land. The darkness was of Satan; it was coincident with the ultimate in the suffering of the Son of God.

And now, ere we ask the most difficult of all questions concerning the transaction of the darkness, in preparation for that inquiry, let us look once more at that at which we have already glanced, the passing of the darkness. In order that we may see, that we may understand, let us listen again to the four words that passed the lips of the Lord beyond the ninth hour when the darkness was passing away, and the light of material day was again breaking through on the green hill and on the Cross and on all those Judaean lands. Notice reverently, then, the four cries that escaped His lips, and divide them, as they most certainly are divided, into two groups, the first two and the second two.

The first cry was the expression of a backward thought. "My God, My God, why didst Thou forsake Me?" It was the call of Jesus of Nazareth as He emerged from the darkness, and from all that happened therein, of which no single word is actually written. It was in itself a revelation, like a flash of light piercing the darkness. "My God, My God, why didst Thou forsake Me?"

In the next word we have the expression of His immediate experience, of that of which in His humanity He became then supremely conscious, "I thirst."

Almost immediately following it we have again an expression of His immediate experience, that of which in the essential mystery of His Being He was conscious, "It is finished."

The final word described a forward glance. As the first word beyond the darkness expressed the backward thought, "My God, My God, why didst Thou forsake Me?" the last word expressed a forward confidence, "Father, into Thy hands I commend My spirit."

We have listened to these words simply in order that we

may try to be near Him as the darkness passed, and with all reverence, by listening to Him, appreciate something of the thinking of His own mind. A backward thought, "My God, My God, why didst Thou forsake Me?" and immediate experience within human limitations, "I thirst"; then spiritual accomplishment, "It is finished"; and then the future, the glorious future, "Father, into Thy hands I commend My spirit."

Then He died, not of a broken heart, not of human brutality, not of murder by human hands; but of His own volition He yielded up the Ghost, and His Spirit, commended to God, passed to God. The death that saves was not that physical dissolution, but the infinite spiritual mystery of the three hours and the darkness, which being passed, He Himself did say, "It is finished."

In all that remained of the story beyond the hours of darkness we have no record of any word uttered by the foes of Jesus. They were not present, or they seem not to have been, during that time. Indeed, it is something to be meditated with thankfulness of heart that no rude hand ever touched the body of the dead Christ, that after the darkness, and beyond the death, and beyond the dismissal of the spirit, they were loving disciple hands that took Him from the Cross and wrapped Him round, and buried Him, giving Him the temporary resting place of a garden tomb. In death He was wonderfully preserved from all dishonor. The foes of Jesus seem to have withdrawn. Satan seems to have been absent.

Where was Satan? There is no answer in the records of the evangelists, and so I pass on to apostolic writings, and I find this written concerning Christ: "Having put off from Himself the principalities and the powers, He made a show of them openly, triumphing over them in it." In the deep darkness, and in the midst of the silence, He triumphed over the forces of evil, the principalities and powers, and made a show of them openly by the Cross, putting off from Himself all that assaulted Him in, and by, and through the darkness.

As the darkness passed, we glance once again at that at which we have already looked, the attitude of the people. They were arrested, they were touched with pity; there came illumination to them concerning the dying and the dead One, and a great fear possessed them.

So, finally, we come to the most impossible subject of all, that of the transaction within the darkness. We admit that this can have no final exposition. We admit immediately that any even partial thing that may be said is incomplete. Every aspect of the infinite whole is larger than we can know. Every theory is of value, but all theories fail. This is not the place, nor would it be within the highest purpose of our worship, to attempt to prove that statement; but at least I may be permitted to say that, so far as I know, I have been reading through five and twenty years with ever growing gratitude great books on the Cross, and from each one I have gained something and every one I have at last laid down, saying as I did so, Yes, yes! All that, but more; something not reached, something not spoken!

God cannot finally be expressed in finite terms. "The stone which the builders rejected is become the head of the corner. This is the Lord's doing; it is marvellous in our eyes." It cannot be explained; it is the perpetual marvel. God must pity any man who thinks he understands this Cross completely. God have mercy on any child of God if the day comes in which he has not to sing, "Love so *amazing*, so divine."

When the amazement dies out, it is not that the Cross has been analyzed, but that the gazer upon it has become blind.

Yet we may gain some light from the words of the Lord as He emerged from the darkness, and the darkness itself was suggestive. We remember the word we have already read from Matthew. "The people which sat in darkness." Into that darkness the Son of God experimentally passed. "If thine eye be evil, thy whole body shall be full of darkness. If the light that is in thee be darkness, how great is that darkness!" That darkness had passed into His heart, when He said, "My God, My God, why hast Thou forsaken Me?" "The sons of the kingdom shall be cast forth into outer darkness." The Son of God passed into that outer darkness.

That does not answer the inquiry as to what happened. I have no answer for that. Only this I know, that in that hour of darkness He passed into the place of the ultimate wrestling of evil in actual experience. There is light as I hear the final word, "Father, into Thy hands I commend My spirit," for the word is a word which declares that whatever the transaction was, it was accomplished; that whatever the dying indicated, it was done.

But let us go a little further back, before the darkness, and listen to the chief priests who joined in the hellish clamor that beat on the suffering soul of the dying Saviour. Among other things, they said this, "He saved others; Himself He cannot save." That brings me nearer than anything else. Those were wonderful hours of the transmutation of basest things to high and noble things. That was the last taunt of His enemies; it has become the most illuminative word about the Cross.

"He saved others; Himself He cannot." So they laughed at Him. But hear it again, as a truth sublime and awful: because He saved others, He cannot save Himself. In order to save others He will not save Himself. Said the rabble, and said the rabbis joining in the unholy chorus, "Let Him come down from the Cross." He did not come down from the Cross, He went up from the Cross. The great Priest Who already had burned the incense in the holiest place bore the symbolic mystery of His own shed blood into the holy place, but ere He could do so, He passed into the darkness and abode in the silence three hours—a human measurement in order that we may somehow understand—and in those three hours He could not save Himself, and that because His heart was set upon saving others.

But why, why, why could He not save Himself? My question descends to the level of common, everyday human experience and capacity at its highest and its best. He might have saved Himself. He might never have gone to Gethsemane's Garden. He might even in Gethsemane's Garden have asked for twelve legions of angels, as He Himself did say. He might with one glance of His shining glory have swept the rabble from about the Cross and descended to the deliverance of Himself. If He had spoken in terms of power He might have saved Himself. Why, then, was it that He could not save Himself?

Because He is God, and because God is love, and love is never satisfied with the destruction of a sinner, but with the saving of a sinner. Love never finds its rest with holiness and righteousness vindicated by the annihilation of the things that oppose. Love will find its rest only when those who have been swept from righteousness and holiness are restored thereto and are remade in the image of the Father, God. That is why.

Yes, but once more. If that be true, then on the ground of the mystery of the compulsion of the ineffable love of God in Christ could love find no other way? Love could find no other way because sin knows no ending save by that way. The conscience of men demands that, the experience of men demands that. I base the twofold affirmation on the testimonies of the centuries and the millenniums. I base the affirmation on what I know within my own soul of sin.

Someone may say to me, "Cannot God forgive out of pure love?" I shall answer, "If He can, I cannot." If he could forgive me for the wrongs of which I am conscious, and that have left behind them their stain and pollution—if He could forgive me by simply saying, Never mind them, then I cannot so forgive myself. My conscience cries for a cleansing that is more than a sentiment of pity. Somehow, somewhere, in order that I may have forgiveness, there must be tragedy, something mightier than the devilish sin.

I do not know what happened in the darkness, but this I know, that as I have come to the Cross and received the suggestions of its material unveiling, I have found my heart, my spirit, my life brought into a realm of healing spices, to the consciousness of the forgiveness of sins. And there is no other way and there is no other gospel of forgiveness.

In the darkness He saved not Himself, but He saved me. He declined to move toward His own deliverance in order that He might loose me from my sin. Out of the darkness has come a light. The word spoken to Cyrus long ago has been fulfilled in the spiritual glory to the Son of God, "I will give thee the treasures of darkness." And because fulfilled to the Son of God by the Father Who loved Him, and wrought with Him through the mystery of His forsaking, the word has been fulfilled also to the sons of God who are born not of blood, nor of man, nor of the will of the flesh, but of God. He gives us the treasures of darkness.

From the sixth hour until the ninth hour there was darkness over all the land, and from the darkness have come the treasures of pardon, and peace, of power, and of purity.

CHAPTER XVI

HALTING

How long halt ye between two opinions? If the Lord be God, follow Him; but if Baal, then follow Him.
                                    I KINGS 18:21.

AHAB WAS KING OF ISRAEL. THE KINGDOM WAS IN A MOST deplorable condition, perhaps at a period darker than any other in its history. Ahab was a veritable incarnation of evil, and his influence, together with that of Jezebel, had been blighting and spoiling everything of essential greatness. Clouds and darkness were over all the land. Images of Baal and Ashtaroth gleamed in the valleys. Temples of idolatry were erected everywhere, and the altars of God were broken down. Then, while such darkness reigned throughout the land, while it seemed as though no cheering star gleamed through the blackness, as suddenly as the falling of a thunderbolt, there appeared on the scene one of the most remarkable and fiery of all the prophets.

In the previous chapter we have the beginning of the story of the mission of Elijah. "And Elijah the Tishbite, who was of the sojourners of Gilead, said unto Ahab." That is the introduction of this man. We know no more of him than this, a Tishbite, and we are not sure even until this day what that may mean. It is even suggested that he was a man of another nationality, not of the chosen seed. Be that as it may, from somewhere, no one knows where, somehow, under what influence none can tell, this man broke in upon the condition of affairs with a message that was fiery and forceful, terrific and timely, a veritable message of God, a message that was brief, a message that was a message of judgment, a message that made no apology, and offered no conditions, and suggested no compromise.

It was briefly this: "As the Lord, the God of Israel liveth, before Whom I stand, there shall not be dew nor rain these years but according to my word," and, having uttered it, Elijah vanished.

But the Word of the Lord, which is ever powerful, which is never void, but ever thrills with energy, wrought out into actual and terrific fulfilment, the word of judgment, that there should be no rain and no dew for three years, and the people who, in material prosperity, had forgotten God—no, infinitely worse, had defiantly rebelled against God—were brought back face to face with God through the process of a judgment which had been foretold by the prophet. Elijah was cared for, first, at the brook, and then at Zarephath, until the time foretold having passed away he appeared again on the scene, first to Obadiah, and then to Ahab.

Our story is that of the hour in which Elijah faced Ahab. It is a wonderful story, dramatic and startling. Ahab, at last, stood face to face with the man whose prediction, having been fulfilled, had wrought such havoc in the condition of the nation. He asked him, "Is it thou, thou troubler of Israel?" And with quiet, calm dignity the answer of the prophet was given, "I have not troubled Israel; but thou, and thy father's house, in that ye have forsaken the commandments of the Lord, and thou hast followed the Baalim." And then addressing himself still to the king, in the language of a superior, with the note of authority, he said, "Gather to me all Israel . . . and the prophets of Baal." The king, who, in his first words, manifested the anger that was in his heart, and the murder that lurked there, made no difficulty, but, under the tremendous power and will of the prophetic command, backed by the authority of God, gathered the people together.

The story is better written than I can ever tell it. All I stay to do for one moment is to notice the different classes that were gathered on Mount Carmel in that wonderful moment in the history of the people. On the one hand were the prophets of Baal, four hundred and fifty; and the prophets of the Asherah, four hundred; and all those who followed their teaching and worshiped at their shrines. On the other hand, stood the one lonely messenger of God, Elijah, confronting the prophets of a false religion, confronting the corruption of a corrupt court, confronting that most terrible of all things, an undecided mob. On the one hand, men who are decided in their worship of Baal; on the other, a man who is decided in his worship of Jehovah; and then that great company of the nation, waiting for leading, undecided, a mixed multitude, many of them never having confessed openly their allegiance to God, even though in their heart they were loyal to Him, for while Elijah said "I, even I only, am left," elsewhere we are told that God replied, "Yet will I leave Me seven thousand in Israel, all the knees which have not bowed unto Baal, and every mouth which hath not kissed him." And beside that seven thousand, the great multitude of the people who knew the will of God, who had been nurtured in the very atmosphere and enforcement of His law, but into whose heart there had come the lusting that is at the base of all false worship—a great crowd, undecided, uncommitted, halting, wavering, taking neither one side nor the other.

It was to this multitude that Elijah spoke, "How long halt ye between two opinions?" *Between* opinions, that is, without opinion. A man who is between two opinions is devoid of an opinion. How long halt ye there? said the prophet. Now listen to him. "If God be God, follow Him; if Baal,

HALTING

then follow him." I think I hear the fervor and the passion in the prophet's voice. I think I know how he felt that day. I think, if I may put this old Hebrew and stately language into the language of the present day and the language of my heart, it is as though the prophet said, Take sides at all costs. Let us know where you are by one thing or the other; find your God, and follow. I think I hear the prophet saying, as he looked out on this great crowd, wondering over the discussing and philosophizing and arguing, "If God be God, follow Him; but if Baal, then follow him." Build your altar, burn incense, and go the whole way. "If God be God, rebuild His broken altar, and follow Him." It is the prophet's protest against indecision. "How long halt ye between two opinions?"

The times have changed. We do not gather now on Mount Carmel. The prophets of Baal are not among us as they were there. Our altars of God are not the same as were the altars raised of old. All the accidental robing has passed, but essential men are still here. All that is merely Eastern has gone out of the story, but the living vital principles abide. And as God, Who alone is able to do it, sifts and divides among us we fall on different sides and into different positions just as did these men of old. The local coloring has passed away, but the central truth abides. There are those who are definitely and openly and positively worshiping God. Thank God for the company. There are those—alas, that it is so, and yet it is true—who are openly and definitely and positively worshiping at other altars, for every man is worshiping, every man has some deity enshrined in his heart and life. Every man has some master passion of his life to which he burns incense as the days come and go. There are those who are worshiping at the altars of idolatry, at the altars of pollution, at the altars of sin. But there are also very many who are not definitely and positively and avowedly committed either to God or Baal, either to purity or impurity, either to right or to wrong. The choice has not yet been definitely made. They have not yet said, God is God, we will follow Him until we see Him. They have not yet said, Evil is God, we will follow it until we see it unmasked in perdition. They have not said these things. They are standing and halting and waiting between opinions, with opinion unformed, with decision unmade.

"How long halt ye between two opinions?" I make the same appeal as did the prophet of old. "If God be God, follow Him; but if Baal, then follow him." If the God Whom I declare to you be indeed the One Who can best fill that place in your heart which clamors to be filled, if He be the One Who can best guide, direct life, enoble you, crown you, follow Him. But if evil can best satisfy you, if you have come to the decision that you can best be fitted and fashioned and formed and satisfied by evil, then follow evil. Only do one thing or the other. In the name of God and humanity, for the sake of God and humanity, take sides, and let us know where you stand. The man who is turning his face toward evil and pollution with all his heart and soul and mind is not doing half so much harm in the community as the man who is taking on his lips for discussion the language of sacred things, while in his heart he refuses to follow them to an issue. That is the kind of statement that some of you resent. I shall repeat it and emphasize it. Here is a man who has given his whole life to the clamant cry for stimulants; here is a man who is a drunkard. That man's influence on the children of the district where he lives is not half so pernicious as the influence of the father of the children who plays with the thing that may damn his child. Think of it. I will take my boy in the freshness of his boyhood's days by the hand, and I will lead him along some street, and there in the gutter lies the man absolutely abandoned to drink, bloated, bruised, and degraded, and my boy looks there at that man, and he is warned. But it may be there lies in the life of my boy some hidden fire, which once ignited, will burn him to ruin, and he sees me indulging, not decided as to whether it is right or wrong; he tries to follow me, and may be ruined. I know that is extreme, but it is true.

You are undecided. You have never come to a definite decision either for God or for evil. There is a man in your store, in your shop, in your place of business, who is "going the whole pace," to quote a phrase with which every man here is familiar. The influence of that man on the other men is not half so pernicious as the influence of the man who discusses and does nothing, affects to believe in the Gospels of the New Testament and never obeys them, speaks patronizingly of God Almighty and of Jesus Christ and in life rebels against God. That is the man who is harming others by his influence, the man who drifts and is not decided, and is willing to discuss, but never to do; to philosophize, but never to surrender; to argue, but never to commit his life to Jesus Christ. Oh, these men and women who are uncommitted, these men and women in our churches and our pews and in our services who come and go, drifting, drifting, until they block the river way and hinder others. In the name of God, I appeal to you, do one thing or the other. If God be God, follow Him. If evil be the true master of life, follow it. Let us have the line of cleavage clearly defined.

If you want to form your decision and cease your halting, if you want to decide whether it is to be Baal or God, sin or Jesus Christ, come back for a few moments and look at the picture in the chapter in which our text is found. If you look carefully you will see the service of sin exemplified in the prophets of Baal; you will see the service of God exemplified in Elijah. I will come, in conclusion, to the same appeal with which I started, I will ask you to halt no longer, to make your choice, and to join with the men who worship Baal or God.

Look at the picture. I never read that story without feeling how graphically it sets before my vision the truth about the men who are serving sin, and serving self, and serving Satan. I look back at these prophets of Baal, and there are different points from which I view them. I see in them, first, a point for *admiration;* I look at them a little more closely, and I see a point for *sarcasm;* I look at them again, and I see a point for *anger;* finally, I look, and I see a point for *pity.*

I look to-day at the men who serve sin with high hand and outstretched arm, and I see exactly the same things—a point for admiration, a point for sarcasm, a point for anger, and a point for pity.

A point for admiration? someone says to me. What do you mean? I am not dealing with the halting multitude. There is nothing to admire in them. I am dealing with the prophets of Baal as they exemplify what sin is. What is the point for admiration? It is the courage, the daring, the enthusiasm, the force that these men put into their business. And I do not hesitate to say that I admire it. It was a daring thing for these men to accept the challenge of Elijah at all. And then there was no half-heartedness. All day they cried, "Oh, Baal, hear us." And there was no voice, no answer. And again they cried, and I watch them as the day wears on leaping in frenzy on the altar, stirring up the passion of their inner life with knives. I look at their zeal, at their earnestness, at their determination, and I admire them.

I look at the men who are sinning hard, and I admire them. I have a great deal more hope of winning that man who serves the devil well than the man who stays half-way between God and the devil, and does not know which to serve. Oh, the passion men are putting into sin!

But I look again, and I see a point for *sarcasm.* It must be a tender sarcasm. Jesus had a great deal of sarcasm about Him. You cannot read the records of His life without finding it. God grant that our sarcasm may always be like His, very keen, but very tender, based on love, and yet flashing like a searchlight. Listen to Elijah. He looks at the men when the noonday has arrived, and he says: "Cry aloud: for he is a god; either he is musing, or he is gone aside, or he is in a journey, or peradventure he sleepeth, and must be awaked." All of which means this, your gods are all very well until you are in trouble. Your gods will do when you do not need help, or to feel a presence, or know a power. Baal is all right so long as you are not face to face with a crisis. But get there, and you will know the folly of the whole business. Cry aloud, perhaps he is sleeping. Think of the sarcasm of it. Men driven wild with a frenzy of desire, and their god asleep!

You who make sin your god, who worship it, and serve it, because of what you get out of it, wait a moment. There is a day of crisis coming. It may come in different ways to you. It may come as bereavement, when the house is darkened, and the heart is sad, and some little child is put down into the grave. It may come as poverty, when riches take to themselves wings and fly away. It may come as death, when you yourself know that you are passing away. Now, oh, bereaved man—think me not unkind, for in God's name I would only drive you to truth—oh, poverty-stricken man, with nobody who cares to help you in the day of your adversity; oh, dying man, with the shadows creeping round you, cry aloud to your god, ask sin to help you now. You see the folly of it. You dare not. The thing for which you have sacrified your loyalty, the thing for which you have turned your back on God and Heaven and life, cannot help when the crisis comes. Where is your comfort, oh, bereaved man? For your own sake play the man, do not turn your back on Jesus Christ and sin against Him and crucify Him, and then when your child dies want His words to be uttered about resurrection. See this thing through. If you are going to turn your back on my Master to-night see it through. Oh, the unutterable folly of it, that a man will take his life, spirit, soul, and body, and pour all out in worship of the thing that never gives him an answering word of pity or of power when the crisis comes. And yet again I look at these men, and I find there is a point that demands my anger. It is the wilfulness of their folly. These people, many of them, who had become the prophets of Baal, and all such in the nation as had listened to the teaching, and followed the guidance of the prophets of Baal, who were they? They were the people who had such a wonderful history, people who belonged to the upper and the nether springs, people who possessed the oracles of God, and yet were deliberately choosing Baal because he gave license to passion and self.

The picture is repeated to-day. I look out on the servants of sin, and sometimes it seems as though the very anger of the heart becomes hot. Why? For the same reason that God is angry with men, because in their folly and perversity and wilfulness they deliberately choose the things that ruin them. Oh, yes, but let the last note be sounded.

I look at these prophets, and I find there is a point for pity. See the effect on them of their own sin. Admire the passion, if you will, as it burns. Be as sarcastic as you will, that in the presence of crisis there is no help. Be as angry as you will over the unutterable folly of wickedness, but look at them after the long, weary day, fainting, wounded men. You cannot look at the prophets of Baal in their weariness and their wounding without pitying them.

You will at once see how this applies to us. The Godly heart, the Christly heart always feels a great pity for the sinner. Oh, these wounded men, these hardened criminals, these ruined lives! Oh, these men, with physical constitution spoiled, and with mind diseased, and spiritual capacity paralyzed and dead! Oh, weep over them! Oh, the pity of it! Oh, dear man, that thou shouldest put passion into the business of destroying thyself! Oh, that thou shouldest take the Divinely bestowed powers of thy wondrous manhood, and burn them up only to burn thyself! Oh, the pity of it! The service of sin, there it is, passion without principle!

For a moment look on the other side, and in that one lonely man, Elijah, see the service of God exemplified.

First look at his *boldness*. Did we say it was a bold thing for the prophets of Baal to accept his challenge? It was a far bolder thing for one man to challenge eight hundred and fifty. He stood alone. He had an avowed purpose to attack idolatrous worship, and he stood confronting the king whose court was corrupt, and all associated with him.

It is not a blustering courage, a courage characterized by foolhardiness. It is not the courage that whistles in the dark. It is the courage that is quiet and *calm* and strong, calm when Elijah challenges the king as the troubler of Israel, calm in the waiting of the long day, calm in the final crises and in the midst of all circumstances. But these are only outward things.

Mark not merely the boldness and the calmness of this servant of God; but discover the reason of the boldness, of the calmness. At last the prophets have done, and have failed. At last his own sacrifice is laid on his altar, and with magnificent daring he has saturated the whole sacrifice and altar with water until the very trench is full of it.

If you want really to see Elijah, you must see him now; see him as he comes quietly forward toward that altar in the presence of all those people, and hear him as he says, "Oh, Lord, the God of Abraham, of Isaac, and of Israel, let it be known this day that Thou art God in Israel and that I am Thy servant, and that I have done all these things at Thy word. Hear me, O Lord, hear me, that this people may know that Thou, Lord, art God, and that Thou hast turned their heart back again." Then the fire fell. Here we are at the heart of it. Elijah quietly built his altar, placed his sacrifice, and then lifted his voice to God, and the moment the cry of His servant reached the ear of God the fire fell.

I am not surprised that Elijah was bold now. I am not surprised that Elijah was calm now. He is seen now as the man who lived by faith, in touch with the secret forces. He is seen to be a man who had communion with God. He knew how to move the hand that holds the world, to bring deliverence down. He lived, not in the power of things seen, but in the power and possession of the unseen. The prophets had cut themselves, and cried in an agony to a god who did not answer, because he did not exist. In the calm of eventide, without frenzy, with quiet bold dignity, this man spoke and fire fell.

This is the picture of the life of the Christian man. That is what we are asking you to choose. You can be bold, you can be calm, you can be courageous, and why? Because if you worship God your life is linked to Omnipotence, your life is linked to Omniscience, your life is linked to Omnipresence.

I will say no more to you save this: I speak here as in God's presence. I have chosen. I will follow God. I will be a Christian man, and now I know that this life of mine is linked to the infinite wisdom of God, and this, if I will but use it, will guide me until time shall blossom into eternity. I, so weak and frail that the slightest breath of temptation will make me sin, if I try to fight it alone—and I speak the thing I know—I am linked to the power of God, and "I can do all things in Christ, Who strengtheneth me." And I that am often lonely if I trust to other friends and other helpers, my life is linked to God, Who is always just where I am. At home, He is there; in the railway train, He is there; in the place of joy, He is there, and His laughter mingles with mine; in the place of sorrow, He is there, and His heart is moved with pity and with help. I am never away from Him.

How long halt ye? How long? How long? I pray you, if sin be the god, follow it. But, oh, if this God be God, if this be life indeed, follow it, follow Him. How long? How long? And why should not the answer be given now, even as my last words are sounding in your ears? God grant that in the hearts of men and women the answer may go up. No longer. Here I choose, and I will give myself to Thee, soul and body Thine to be, wholly Thine forevermore.

CHAPTER XVII

THE UNSTRAITENED CHRIST

The former treatise I made, O Theophilus, concerning all that Jesus began both to do and to teach.
ACTS I:I.

THIS AT FIRST SIGHT APPEARS A STRANGE OPENING TO A book, and yet it is perfectly natural when we remember that the writer had already written another pamphlet, which we know as the Gospel according to Luke. It is to that he makes reference when he writes, "The former treatise I made, O Theophilus, concerning all that Jesus began both to do and to teach."

To this link of connection I desire to draw your attention, in order that we may understand the true character of this book of the Acts of the Apostles, and from such understanding deduce certain lessons of profound and paramount importance to the whole Church of Jesus Christ.

First, Luke does not say in speaking of his previous pamphlet, "The former treatise I made, O Theophilus, concerning all that Jesus did and taught." He says, "The former treatise I made, O Theophilus, concerning all that Jesus *began* both to do and to teach." The story of Luke, as he gives it to us in the Gospel, is the story of the beginnings of the doing and teaching of Jesus.

Over twenty years ago one of the most brilliant of our journalists went to see the representation of the Oberammergau Passion play. When he came back he wrote an account of what he had seen, and he called the little book, "The Story that Transformed the World." I have no desire to be hypercritical, but while I greatly enjoyed reading the book, I join issue altogether with the suggestion of the title, that the world has been transformed by the telling of a story. I do not mean to say that the world has not been transformed. I hold that it has been transformed as the result of the coming of Christ, and the message and ministry of Christ in every successive century, but what I do say is that this transformation has not been brought about by the telling of a story. There never was such a story as the story of Jesus. Never was story so pathetic, so tender, so beautiful, so strong. But I do not hesitate to say that if there had been nothing more than a story it would have lost its power long ago. Men have not been remade, and nationalities reborn, and human society permeated with new influences and new thoughts and new conceptions by the telling of a story. How, then, has the world been transformed? The answer is suggested by the underlying truth contained in my text. The story is the story of the things He began to do and teach. The world has been transformed by the things He has continued to do and teach. The world has not been transformed by the telling of the story of a death and a life transcendently beautiful nineteen centuries ago. The world has been transformed by the living presence of the living Christ in every successive century. He began to do, and, thank God, He has never ceased doing; He began to teach, and, thank God, He has never ceased teaching. Christ did not pass away from the world when He ascended; He has been here ever since, and through every successive century He has been busy doing and teaching. Thus has the world been transformed. This congregation is not gathered round the memory of a Christ Who was. It is gathered round the presence of a Christ Who is. We are not here because of the pathetic and majestic and radiantly beautiful story of what happened nineteen centuries ago. We are here because Christ is here, the same living Lord, by the power of His Holy Spirit, doing things among men, still teaching men, even as of old.

What, then, is the book of the Acts of the Apostles? It is the first fragment of Church history. It is the first chapter in the story of the things that Jesus has continued to do and teach.

Let us go back to the Gospel of Luke, to something that Jesus said while He was still among men:

> I came to cast fire upon the earth, and what do I desire? I would that it were already kindled! But I have a baptism to be baptized with, and how am I straitened till it be accomplished! (Luke 12:49, 50).

In these words our Lord declared that He had come to the world to pour on men a baptism of fire; He declared the supreme wish of His heart was that that baptism might be poured out, that that work might be accomplished; but He also declared He could not send the fire until He Himself had been baptized with a baptism toward which His face was set. What was that baptism? The baptism of the Cross. So that Jesus, in effect, stated that He could not do His greatest work until after the Cross, that He was straitened, limited, confined, and only beginning His doing and teaching. He could not carry either to consummation until He Himself had been immersed in the great baptism of death, the mysterious passion baptism of the Cross.

In the book of the Acts of the Apostles I stand by the side of Jesus and listen to Him after His baptism, after the Cross, and I do not hear Him saying, "I am straitened." I hear Him saying now, "John indeed baptized with water; but ye shall be baptized with the Holy Ghost not many days hence." The Cross being accomplished, the greater work begins.

From this beginning the book runs on. In the second chapter we read, "And when the day of Pentecost was now come, they were all together in one place"; and the rest you know: the fire baptism came, and in its coming the little group of disciples were made one with Jesus as they never had been one with Him in the days of His flesh. Peter and James and John and the rest never knew Jesus perfectly until He was dead, buried, risen, ascended, and had poured on them the gift of the Holy Ghost. Then their eyes were opened, then their ears were unstopped, then their heart lost its frost and flamed with fire, then Peter ceased to be anxious about keys. He was prepared for the Cross, if by any means he could suffer and serve with Christ; and in the little company of disciples baptized with the Holy Ghost and fire Jesus found an enlarged sphere of operation. He began the mightier works which He could not do before, but which He had promised they should do when He had gone to the Father.

I love the Gospel story, for it gives me the beginnings of things, but when I come to the Acts of the Apostles I feel myself in the tremendous movement of the larger Christ, of the more infinite power, no longer straitened, confined, and shut up within Himself, but liberated through His passion baptism. Here I see Him moving to the greater works.

That is the significance of this introduction. Let us now look at it from another standpoint. If, indeed, I have in the Gospel the story of what Jesus began to do and teach, and if in the Acts of the Apostles, and all Church history, I have the story of what He continued to do and teach, it becomes manifest that there will be no practical and radical difference between the principles on which He began to do and those on which He has continued to do. In the Gospel I learn what is the passion of His heart, what is the intention of His purpose, and what is the manifestation of His power; and I may test my work, my responsibility, by asking the question, Am

I living and serving on the same lines as did the Christ? What He did, He does, only with increased power. He began and He continues on the same lines.

I sometimes hear people say that what we need in Christian service is to see to it that we are on parallel lines with Jesus Christ. Again, I do not want to be hypercritical, but it is a very weak geometrical illustration. Parallel lines are lines which never come together. We do not want to be on parallel lines with Jesus. We want to be on His lines exactly. The perfect geometrical figures illustrative of the methods of God are always those of the pyramid or the square or the circle.

In this case take the circle. At the center is Jesus. In one of those inimitable sermons of Joseph Parker on Jesus in the midst, he spoke of Jesus as in the midst of the doctors, as crucified in the midst of thieves, as in the midst of two or three gathered together in His name, and, finally, as in the midst of the throne, a Lamb as it had been slain. Always in the midst, always at the center. Go back and take one prophetic word of the past, the word of Isaiah, "Look unto Me, and be ye saved, all the ends of the earth"; in the center, God manifest in Christ; the circumference, "all the ends of the earth." Or come once more to the first chapter of the Acts of the Apostles, and there find the same great figure. He stands, the center of a very small group of disciples, and they do not understand Him. They are asking foolish questions about the restoration of the Kingdom to Israel. Jesus is the center. What is the first circle? The disciples. To this first circle of men gathered round Him He says, "It is not for you to know times or seasons, which the Father hath set within His own authority. But ye shall receive power when the Holy Ghost is come upon you, and ye shall be My witnesses." Where? Now watch the circles widening round Him. "In Jerusalem," that is the city close at hand; "and in all Judæa," that is the suburbs; "and in Samaria," that is the country lying out further still. Where does He finish? "Unto the uttermost part of the earth." Those are the circles which sweep around the Christ. How am I to serve the Christ? By serving Jerusalem. How am I to serve Jerusalem? By serving Judæa. How am I to serve Judæa? By serving Samaria. How am I to serve Samaria? By serving the uttermost part of the earth.

Do not forget that we have never obeyed Him yet. The vast part of the world has never heard the Gospel. How shall we fulfil all these responsibilities? By getting on parallel lines? No, by getting on the same lines of service. The radii of a circle may be carried far, but they are the same lines at the uttermost circumference as those which rest in the center.

This is the truth which lies like a burden on my heart to-day, the great truth I want to bring to others, not so much for instruction as for encouragement. All He began to do He is still doing, and we are His fellow workers; all He began to teach He is still teaching, and we are His messengers.

In looking back at the story of Jesus as we have it in the Gospels, I find general principles of present value. When Jesus began, He attracted the multitudes; when Jesus began, He was attracted by the multitudes; when Jesus began, He knew the multitudes; when Jesus began, the multitudes knew Him.

First, Jesus began to attract the multitudes. Than this nothing is more obvious. Wherever He came in the days of His public ministry the crowds came too. He was weary and crossed the sea, and when the boat reached the other side of the lake they found waiting for Him vast multitudes who had run round the shore, outrunning the boat, in order to be there when He arrived.

On another occasion He said to His disciples, "Let us go into a desert place, and rest a while." They never reached the desert place; they got into the boat, and crossed the lake; but when they got to the other side vast multitudes were waiting for Him. They thronged Him, they "pressed Him," to use the expression of Mark.

The crowds who came to Jesus in the days of His flesh were not crowds composed of one particular class of people; rulers were in the crowds, fishermen, Pharisees, and publicans were in the crowds. There is a very popular fallacy abroad in the world that Jesus attracted persons of only one class, the poorer people, the working people. It is not true. Now some of you are thinking that "the common people heard Him gladly." Yes, and no! That passage has been much misquoted. To begin with, the Bible never insults that class of people by calling them common in our sense of the word common. That phrase occurs in the Gospel of Mark, and nowhere else. Read Mark's Gospel and put a pencil mark under this phrase "much people." It runs all through the Gospel. Mark seems to be a man always listening to the tramp of the crowds as they thronged on Jesus. Once, in the course of translating the Gospel of Mark, both King James's translators and the Revisers, for some reason, have rendered the same Greek phrase "much people" "common people"; it is exactly the same phrase. "Common" does not mean poor people, working people. It means all sorts and conditions of people, the mixed multitude, the common crowd. It is quite time we got rid of this fallacy; I am quite willing to grant that there were more poor people than rich, because there are always more poor than rich in the world, always more illiterate people than learned. But Jesus Christ attracted all sorts and conditions of people. He was the great Center of attraction. The one thing people could not do with Him was to let Him alone. Wherever He came they came, and they thronged after Him in the country places, in the cities, along the highways.

These were the beginnings. Has that ceased to be true? Has Jesus lost His power to attract, and to attract all sorts and conditions of men? I want to say to you, and I want to say it quietly and finally and deliberately and without apology, that Jesus Christ is just as attractive a personality in the twentieth century as He was at the dawn of the first in old Judæa. He still attracts men and women to Himself.

The problem of the empty church in the midst of a vast population in London, or anywhere else, has a deeper problem still underlying it, the problem of an absent or a hidden Christ. I do not care where it is, I do not care what is the class of people round about it. Find me any empty church in any populous district, and let Jesus Christ be seen and known and preached there, and men will still crowd to Him just as they always crowded to Him. I am not criticizing the ministry, I am criticizing the Church, and I say that wherever you find me the problem we are discussing in conferences and synods, it is not the problem of how to get the crowds into the church, it is the problem of how to show Christ in the church. He will get the crowd; He attracts men always.

Jesus may be hidden by priestism, by ecclesiasticism, by the sordid selfishness of people who take His name on their lips but lack His love in their hearts. He may be hidden by people who deny His Spirit in the way in which they refuse to welcome the outcast if the outcast enters the church. But let the great, warm, loving heart of the Christ be shown, and the people will come. The things which hide Him eventually drive Him out. But let Him be present, managing the whole business, impulsing all the service, shining through the lovelit eyes of His own children, teaching in gentle language the broken-hearted sinner that comes within the building; let but Christ be seen in His people, let but Christ be manifested, and men will crowd to Him. Jesus is not the Saviour of a caste. He was never attracted by the broad phylactery or the wide border of the garment. He was never repelled by the beggar in rags. I was going to say He never saw the phylactery and rags, and yet He saw everything. In some senses, it is true, He did not see the garment, for, looking at the man, He did not see the accidental trappings of his birth; He saw the immortal soul that dwelt in his house of clay, and when He sees men through our eyes, and touches men with our hands, they will come with their woes and sin and sorrow.

It is not only true that He attracted the crowds, it is also true that He was attracted by the crowds. Where the crowds were He went. What drew Him to the great feasts in Jerusalem, the feast of Tabernacles, the Passover feast, and all the rest? I do not hesitate to say it was the crowd that drew Him, not the ceremony, which was effete, worn out, spoiled by the ritualism and the rationalism of His age. "When He saw the multitudes, He was moved with compassion." And I say it reverently of my Master, and yet it is true, He could not keep away from the crowds. I see Him one day, tired, going into a house to rest, and immediately after there is this very remarkable statement, "He could not be hid." Why not? Read on, and you will find why. Outside is the crowd, and in the crowd one poor woman is in need, and the sorrows of the woman and the surging sorrows of the crowd dragged Him from the house in order that He might help and serve. Oh, yes, and He was attracted by them as they were, sinful souls and ungrateful. He saw them not only as they were. He saw them as they might be, and He loved them in the midst of their sin and degradation, and what repelled others attracted Him.

Has Christ changed? Nay, verily. The most attractive center to Jesus Christ is not the church half empty. But the theater if it is full. I know men and women are there for amusement, sinning their life away. Thank God when a church has wisdom enough to say, We will reach these people. It shows the Church has caught the Spirit of the Christ. He is attracted by the people. There comes back to my mind a quaint old piece of poetry. It teaches a great lesson in simple form:

> The parish priest of austerity
>   Climbed up in a high church steeple,
> To be nearer God, so that he might hand
>   His word down to the people.
> And in sermon script he daily wrote
>   What he thought was sent from Heaven;
> And he dropped it down on the people's heads
>   Two times one day in seven.
> In his age God said, "Come down and die,"
>   And he cried out from the steeple:
> "Where art Thou, Lord?" and the Lord replied,
>   "Down here among My people."

That is the profound lesson of the life of Jesus. He did not climb away from people to drop the Gospel down on their heads. He is in the midst of the wounding and the woe and the weariness of this present day. Wherever you see a crowd of people the Christ is there. In the Labor Church He is there, not as the Head of the Labor Church, but He is there because men are there; in the fashionable West End, with its veneered rottenness and its cultured devilry, because He loves the people; in the East, with its overwhelming despair and its terrible wail of suffering and sorrow, He is there. They abuse Him; it does not matter, He loves them. Where the crowds are the Christ is. If we want to live near to Jesus we must get near the crowds, get close by their sorrows, and feel them; near their tears, to dry them; under their burdens, to lift them.

Do not talk to me about coming revivals. The revival has come when the Church has caught the compassion of Christ, and is near the sorrows of the world to lift and heal them.

I go back to my book of Isaiah, and I read that the ancient people of God said, "Awake, awake, put on strength, O arm of the Lord." And how did God answer them? He answered by saying, "Awake, awake, put on thy strength,

O Zion, put on thy beautiful garments, O Jerusalem." It is as though God said to His people, Do not ask me to awake; I have never been asleep. You must awake! And while to-day we cry, "Awake, O arm of the Lord," I hear the answer, I have never been asleep. I have never slumbered. It is you who must awake!

Let me take a step further. Not only is it true that Jesus attracted the crowds, and was attracted by the crowds; it is also true that He knew the crowds. He knew their possibilities; He knew their agonies. Jesus never upbraided the multitudes. He did upbraid the men whose false philosophies were ruining the multitudes; but He never upbraided the multitudes. He knew them in their sin and sorrow, knew them in their capacity, knew them perfectly. You remember the great word in the close of the second chapter of John's Gospel, "Many believed on His name, beholding His signs which He did. But Jesus did not trust Himself unto them, for that He knew all men, and because He needed not that anyone should bear witness concerning man, for He Himself knew what was in man." Every broken heart that came to Him, He knew it and all its sorrow.

He knows the crowds to-day. It was Charles Kingsley who said, "We may choose to look at the masses in the gross as subjects for statistics, and, of course, where possible, for profit, but there is One Who knows every temptation of each slattern and gin-drinker and street boy." Yes, He knows. But you say, Why emphasize it? Because I want to remind you that, knowing all, He loved men, thought they were worth dying for. Oh, God, help us to realize it. When you are tempted by some article in some brilliant magazine to think that the people are not worth living for and dying for, get back to the Christ, and remember that over all the woe and misery of London the shadow of the Cross is the greatest light that shines, as it tells us until this moment, whatever the people may think of Him, He reckoned that they were worth dying for. God help us to have the same estimate.

Finally, my brethren, not only is it true He knew them; it is true they knew Him. Not perfectly, I grant you, but they knew Him by name, by hearing, and by sight; and the more the multitudes of His day came to know Him with that keen, acute, mystic consciousness, the more they were dissatisfied with any save Himself. The Pharisees said, "The world is gone after Him." One came to Him when He came down from the mount of transfiguration, and said, "Master, have mercy on my son, my only begotten son; a devil vexes him sore, and I brought him to Thy disciples, and they could not cure him." But the man knew that Jesus could, and this consciousness of the power of Christ swayed the multitudes all through that region. You say that is changed. No, it is not. The multitudes to-day know the living Christ of God. Believe me, you cannot deceive humanity. They still know the difference between the method of the philosopher and the living, warm, powerful Christ; the multitudes know the difference between a stone, polish it as you will, and bread. And you may preach the Christ, Who is the Founder of a system of ethics, until your church is empty, and you may preach a cold, passionless Christ, Who is the ideal of perfection, until men are driven away by your preaching. But preach the Christ of the Cross and the warm mystery of His shed blood, and that Christ still attracts men, and saves men; and men know Him, and you cannot deceive the multitudes.

He began, and I hear Him speak as He begins. What does He say? "I am the Light of the world." But He is going away, and yet He is going away to come again, and to carry on His work. What does He say now? "Ye are the light of the world"; that is to say, we of the Christian Church, we of the Christian faith, are the instruments through which Christ elects, in great grace and mercy, to carry on His work.

Jesus wants to get to men through us. Are we at His disposal? It is a cheap and sentimental Christianity that sings songs about Heaven and hopes to get there. Are we saints, separated to Him? Are our feet ready to run on His errands? Are our hands ready to minister to His bidding? Are our eyes ready to flash with His love? Are we ready to suffer, to serve, and die with Him? That is the question.

He wants to get men to Himself through us. Are we likely to attract them? I am only asking the question; God help us to answer it alone. Is it possible that the men you pay wages to will be attracted toward the Christ through you? Dear Sunday-school teacher, has Jesus a chance to make the children in your class see how lovely He is?

He is waiting for our feet to run on errands, our hands to touch men with His love, our voices to sing with the tone of His infinite compassion, the Gospel of His grace. Are we at His disposal? That is the question of the hour. May God grant that we shall be able to carry on His victories until even His heart is satisfied.

CHAPTER XVIII

BURDENS: FALSE AND TRUE

All things have been delivered unto Me of My Father; and no one knoweth the Son, save the Father; neither doth any know the Father, save the Son, and he to whomsoever the Son willeth to reveal Him. Come unto Me, all ye that labour and are heavy laden, and I will give you rest. Take My yoke upon you, and learn of Me; for I am meek and lowly in heart; and ye shall find rest unto your souls. For My yoke is easy, and My burden is light.
MATTHEW 11:27-30.

IN ALL PROBABILITY NO WORDS THAT EVER FELL FROM THE lips of our blessed Lord have more remarkably and profoundly taken hold on the heart of man than those of the last three verses of this paragraph.

There is something here that charms the heart of man, not in one age, but in every successive age, and not among one class of people, but among all classes of people. It is a remarkable and arresting fact that it is impossible by translation to rob these words of music, or to weaken their appeal. In every zone, frigid, temperate, and torrid, they have the same effect.

We are driven to ask, Why is it that this passage has so remarkably taken hold of the heart of the human race that wherever the Bible comes, and the words are given to the people, they are almost invariably taken out and committed to memory, and passed from mouth to mouth until men everywhere who know anything about the Bible know these words? Why have the words so profound an effect?

It may be said that their attraction is due to their simplicity; but that does not touch the deepest reason, for the simplicity of superficiality may charm for the moment, but it does not live. The general answer I make to this inquiry is: The words have had a profound effect because they are profound words. This is not merely the language of a tender and beautiful sentiment. Sentiment is an excellent thing; God have mercy on the man that affects to disapprove sentiment. But sentiment does not live century after century. You must create new sentiments if you would move men by sentiment. Something infinitely more than a soft lullaby that appeals to the tired side of humanity is needed to grip humanity's heart and hold it; something infinitely more than what I have already described as a wooing winsomeness is needed to take hold of the heart of a man as he fights his battles and bears his burdens and feels the strenuousness of life. And the infinitely more is here in this call, or it would long ago have been forgotten.

That which has made these words live is revealed in the verse that comes before them. The profundity of the invitation is not understood if you begin with the words of invitation. Immediately before this, Jesus uttered stern words; He upbraided the cities in which most of His mighty works were done. Suddenly He ceased, and, standing still in the midst of the crowd, He lifted eyes and heart to God, and spoke no longer to men, but to God. "I thank Thee, O Father, Lord of heaven and earth, that Thou didst hide these things from the wise and understanding, and didst reveal them unto babes; yea, Father, for so it was well-pleasing in Thy sight."

Having thus spoken to His Father, He turned back to the crowds, and said, "All things have been delivered unto Me of My Father; and no one knoweth the Son, save the Father; neither doth any know the Father, save the Son, and he to whomsoever the Son willeth to reveal Him. Come unto Me . . . and I will give you rest."

Most reverently and carefully may I put this into another form? Jesus upbraided the cities that had not known Him, the cities that had been blind to His presence, deaf to the music of His voice, unconscious of their day. Then, suddenly turning to God, He said, "I thank Thee, O Father," that these things are revealed to the children, and the simplehearted and the men that lack understanding. Turning back to the people, He declared: God has put everything in My hands. He has committed all things to Me, and yet men do not know Me, no one understands Me; My Father understands Me. But it is also true that no man understands the Father but the Son, and the man to whom the Son will reveal Him. And to whom will He reveal the Father? "Come unto Me, all ye that labour and are heavy laden, and I will give you rest." What rest? The rest of the revelation of the Father, the one and only rest that man needs, the rest that comes to the soul when God comes to the soul and the soul comes to God.

Jesus Christ thus virtually said to men: All your restlessness is Godlessness. All life's fitful fever is the result of the exiling of God; all the tempest-tossed experiences of men are due to the fact that they do not know the Father. Jesus, looking at the multitudes, sorrowing and suffering, tempest-tossed and driven, restless and tired, weary and heavy-laden, said to them, in effect, If you could know God all your restlessness would cease; but you cannot know Him except through Me. But if only you will come to Me I will reveal Him to you, and you will find your rest.

That is the reason why the verses live and the music wins its way through all the centuries. Jesus is not saying to men: Never mind, do not trouble, it will soon be over; He never deals with sorrow and trouble that way. He is saying to men:

Get right at the foundation of your life and the surface will be right. He does not come to men and say to them: Cheer up, it is all right; I sympathize with you, I pity you. That is not the way Christ deals with the restlessness of human life. It is not pity He offers men, it is power. His gift is not an opiate that puts them to sleep and makes them forget; it is life that wakes them, and makes them triumph. Get right with God, and the only way in which you will get right with God, says Christ, is by coming to Me.

Having seen the setting of the words, let us examine them in that setting and in that relationship.

Confining ourselves from this moment to the actual words beginning, "Come unto Me," I shall ask you to notice three things. First, that Jesus here makes His appeal to something that is a necessary part of all human life. Second, that in the words of His great appeal Jesus separates humanity into two camps. And, finally, that the call of Jesus is a call in which He appeals to this underlying fact of life, and invites men from a false position into the true.

I do not care for the moment whether you are a Christian man or no, whether your life is godly or godless, pure or impure, restful or restless; there is an essential fact in human nature, and it is to that fact that Jesus makes His appeal.

In order to find it, I am going to take you to my second division first. I shall return to it for consideration in detail at a later stage. Jesus divides humanity into two camps. Notice carefully these words, "Come unto Me, all ye that labour and are heavy laden"; that is a description of one class of people. Pass to the end of the verses, "My yoke is easy, and My burden is light." That is the condition of the other class. Mark the contrast: People that labour and are heavy laden; a Man Who says, "My yoke is easy. My burden is light." Remember that when Jesus said, "My yoke is easy, and My burden is light," He did not mean the yoke He was going to give us and the burden He was going to impose upon us. He did mean that also, but fundamentally and primarily He was speaking out of His own experience. The yoke I wear is easy, the burden I bear is light. "Labour." "My yoke is easy." "Heavy laden." "My burden is light." The contrast is self-evident and arresting.

Now we will find our way into the discovery of that which is common in human life by looking at those contrasts. What is common to both conditions? There are people who labor and are heavy laden. Here is a Man with an easy yoke and a light burden. It is a great contrast, but the common quantity is a burden. These people are carrying a burden. This Man is carrying a burden.

When that is seen, there is discovered the underlying fact in human life to which Jesus appeals. No human being lives without carrying a burden. I am not now speaking of the burden of sorrow, of the burden of care, of the burden of grief, of the burden of trial. When Paul was writing to the Galatians, toward the close of the letter, in very close proximity, he said two things: "Bear ye one another's burdens, and so fulfil the law of Christ," and then, "Each man shall bear his own burden." That is not a contradiction. Whereas the word "burden" in neither case is incorrect, as a matter of fact, the apostle did not use the same word; the words that lie behind are different words. Those who are familiar with the Greek Testament will remember the fact, but to those who are not, if I simply utter the words that lie behind, you will see the difference in the sound—*Baros* and *Phortion*. The first word means a burden of sorrow, of pain, of difficulty, of trial. We are to bear one another's burdens of that sort; but the second burden is the burden of responsibility. Every man must bear his own burden of responsibility; no man can carry his brother's responsibility. No man can live and work under the impulse that drives his brother man.

What, then, is this burden of responsibility? It is the master passion of life, whatever that may be. It is the conception of life that dominates it, drives it, sends it through the days. It is the aim that a man has in life, the thing that has taken hold upon him, and is molding him; it is the conception that lies at the back of his will, creates the reason for its decisions, and, therefore, is the motive power in his life.

There is no man who has not such a reason, has not such a master passion; it is present in every life.

A great many men have never named it, have never taken time to ask what is the all-inclusive conception of life that drives them through the days; but if it has never been written down or found, it is there. In these days of psychological investigation we hear men correctly talking of a subconsciousness; and the burden may lie in a man's subconsciousness, but it exists.

I do not want to lead you into any metaphysical disquisition, but in the name of God I want you to find out the deepest thing in your life. I want to deliver you from surface living, and therefore I beseech you to recognize this deepest, simplest, profoundest thing. Back of your life there is a reason, a motive, an aim, an impulse, a master passion: the conception of life that is mastering you and driving you, making you rise in the morning, toil through the day, rest at night. Back of all the externalities is some dynamic, and this is so in every life.

A friend of mine once said to me, when I had said something like this in preaching, I do not think you are quite right about that. I think there are men who have no aim in life, no motive power, no master passion. And I said, Well, tell me of one. And he named someone whom we had known for long years. Look at So-and-So. You know as well as I do that he has just drifted through the years, and done nothing in the world, simply because he has no aim in life. And I said to my friend, The man you quote is a forcible argument in favor of my position. And he said, But surely his trouble has been that he has had no aim in life. I replied, His aim in life is to do nothing. And it is a most remarkable thing how hard some men will work to do nothing. This man had one conception —to shift responsibility and shirk work. Mean and contemptible, but there it was, the master passion that made him shiftless and lazy.

We all have a master passion, and that is the matter with which Jesus is dealing in these old sweet words. He is getting underneath the external action, and underneath the surface thinking. He is getting down to the deep subconsciousness of life, putting His hand on the thing that molds and makes all the externalities, and He is saying to men, in effect, If you will get the right master passion you will have rest. If only you will find the right motive, the right aim, the right reason, then the friction will go out of your life, peace will take its place, and you will find yourself at the secret source of all strength.

Now let us pass again to the second point for more careful examination. Jesus divides men into two camps. On the one side are people trying to carry a burden too heavy for them, and the yoke in which they are attempting to carry this burden galls and frets them. All life is a weariness because they are attempting to carry a burden that they were never meant to carry. Jesus looks on them in pity and declares, "My yoke is easy. My burden is light."

Let us endeavor to discover these different burdens.

What is this burden that Jesus described as light? What was the master passion in His life? What was His aim, His motive, His impulse, the reason for everything He did, every journey He took, every word He uttered, all the output of life, in thought, and speech, and deed? There was one unswerving principle at the back of the life of Jesus, one master passion that always drove Him. I take you back for a concrete and wonderful answer to an Old Testament prophecy concerning Him, and then ask you to hear how through His life the music was always true to the chord of the dominant.

In the roll of the book it is written of me;
I delight to do Thy will, O my God.

That was His master passion. Take His life for a moment, a fascinating and delightful study, which we can only glance at, but of which we may see enough as we go to learn the truth. The first recorded words of Jesus are, "Wist ye not that I must?" Now listen. That is what I want to find out. When a man says, I must, I am getting at the deepest thing in his life. It is not when a man says, I ought, or I would like; that does not matter, but I *must*. "I must be about my Father's business." There the master passion flamed out. His Father's business for Him at that moment was that He should go home and be subject to His parents, that He should learn the trade of His reputed father, Joseph; and then that He should remain for eighteen long years in the seclusion of the carpenter's shop, doing what men call "the daily round, the common task."

Then He passed into public life, and again we listen to some of the things He said: "My meat is to do the will of Him that sent Me." "I can of Myself do nothing." "The Son can do nothing of Himself but what He seeth the Father doing." "I do always the things that are pleasing to Him." "I . . . have accomplished the work which Thou hast given Me to do." "It is finished." "Father, into Thy hands I commend My Spirit."

Oh, ye masters of the modes of music, tell me, is not that harmony? The will of God, the master passion operating through all Jesus' days and doings. Back of Calvary, and back of the carpenter's shop, back of the infinite teaching, back of the sweet human life, back of the majestic marvelous unveiling of God, and back of the tender patient unveiling of man, the will of God was His master passion.

Now listen and be astonished. He says, "My burden is light." Some of the simplest things Jesus said are the most startling if only we take time to listen to them. My brother, you have been saying in your heart, I would like to be a Christian, but I cannot be one because it is such hard work; it is very hard work to please God always. Jesus says it is not. He says it is easy; and let me say it very kindly, I would rather believe Him than you. I would rather believe Him, because He always did it, and you and I have not always done it.

This is one of the superlative notes of the Gospel which needs to be delivered to-day. Jesus says that the light burden is the will of God, says, in effect, that it is easier to please God than not to please Him. My testimony by the side of His is very imperfect, but I have discovered that it is far easier to please God than any man.

I would rather please God because the law of God conditions human life according to its first intention and its true possibility. Oh, but a man says, if I am going to be a Christian everything will go against the grain. Nothing of the sort. Everything will go with the grain. You have been going against the grain all your life. Our Lord will take hold of the inherent and created capacity, and put it into its right relationship with God. When a man is born again all the essential facts of his first birth are found and realized and crowned. The second birth of a man is finding the first birth, and putting it into true relation with God.

And now let us look at the other camp. Jesus said, "Ye that labour and are heavy laden." What are the burdens they are carrying? Let us try to find out. We need not go back to Palestine. Some of you have been honestly exercising your heart and mind in the last few minutes. You have been saying, Well, what is my burden? The preacher says that perhaps we have never found it out. What is it? Some man is getting down to the undercurrent of his life, and is trying to find out. What is it, my brother? Well, says one, if I am honest, the master passion of my life is money; I am living for money; I am living for wealth. I am thinking and planning and working and toiling for money; that is my master passion. Some other says, I care nothing about money; but, if I am to confess the truth, the thing that is driving me is the passion for fame; I want to be known, I must make a name among my fellow men; that is the goal toward which I am running. Yet another says, No, I care nothing for money simply for the sake of money, and fame never attracts me; but if I had to confess, the master passion of my life is pleasure. I want pleasure, enjoyment, a thrill, and a sensation; I must have it; that is what I am working for; if I work hard it is that I may earn the wherewithal to secure pleasure. Oh, what thousands are living for that to-day! They work hard, and the goal is always the pleasure that is to come presently. Still another says, I care nothing for money, nothing for fame, nothing particularly for pleasure; all I want is ease and quietness and to be let alone. If you will just let me alone, that is all I ask; I want to go through life peaceably and quietly, not to be perplexed or bothered.

Now let us be very careful. As a matter of fact, none of these constitutes the burden of any human life. Money, pleasure, fame, ease—not one of them is a burden. You have not thought deeply enough; you are confounding the yoke with the burden. These are the yokes in which men are trying to carry burdens, but the burdens lie deeper.

Will you let me cross-examine you for a moment? What do you want money for? Why do you want money? For whom do you want it? Want it for? Of course, I want it for myself. Exactly; now you have named your burden. For *myself*. Of course, there may be a man who says he wants it for someone else. Well, he is so rare a specimen that I will not discuss the question with you. I am dealing with the average man, the man who wants money for himself. Or this man who says, I want fame. I am not seeking fame for anyone else. It is my name I want to be carved into the granite. Or this man who is seeking for pleasure; he seeks it for himself. And the man seeking ease, the answer is always the same: *self*.

There are only two burdens that men can carry. One is the will of God, and the other is self. The life of every man, woman and child having come to years of discretion and understanding is centered around God, or around self. Self is very subtle, very insidious, hides itself in all sorts of masks, dresses itself in all garments; but if God is not at the center of your life, man, you have put yourself on the throne. There are only two burdens but thousands of yokes.

Now listen again to Jesus. He says you are heavy laden if you are living for self. What does He mean? He means that it is very difficult for any man to please himself, very difficult for any man to satisfy himself. Difficult? I dare venture to go further, and say my blessed Lord meant that no man can satisfy himself. A boy at school dreams of the day when he will be able to please himself. I know that I did; I know I thought when I was once out of school, and away from discipline, I could please myself. And I have found out that I pleased myself more in those days than I ever have done since.

Can you find me a self-satisfied man anywhere? You say, Yes, quite a number of them. Self-satisfied men? Yes, have you never heard of one? I have heard of many, and never seen one. Oh, but if you only knew this man whom I know, he is just that; he is self-satisfied! Get in to his inner life, and you will find that the man most self-satisfied in outward manifestation is always uneasy lest some other man should not think of him as he thinks of himself. He is never at rest.

Oh, men, oh, women, hear me; I would not trifle with this tremendous and awful truth. If you want to know what hell is enthrone yourself, try to please yourself, live for yourself long enough. The lady in the West End, she lives for self, talks about ennui. And what is ennui? Hell! The poor soul in the East End, when that soul lives for self, speaks only of despair. And what is despair? Exactly the same thing as the other, only at one end of London they give it a French name; but it is the same thing. It is the worm that dieth not, gnawing at the vitals of the life. It is the fire that is never quenched, burning at the center of the soul. Live for self, and you are trying to carry a burden that crushes you as you carry it. Jesus says, Mine is a burden that is light; take Mine, it is the will of God.

You will not find any woman of culture and refinement who is devoting her life to God who talks about ennui. My dear sisters, if you are suffering from ennui give your heart to Christ, and come and give your life to sevice, and I will cure you of ennui. I will cure it by putting your life in contact with the suffering of some poor fallen sister, and as you begin to take that poor fallen life, and care for it and love it, the peace of God will flow through your life. My dear brother, troubled with restlessness, anxious when there is a fall in the market where you wanted a rise, or a rise where you wanted a fall, give your heart to Christ, and bring your business acumen and your splendid possibilities and say to Him, Lead me into the will of God, lead me where God wants me, and you will find that the peace of God, as a river, will come surging through your life, and the song of the everlasting rest will be the anthem of all your days. Live for yourself, and you are heavy laden. Live for God, and life is a rapture, and the burden is light.

Finally, Jesus called men from the false into the true. He said, "No man knoweth the Father, save the Son." "My burden is light." I know my Father, and because I know my Father I delight to do His will, and that makes life restful. And to the heavy-laden people He declared, You are trying to please yourselves because you do not know My Father.

"No one knoweth . . . the Father, save the Son." You will never try to please God until you know Him.

> Oh, God, of good the unfathomed sea,
> Who would not give his heart to Thee?

That is the language of a man who had come to know God. And when a man comes to know God, he yields Him everything. And how did I get to know Him?

> I heard the voice of Jesus say,
> "Come unto Me and rest."

I came to Him, and He revealed the Father to me, and when I saw God in Jesus there was nothing left that I did not yield to Him.

Let the last word be of the simplest. What is this that Jesus said? He said, "Come unto Me." Oh, thank God for those little words. There is no room for pope, or priest, or pastor, or preacher, or penitent form. There is room for nothing but Christ and the soul. Get to Him, man, get to Him. Get to Him now, come to Him Whom you know so well theoretically, and say:

> Just as I am, Thy love unknown
> Has broken every barrier down;
> Now to be Thine, yea, Thine alone,
> O Lamb of God, I come.

And to whoever will do that, He will reveal the Father, and you will find God through the Son, and your whole life yielded and trusted and reposed in Him, you will accept His will as your master passion.

What then? Rest, sweet rest, deep rest; rest in the midst of the battle, rest while the testing and the trial and the triumph press, rest all the way until the final rest be won.

CHAPTER XIX

LIKE GODS OR GODLIKE

They that make them shall be like unto them.
                                                    PSALM 115:8.
We shall be like Him.
                                                    I JOHN 3:2.

IN THE CHAPTER OF "CONFORMITY TO TYPE" IN HIS "Natural Law in the Spiritual World," Henry Drummond wrote:

> The protoplasm in man has a something in addition to its instincts or its habits. It has a capacity for God. In this capacity for God lies its receptivity, for it is the very protoplasm that was necessary. The chamber is not only ready to receive the new Life, but the Guest is expected, and, till He comes, is missed. Till then the soul longs and yearns, wastes and pines, waving its tentacles piteously in the empty air feeling after God if so be that it may find Him. This is not peculiar to the protoplasm of the Christian's soul. In every land and in every age there have been altars to the Known or Unknown God. It is now agreed upon as a mere question of anthropology that the universal language of the human soul has always been "I perish with hunger."

What Drummond declared in that remarkable passage as "now agreed upon as a mere question of anthropology" I desire to emphasize in order that we may consider in the light of it these two passages of Scripture, which immediately suggest a somewhat remarkable and startling contrast.

There is a master passion in every human life, some one principle which at least professes to render the life consistent and cohesive, and drives it in some given direction. That truth may be stated in another form. Man cannot live without a God. The origin of the word "God" is etymologically obscure. The simplest use of the word, so far as we are able to trace it, is one which suggests a Supreme Being, and, consequently, a Supreme Authority over human life.

The term "God" has been applied to erroneous conceptions of Deity, as to nature, interest, power, and activity; but underneath all the mistakes the word "God" suggests a Being superior to men, a Supreme Being, who, therefore, whether His authority be exercised righteously or unrighteously, mercifully or cruelly, beneficently or tyrannically, yet has power over men.

The recognition of that essential and simple thought concerning God has produced very many different attitudes on the part of men toward God, attitudes depending on the conception of the character of God which they may have entertained.

There is no living man or woman or child who has come to years of understanding but that has, in some form, in some fashion, a God. They may decline to use the word "God"; but the fact remains, no human life can continue without some conception of a Supreme—we need not say "Being." We may say force, or power, or motive; but the supremacy is the quality of importance.

In the passage quoted, Drummond declared that this is because human nature is made from its very beginning with a capacity for a God, and consequently lives in the experience of a clamant cry after God. That I take to be the statement of a simple truth from which there can be no escape.

Out of that conscious necessity for God has arisen all

forms of worship. If we go back to the old days of widespread idolatry, or if we examine the great systems of idolatry which still exist; though we have a thousand and one varied expressions of idolatry, we find on examination that they fall into three main divisions, which our Old Testament Scriptures deal with: the worship of Baal, the worship of Moloch, the worship of Mammon. We to-day may affect to smile at those old ideas, but they still exist. There are thousands of men worshiping Baal in London, thousands of people bowing at the shrine of Moloch in this city at this hour, and how many are worshiping Mammon?

What does it mean when a man worships Baal? It means that he must worship something. What does it mean when a man offers his sacrifice on the shrine of Moloch? It means that there is that in his nature which drives him to the activity of sacrifice. What does it mean when a man worships Mammon with all his heart and all his soul and all his mind and all his strength? It means that he must exercise heart and soul and mind and strength in one supreme and all-inclusive act of worship in some form. Man is by nature and instinctively, whether he will or not, religious. I did not say good. I did not say pious. I did not say holy. I did not say righteous. I said religious.

Religion is that which binds a man. Every man is bound somewhere, somehow, to a throne, to a government, to an authority, to something that is supreme, to something to which he offers sacrifice, and burns incense, and bends the knee. I glance back for a moment to those old systems, and I see men worshiping Baal, the god of nature; Moloch, the master of the emotions; Mammon, the deity of will power. Though the method of the worship has changed, and though the faces of the worshipers are others than those of old, and though the language of the worship is not what it was, the essence is the same, and the common fact of worship comes thrilling and thundering, vibrating and sounding through the ages, expressing itself in a thousand new ways with every new-born generation. Through all the long history of the human race men have worshiped. The common principle throughout all this great fact is that man has capacity for God, must have a god, must bow the knee in some form at the altar of his god.

In the light of that great underlying truth I return to our two passages of Scripture.

The psalmist was dealing with idolatry, boasting and vaunting in holy joy in the fact that Israel trusted Jehovah, and putting into contrast to that trust of Israel in Jehovah the trust of men in the idols that they had created for themselves. In a passage of fine scorn he spoke of these idols: mouths that speak not, eyes that never see, ears that hear nothing, noses that smell not, hands that never handle, feet that never travel, throats through which no speech comes. He was describing idolatry as it manifested itself in his day and in his age; and having described it, he said these idols were made by men, and they that made them were like them.

John was speaking in exquisite tenderness of the new relation between man and God, which is the result of the mission of Jesus; and the music of the whole passage thrills through the mind of every child of God who knows it. "Beloved, now are we children of God, and it is not yet made manifest what we shall be. We know that, if He shall be manifested, we shall be like Him."

"They that make them shall be like unto them." "We shall be like Him." These two statements constitute a great contrast, but they contain a common principle. The common principle is that every man becomes like his God. You must have a God. You have a God. You are growing like Him! If your god is false, you are becoming false; if your God is true, you are growing in truth; if your god is hard, you are becoming hard; if your God is tender, you are becoming compassionate. The principle is described in these two passages as working in two opposite directions to two opposite results. Insensate gods create insensate men. The one living and eternal and loving God makes men living and eternal and loving.

Let us look at these things carefully by taking these texts and examining them a little more closely. We will consider *first*, the men who become like their gods; and, *second*, the men who become Godlike.

First, then, the men who become like their gods. And here we need not refer to the idolatry of the past save as it reveals perpetual principles. I have no care to attack and denounce and combat the idolatry of Eastern lands. Henceforward I refer only to the idolatry described by the psalmist as manifest in his day, that we may discover that though the garb is changed and the language altered, the essence is the same in our day and in our land as it was in Syria. The very essentials of idolatry which expressed themselves in strange and crude forms in days long gone exist in our own days.

The worship of Baal was the worship of nature, and when man begins to worship nature he finally enters into the holy of holies of nature to its most mystic center, to its most mysterious realm; and consequently the worship of Baal in those olden days finally became a worship which expressed itself in ways that must be nameless in the congregation of the saints. We still have this deification of the intellect in the days in which we live. Men who own no allegiance to the throne of our God enthrone in His place human intellect, indulge in philosophies, follow speculations, are given, as the apostle said in writing to Timothy, to "fables and endless genealogies," consult together concerning the long-continued and perpetual emanation of life, attempt to knock at the door of the deepest heart of Nature and fathom its profoundest secret, ask for the solution of the riddle of the universe. That is idolatry. It is the deification of intellect, and when a man says, I will refuse to worship or believe or bow the knee in the presence of anything that does not come within the grasp of my own mind, and that cannot be encompassed in the reach of my own thinking, that is Baal worship.

There are other men who deify their emotional nature, and strange as it may be, the idolatry that deifies the emotional nature always descends to a lower plane than the idolatry that deifies the intellect. Not that the emotional nature is lower than the intellect, but that it is higher, and the higher the faculty the lower its sweep if you degrade it. It has often been said, and I for one feel that it is true, that a woman is capable of a far deeper degradation than a man; and that is not to reflect upon womanhood but to say that the finer fabric, when once thickened and coarsened, becomes more vulgar than the texture of that which is coarser in itself. And what is true by way of illustration is true in this matter. When man burns incense to his emotional nature the outcome is lust, in the most debased sense of that word. Love is the true deity of the emotion; but if a man lets emotion master him lust is the result. And careful as I would be to make reference to such subjects here, there are times when the prophet must speak. On every street men are worshiping Moloch, and it eventuates in the most awful cruelty that it is possible for the heart of man to conceive. Love prostituted becomes hatred. Adoration debased becomes loathing. You have but to have eyes lit with God's love, and hearts tender with His compassion, to see the most awful and devilish cruelty being practiced in the glare of the London streets every day that you live.

There are also those who worship Mammon, moved by the passion for power that makes a man want to possess wealth. Men who desire to possess wealth simply for its own sake are very few and far between, and they are always men who have lost their reason. That is not the worship of Mammon. I have a pity for the man that piles up golden sovereigns and puts his fingers into them. But there is another man who grinds and drives and schemes and plans for the same gold, not in order that he may put his fingers into its yellow glitter, but that he may drive men and make them serve him and obey him. Infinitely more cruel than the worship of the intellect or the worship of the emotion is will worship. Jesus said once to men, "Ye cannot serve God and mammon." The devil of the Middle Ages was painted with horns and hoofs and a tail and fire coming from his mouth. That devil is dead, because he never really existed. The devil to-day enthrones himself most often behind Mammon, the greed for power, the lust for possession that deadens and hardens every aspect of human life. The love of money is a more terrible thing than the drink traffic. Kill the love of money and you will sweep the drink traffic out in six months. This worship of Mammon is a more terrible thing than the awful prostitution of our streets. If only I could burn up the love of money in the hearts of landlords I would close all the houses of ill fame. It is not the girl on the street with whom I am angry. It is the man who is behind the business and makes possible the continuance of the vaunted and flaunting sin by reason of his damnable love of gold. That is the worship of Mammon. And it is everywhere. I never walk down London streets without seeing an altar besprinkled with blood, a worshiper debased and degraded!

Yet look again, oh, look again, and see this: the horror of the whole thing is due to the fact that the capacity which prostituted works ruin is a Divine capacity. The thing in the man that drives him to the deification of his intellect, to the enthronement of his own emotion, to the love of power, what is it? Oh, God, open our eyes to see it. It is the cry of the soul after God with parched lip, and breaking heart, and throbbing brow. Though he does not understand his own language, he is saying everywhere, "When shall I appear before God? Oh that I knew where I might find Him."

But pass on. When a man makes a god for himself he always constructs his god on the pattern of himself. Take the older forms of idolatry, or the more recent forms to which I have been referring, and what is man doing when he worships? He is making a god on the pattern of himself. You cannot find me a single idol in the world to-day but that if you will come back from that deity and narrow the lines that enclose it you will find the man who made it. Every deity that a man makes for himself he makes on the pattern of himself.

I will imagine that I am back among the old idolators whom the psalmist described. I must have a god, I must have something that represents to me the thought of authority, of supremacy. I will make my god of gold, of silver, or out of a tree; and I set to work with carving instruments to make my god. How shall I make it? I must give him a mouth. Why? Because I have one. I must give him ears. Why? Because I have ears and can hear. And so through all the gamut of the senses, whenever a man makes a god he makes it on the pattern of himself. "They that make them" make them on the pattern of their own personality.

So to-day. The moment you see a man deifying his intelligence you say, What does he know of intelligence? He knows that he knows, and he deifies the capacity for knowledge. He lifts a part of himself out of himself, and he says, That is supreme. I worship that. Or a man is deifying his emotion, and you say, What does he know of emotion? He says, I can love, I can hate. That is the greatest thing. I will worship love and hate. I will give free rein to the sweep and the thrill and the throb of myself. It is always himself enlarged that he worships. And when a man worships Mammon, what is it he worships? His own will power. He says, That is the thing, to be able to will, and see it done; to wish, and to achieve; to decide, and see it carried out. It is a true instinct, and it is part of the man, and he enlarges it and worships it. Every man makes his god on the pattern of himself. That is the first thing.

Look once again. Whenever a man makes a god on the pattern of himself he makes something less than himself. A man says, I will create a god. I will give to this god a mouth and eyes and ears and nose and hands and feet and throat, all greater than I. A mouth that can utter a more authoritative speech. Eyes that can see greater distances. Ears that can hear minuter sounds, more feeble vibrations. A nose that can scent with a more remarkable accuracy. Hands that can encompass more work. Feet that can travel greater distances and more swiftly. A throat out of which the thunders roll instead of the puny speech that is in my throat. And see, he says, now I have made something greater than myself.

Yet he has not done so! Let the psalmist interpret the result. Listen to his fine scorn. A mouth, greater? Infinitely less, it cannot speak. Eyes, greater? Infinitely less, they cannot see. When a man builds a god on the pattern of himself he makes something less than himself.

Bring the thought into our present age, and what have you? A man deifies intelligence, but what is this that man deifies? He deifies his own capacity, and he says the ultimate knowledge is the great thing. And where does he end? In agnosticism. And what is agnosticism? A confession of ignorance. I start to worship the ultimate knowledge, and when I have worshiped ultimate knowledge long enough I say, I cannot find it. I am an agnostic. I am ignorant. I went after the ultimate, and all I found was its hollow laugh of mockery as it evaded me through the mysterious door of the protoplasmic germ. That is the end of it.

Or a man deifies his emotion, and he says emotion is the great thing, a thrill, a throb, a passion, an excitement, and he worships it. How does it end? He built up something in himself that was real, and when he had constructed it, and went to worship it, he found what? Did I say lust? I will repeat it. What is lust? Hunger. A man set out along the line of the worship of an enlarged capacity for mere emotional satisfaction, and he found the opposite of satisfaction—hunger, panting desire, and no water; perpetual craving, and no bread. And here again I speak carefully, if you will bring down that one fearsome illustration of the worship of Moloch that I have more than once referred to, it is a patent commonplace, almost too shocking to mention, but awfully true, that the end is the same awful desire that can never be met, and that is hell begun ere hell is reached.

Or if a man shall deify Mammon because he would worship his will, what is he doing? Constructing something less than himself. He has a will. It is a divine power. He can choose, he can elect; and, in order to elevate it and deify it, and reach out after larger things, he comes at last to a night dark with clouds, lit with the glare of the vivid lightning, and he hears the voice which says: "Thou foolish one! This night is thy soul required of thee!" and the hand that grasped unloosens, and nothing is there, and the will that mastered bends to the blind fate of oncoming death. He has worshiped something he thought higher, and finds it infinitely lower.

But all this is not finality, nor is it the most terrible thing. The most terrible thing is that, when a man deifies something he thought higher, in the moment he discovers it lower he finds he has dragged himself down to the level which he discovers it occupies. The man who worships an insensate god becomes insensate; the man who worships something that looks and never sees, himself presently looks and never sees, listens and never hears.

The worship of anything less than God blinds and blasts and burns to cinders every distinctive excellency in man, until life itself becomes an unutterable weariness. Do not laugh at the man who talks about killing time. Next to killing the Son of God, or killing my fellow man, killing time is the most awful guilt and the direst tragedy. Do you want to kill time? You have lost your power to see. Give me that little child for a minute or two. I will put that little child down in a one-acre field, with nothing but green grass and buttercups and daisies, and the child will weave garlands and make crowns and play at kingdoms, and see everything; and you trot over Europe and sweep round the world and see nothing. You have become like your god. Your worship has degraded you. You may have pored over the musty tomes in your search after intellectual crowning, you may have followed every new call of emotional temptation, you may have planned and schemed to grasp power by the worship of Mammon, but these things give you nothing except their own emptiness, their own inability, and, at last, alas! too late, you will find that all you have gathered is vanity. You may live in a soft, miserable age that does not like the preacher who thunders to you about hell, but I tell you you are lighting the fires for it yourself if you are worshiping a false deity.

But let me pass to the other side. "We shall be like Him." I ought to say it with bowed head. I ought to say it with reverent demeanor. I ought to say it in tones that thrill with a great sense of the infinite Grace. I think that when John wrote it his pen throbbed with the sense of the infinite mystery.

"We shall be like Him." Like whom? A careful exegesis of this text must refer the pronoun "Him" to the Father. "Behold what manner of love the Father hath bestowed upon us, that we should be called children of God. For this cause the world knoweth us not, because it knew Him not"—that is God. "Beloved, now are we children of God, and it is not yet made manifest what we shall be. We know that if He"—God—"shall be manifested, we shall be like Him"—God. The reference is to the Father. Jesus said one day to an inquiring man, "Have I been so long time with you and hast thou not known Me, Philip? He that hath seen Me hath seen the Father." Yes, we shall be like the Son, and, being like the Son, we shall be like the Father.

Notice first the fundamental change of suggestion. The other men were men who made gods; these people are people whom God has remade by new birth. The primal capacities are redeemed, intelligence is illuminated, emotion is inspired, will is dominated. So instead of saying that when men make gods they make them like themselves; I have to change the whole position and say, When God makes men He makes them like Himself.

Moreover, when men make gods they make them less than themselves; when God makes men He makes them greater than themselves. Man was never perfected on the earth, even when he stood in Eden's perfection, and now John has to write, "We are the children of God, and it is not yet made manifest what we shall be." There is something more, there is something grander. The intelligence has been illuminated, and we have seen into the heart of the riddle of the universe; we have not found the protoplasmic germ—we have found God. The emotion has been enkindled, and we do not worship it; but it fastens on the eternal Love, and is hungry never more. We worship will, but we are not foolish enough to worship our own; instead, we sing with sweet old Faber:—

> I worship Thee, sweet will of God,
> And all Thy ways adore;
> And every day I live I seem
> To love Thee more and more.

These are present realizations, but John says this is not all. There is something else. "It is not yet made manifest what we shall be." We are not at the end of the process. We are just beginning. We are learning the alphabet. We do not know all, but we know something. "We shall be like Him." Much as I love the work of exposition, I have no exposition for that. That defies the expositor, that makes the exegete bow in worship. That is the cry of a heart resting in God. That is the language of the soul in whom the wilderness ends, and the eternal morning flames and flashes with glory. There is neither hunger nor thirst, there is no unsatisfied desire. "Like Him," walking in light with Him who dwells in light—that is the highest function of intelligence. "Like Him," acting in love with Him who is essential love—that is the highest possibility of the emotional nature. "Like Him," operating in power under Him who is essential life, and whose will is therefore perfect in its goings—that is the final action of human will.

Oh that I could speak to you one by one. What would I say? I would say this: Who is your god? Who is your god, young man? Who is your god, young maiden? That is your first question. It is the supreme question, but I beseech you, find your answer quickly, and find it truly. Who is your god?

To-day only can you answer that question; to-morrow we shall all know. How shall we know? We shall see the likeness to your god in you. Already it is manifesting itself!

I know that man's God. Who is it? The one only living God. How do you know? See the love in his eyes, the light on his life, see his likeness to the infinite order, see the sweet certainty and peace that make him sing the song of triumph, when the tempests are sweeping round him. I know your God, sir, I can see Him in you.

I know your god also! His marks are already on you. I meet you on the highway, and look into your face, and as God is my witness, my heart often goes out in compassion for you. The brand is there, the shadow of death is on your face, the vacuous stare is there. You are becoming like your god, man! Already it is beginning to be seen.

Listen for a minute, not to me; listen, man, listen to the voice that is speaking within you. Can you hear it? I will tell you what is being said in your heart now: "Show us the Father." That is it. Whatever the desire that is operating in your heart at this minute, that is what it means. You are going back to the thrill of a shameless sin, and the thing you really want is God. The clamant cry that you are trying to answer in a wrong way is the cry of your being after God.

There are some who say, Yes, it is true; what shall we do? I have the answer to that cry in your heart. They are not my words, but I am here by holy ordination, the ordination of the pierced hand on my head to utter them for my Master. Do not hear them as mine, hear them as His. "No man knoweth the Father save the Son, and he to whomsoever the Son willeth to reveal Him. Come unto Me." "He that hath seen Me hath seen the Father." Crown Him and find God. Find God and grow like Him. God helps you now to answer His call and find all that your heart needs.

CHAPTER XX

THE VINE

I am the vine, ye are the branches: he that abideth in Me, and I in him, the same beareth much fruit: for severed from Me ye can do nothing.

JOHN 15:5.

These words are among the most simple, the most sublime and the most solemn which ever fell from the sacred lips of our adorable Redeemer. They were spoken to a small group of men who at the moment were alert with the fear of the approaching departure of their Lord. Where He was going they could not tell, but He had told them again and again that He was about to leave them, and that the pathway of His pilgrimage was overshadowed by clouds, and the method of His going must be that of suffering. These men were listening to Him in the quiet and subduing influences of the night.

The words were spoken, not at the commencement of Jesus' training of the twelve, but at its close. So far as His own mission was concerned, the words of the paschal discourses were resultant words, words into which He gathered all the emphases of His teaching, words in which, as in the case of our text, He uttered inclusive and exhaustive claims. If they were resultant so far as His own teaching was concerned, they were preparatory in view of what the disciples were called to do in the world.

THE VINE

We should remember, further, that these words of our text occur in the latter part of the paschal discourses, after the disciples had been at least hushed into silence and solemnity. The first part of Jesus' teaching on this occasion was broken in upon by the questions and objections, aspirations and difficulties, of perplexed and puzzled men. Peter, "Whither goest Thou? . . . Why cannot I follow Thee even now?" Thomas, "We know not whither Thou goest; how know we the way?" Philip, "Shew us the Father, and it sufficeth us." Jude, How is it that "Thou wilt manifest Thyself unto us, and not unto the world?"

At last the questions were hushed, and the men were still. Then He spoke of the mystery of the coming union between themselves and Himself, and that principally in order to teach them, not the privileges that would accrue to them as the result of the union, but the responsibilities that would rest on them in view thereof.

Often our exposition of the teaching concerning that responsibility has been too narrow in that we have dwelt altogether too exclusively on the personal aspects of this particular text, "I am the vine, ye are the branches." Almost invariably in our exposition of this great teaching of Jesus we have dwelt on the joy and glory of being members of Christ as branches are members of the vine. We have thought of what that means to us in the way of abounding life and intimate relationships. These things are all true, but they do not constitute the final truth; they do not reveal the ultimate meaning of this allegory of our Lord. We have rejoiced in the resources which the figure suggests, and have altogether too largely forgotten the responsibilities which it reveals.

Therefore let me ask you to consider with me, first, the figure of which the Lord made use; second, the use which the Lord made of the figure, and that in order that we may come to a practical application of the teaching.

First, then, the figure of which our Lord made use. It is

difficult to read the chapter without wondering where the Lord said these things. The fourteenth chapter of this gospel ends with the words, "Arise, let us go hence." There can be no doubt in the mind of any natural, simple reader of the narrative that at that point they left the upper room where the earlier part of these discourses had been delivered. Where did they go? It may be that they passed from the upper room, down through the street of the city, and out through its gates across the Kedron toward Gethsemane. If so, possibly on their way they would see the vines growing on the mountain slopes, and in the darkness of the night the fires of the vine dressers, in which withered and dead branches bearing no fruit were burned. Or it may be that they left the upper room and found their way to the great temple, for the Passover period was approaching, and at that time the priests opened the gates of the temple immediately after midnight that worshipers might pass into the courts. At that time the chief and distinctive glory of the temple gate was that of the golden vine, the symbol of Israel. One wonders whether, as Jesus used this figure, they with Him were looking at the actual vine on the mountain side, all gnarled, and showing marks of the knife provocative of fruit, and on the fires lit for the destruction of fruitless branches; or whether, perchance, in the hallowed and sacred courts of the temple they saw the glorious symbol of the national life on the gates.

Whether here or there matters little. That which is of supreme importance and to which I ask your most special attention is that when Jesus commenced this discourse with the words, "I am the true vine," He was not using a figure of speech that was new, but one which was perfectly familiar to the men who listened to Him.

It is in order that we may understand the word of Jesus, so far as is possible, as the men understood it who first heard it, that I read that somewhat long selection of Scriptures, first the song of the ancient psalmist concerning the vine which God had brought out of Egypt and planted in His own vineyard, that marvelous description of its planting, and then of its ruthless destruction, until the sigh and sob of the singer became a prayer for its restoration in the economy of God. Then the two figures of the vine in the prophecy of Isaiah, the first telling of its failure, "He looked that it should bring forth grapes, and it brought forth wild grapes . . . He looked for judgment, but behold oppression; for righteousness, but behold a cry"; the second, the song that tells of restoration in the day of God, the song of a watered garden in which the vine grows, and over which God watches in infinite patience and care. Next in the prophecy of Jeremiah, that wonderful word, so rich in suggestion, "I had planted thee a noble vine, wholly a right seed: how then art thou turned into the degenerate plant of a strange vine unto Me?" Thus the figure of the vine runs through the Old Testament teaching; it was the method of the singer of the song, it was the figure of the utterer of the prophecy, and it was always used in relation to God's ancient people. The vine to the Hebrew was the nation of God.

In the New Testament, we find the Lord exercising His ministry among these very people and at last coming to that solemn and culminating hour, when, in Jerusalem, by parables He compelled the rulers to find a verdict against themselves and to pass sentences upon themselves. The last of these parables was that of the vineyard, the vine, and the men who were responsible for the vine in the vineyard. He asked them, What will the possessor do to these men who have failed to send him the fruit for which He asks? They, caught by the wizardry of His method, passed sentence upon themselves, "He will miserably destroy those miserable men." Then in august and awful dignity He pronounced doom on the nation which had been the vine of God as He said, "The Kingdom of God shall be taken away from you, and shall be given to a nation bringing forth the fruits thereof."

The vine was ever the figure of Israel as the instrument elect for service; its fruit was to fill the whole earth. The vine of Jehovah was not a pleasant plant in His vineyard on which fruit should grow to be consumed for the maintenance of its own life; it was not even to be a precious vine on which should grow fruit which should give satisfaction to the heart of the One Who possessed it; the vine was to be that on which fruit should grow that should fill the whole earth; its fruit was intended for the world. That was the purpose of the creation of the ancient people of God. Seers, singers, psalmists, prophets understood this. They consistently taught that on His vine should grow clusters of fruit that should be for the benefit of the wide world: righteousness and judgment, equity and truth, mercy, love, beneficence; healing for all wounds, rest for weariness, the wine of the Kingdom of God for the gladdening of the heart of humanity. That was the purpose of God in the creation of His ancient people.

After Jesus had thus pronounced doom on the nation because it had failed to bring forth these fruits, He gathered His disciples about Him and said, "I am the true vine." Thus He carried over the figure of the ancient economy into the new. Among all the claims He made, none, in some senses, is quite so wonderful as this. With the songs and voices and messages of the past in their minds, He said to these men, "I am the true vine." By that word He assumed the responsibility that Israel had failed to fulfil. God had made of Israel a nation for the blessing of humanity, and it had failed. He had planted a vine whose fruit was to fill the whole earth, and behind them lay the history of its persistent and perpetual failure. Now standing in the presence of unutterable, final failure, upon which He Himself had been compelled to pronounce doom, He said, "I am the true vine." Among His own disciples He claimed that He had come to fulfill that in which the ancient people of God had failed.

What, then, had He come to do? To bear fruit, the fruit

of righteousness and of judgment in all the affairs of the world. Listen to the keynote of the preaching of His herald, "Repent ye; for the Kingdom of heaven is at hand." Listen to the keynote of His own preaching, "Repent ye; for the Kingdom of heaven is at hand." Listen to the great word of Paul on Mars Hill when he said to the listening Athenians, God "hath appointed a day, in the which He will judge the world in righteousness by the Man whom He hath ordained." That was not a reference to the final day of judgment, the great assize when sentences are pronounced; it was a reference to the reign of right in the world. Our Lord, standing among the disciples, said, "I am the true vine," I am here for the fulfilling of the Divine purpose; from Me shall come the fruit that shall be for the healing of the world, and the satisfaction of its need; through My ministry righteousness and truth shall prevail, and humanity shall find the meeting of its need in the Kingdom of God. "I am the true vine."

If that were all then we should wonder and adore; but that does but introduce us to our text. "I am the vine, ye are the branches."

Are we not at least inclined to think that our Lord said, I am the main stem of the vine, that through which the life forces rise, and ye are the branches? As a matter of fact, He said nothing of the kind. He said, "I am the vine." What is the vine? The root, the main stem, the branches, the tendrils, the leaves, the fruit. The vine is the vine, the whole of it. The vine is not complete in its branches. The vine is not merely the root, out of sight. The vine is not merely the main stem up which the life forces pass to the uttermost reaches of the last and most delicate tendril. The vine is everything. That is the first amazing revelation of this figure of speech. Jesus said, "I am the vine." By that figure of speech He taught the incorporation with Himself of all believing souls, in vital, intimate union. "Ye are the branches." The branches are part of the vine. These men to whom He spoke were members of Himself, in new and mystic fashion, to be consummated presently by the baptism of the Spirit. Speaking allegorically and prophetically of that which presently was to be perfected by the way of His passion, resurrection, and ascension, and the coming of the Holy Spirit, He said, "I am the vine; ye are the branches"; that is, ye are parts of Myself, united to Me in a union so close and definite that I am incomplete apart from you, as you are incomplete apart from Me. As our Lord said in this particular text, "Severed from Me ye can do nothing," so, with reverent and almost awful sense of the solemnity of the fact, it is true that Christ stood there in the midst of the twelve, and said, in effect, Apart from you I can do nothing. Severed from you I cannot produce the fruit for which God has long been waiting! Severed from Me ye cannot produce the fruit for which the world is waiting! United with Me, and I united with you, then "I am the vine; ye are the branches," parts and members of Myself; and in that vine, that new and mystic entity in human history, consisting of Christ in union with His people, fruit shall grow that is to fill the whole world and glorify God. "I am the vine; ye are the branches."

Yet, if the figure is one that reveals the vital and intimate union between Christ and His people for the purpose of fruit-bearing, the whole teaching of the passage shows that continuity of relationship between Christ and men is dependent on their bearing this very fruit. "Every branch in Me that beareth not fruit, He taketh it away," casteth it out to be burned. If the initial fact of union is of the grace of God, the continuity of union is dependent on the realization of the purpose of God.

It is not the burden of my message to you this evening to dwell on the personal advantages that accrue from this union with Christ. I know how fascinating the theme is, how full of value it is. Oh that we may remember it for the encouragement of our aspirations after good, and our seekings after holiness. Abiding in Him I have all resources for the perfecting of that character of holiness which expresses itself in righteousness. That, however, is not the ultimate value of the story. In this great figure of the vine Christ has revealed the fact that the purpose of the Church of God is bearing that fruit for which the world is waiting in its sickness, its sins, and its miseries. I am a worthy member of Christ only as I am a branch from which fruit is plucked for the benefit of the outside world. The life of the believer is the life of Christ by the ministry of the Spirit of God; and the ministry of the Spirit of God in the world, our Lord clearly defined in this same discourse, in the words, "He, when He is come, will convict the world in respect of sin, and of righteousness, and of judgment," referring first to that which wounds and wearies and blasts the world, sin; referring, second, to this very fruit which the prophets had described, righteousness and judgment, "He looked for judgment, but behold oppression; for righteousness, but behold a cry." Said Jesus, When the Spirit of truth is come, He "will convict the world" concerning these things, and reveal to the world that all these things are to be dealt with through Christ, that the sin that ultimately blasts and damns is the sin of rejecting Christ, "of sin, because they believe not on Me"; that the possibility of righteousness comes through the finished work of Christ, "of righteousness, because I go to the Father"; that judgment in the economy of God is already accomplished by the way of the passion of Christ, "of judgment, because the prince of this world hath been judged." Thus Jesus taught them that the Spirit of God Who was coming to be their Paraclete, their Comforter, their Advocate, was coming, not for their sakes alone, but for the sake of the world, that the world might be brought to the truth concerning sin, righteousness, and judgment.

Thus we understand that by His use of this figure, Christ was saying, in effect, to these men, the Spirit will be able to bear His witness to the world only through the members of My Church. The Spirit is able to fulfil His ministry in the world only by bringing men into actual vital association with Christ, and by revealing through them what He is. He is the vine; in Him is all the fruit for which the world is waiting; but it can grow only on the branches; only through the branches grafted into Him and sharing His life can righteousness and judgment be given to the world.

This teaching reacts on the soul like a veritable fire. What shame, what wrong, what tragedy if a branch, if such a thing be conceivable, shall grow clusters of grapes containing the wine of the Kingdom of God, and consume them on itself for the enrichment of its own life. There can be no selfishness so devilish as the selfishness of the man who takes whatever comes to him from Christ, and fails to hand it on to other men. There can be no failure in the world so disastrous as that of receiving into the soul all the light and love and life of God by the bruising and the dying of the Son of God, and expending the sacred virtues and values on one's own spiritual condition. "I am the vine; ye are the branches." The purpose is fruit for the world. These words of our Lord, if most tender and gentle, are yet the most severe of all He uttered, as He teaches in this allegory that if there be a branch that fails to bear fruit for the world it is to be cut out of the vine and cast away.

For the fruit of the Son of God incarnate, for the rightness of His life, for the judgment of His mind, for the mercy of His heart, for the high ideals of His example, for the wondrous dynamic of His passion, for these the world is waiting; all the peoples that sit in darkness and in the shadow of death, are waiting for the Vine of God, and for the fruit that grows therefrom.

Do we understand what this means? In order that the need of the world may be satisfied, the branches are responsible for abiding in the vine, for the maintenance of that relationship with Christ that shall issue inevitably in bearing fruit. Herein is revealed the profound malady of the Christian Church. Here is the reason why we are almost wearied to death with appeals from missionary societies for help. I know exactly the feeling that comes to you when the last appeal of some society reaches you through the post. You fling it down with weariness, and say in actual words again and again, Always these appeals, always these appeals! Why are there always these appeals? Simply because in the vine there are thousands of branches fruitless, withered, not abiding in Christ, not responsive to the propulsion of His life, limiting Him by refusing to allow His great life to sweep through all the soul and have its ultimate and final expression.

When first we saw the vision of the Christ there was the sense of allurement, and we went after Him with the flush of hope on the cheek, the flash of a fine endeavor in the eye; we were heroic and sacrificial, ready Crusaders.

How was it that we lost our first love? Because at some point we became calculating. When the call of Christ was to new heroism, and fresh sacrifice, and larger abandonment, we held back and refused; we began to argue that it was mere emotionalism, and as we stifled emotionalism we quenched the Spirit of the living God, and did despite to the tender emotions of the heart of Christ. That is the story of our failure.

Go through these discourses again and listen to the teaching of the Lord, and attempt to apprehend His outlook on the world. He saw the true order, and He saw the chaos. Listen, as you listen to Him, for the thrill of passion vibrating through His voice, the passion of a great love, the passion of a fierce anger. Observe Him, the Waster, the Destroyer of all that blights humanity; and observe Him the Builder, the Constructor of the city of God. Observe the vision of the

Christ, see with His eyes; share the passion of the Christ, feel with His heart; watch the mission of the Christ and be with Him.

"I am the vine; ye are the branches." Then, if branches, we must be of the vine, and allow the life of the vine to master us, the purpose at the heart of the vine to inspire us, and the method of the vine dresser to have victory over us. Is it not in these things that we have failed?

What did He charge these men as to responsibility? He charged them that in order to maintain fellowship two things were always necessary: first, prayer, and, second, abiding in Him.

When reading this fifteenth chapter have you never felt there was somehow a break in the continuity at a certain point? Does it not seem for a moment as though the rhythm of the method of the teaching is broken in upon? Let me show you what I mean. "I am the vine; ye are the branches: He that abideth in Me, and I in him, the same beareth much fruit: for apart from Me ye can do nothing. If a man abide not in Me, he is cast forth as a branch, and is withered; and they gather them, and cast them into the fire, and they are burned. If ye abide in Me, and My words abide in you, ask whatsoever ye will, and it shall be generated for you." It is there that it seems as though there were a break in the continuity. Why introduce this word about prayer at that point? When you ponder long enough you will discover that the introduction of prayer at that point was essential to the argument. It was a revelation of the true place of prayer in the life of the believer. Let me put it, almost brutally, by saying, Prayer is not a trick by which we get something for ourselves! Prayer is a method by which we abide in such relationship with the vine that we produce something for the world. Prayer is inspired by passion for the Kingdom of God. Prayer is the branches desiring and demanding the life of the vine in order that they may bear fruit according to the nature and purpose of the vine. Prayer is the soaring of the soul to the height of perfect compliance with the will of God, the consuming of the soul with the passion for doing the will of God. The first operation of prayer in the economy of God, therefore, is not demand for what I need, but for what the world needs. In the pattern prayer mark the revelation of method: First, Give us this day our daily bread? No, a thousand times no! First, "Our Father, Who art in heaven. Thy Kingdom come, Thy will be done on earth as it is in heaven." That is the highest plane of prayer. The first law of fruit-bearing is that of prayer which asks for yet more abundant life, for the mastery of the soul by the life of God revealed in the Son of God, and communicated by His Spirit. Dare we pray for that? If we dare to pray in that spirit tonight what will happen to-morrow? I cannot tell. It may be that if some of you begin to pray in that spirit, ere four and twenty hours have passed over your heads you will have abandoned your prospects, stepped out of the profession that is so full of hope, and given yourself to some dark lone corner of the world to pour out your life in sacrifice. Prayer asks for fulness of life that fruit may be manifest; asks for that purging of God that shall make life more abundant!

Once more to utter the thing already said, to abide in Christ is the secret of fruitfulness. How are we to abide in Christ? There are two most simple things I will say. First, abiding consists in the cessation of effort. The one thing you do not need in order to abide anywhere is strength. Weakness is the condition for abiding. I can abide in this pulpit for hours without putting forth any strength. I need strength to get out of it, not to abide in it. Do not be afraid of the homeliness of the figure. I have found Christian people strenuously striving to abide in Christ, and by their very effort separating their souls from Him. Rest in Him, abandon yourself to Him, that He may have His way.

To abide means cessation of our effort, and it means the

acceptation of His effort, relaxing all the life to the Lord Christ and letting His life have right of way. That is abiding in Him.

This does not necessarily mean perpetual, constant consciousness of Christ. It does mean when His voice speaks, we hear; that when He looks, we see; that when He beckons, we go; that when He commands, we act. In order to win the world He is waiting for that kind of obedience.

"Apart from Me ye can do nothing." There is no vision, no passion, no mission apart from Christ. All the failure of interest and effort in regard to missionary work results from poverty of life. The things which sever, what are they? In the unity of the vine, schism. In the individual branches, selfishness and sin. What is the remedy for all missionary failure? Not demonstration, not literature, not raising of funds. What, then, is the cure? Life, more life.

> The vine from every *living* limb bleeds wine;
>   Is it the poorer for that spirit shed?
>
> Measure thy life by loss instead of gain;
>   Not by the wine drunk, but by the wine poured forth;
> For Love's strength standeth in Love's sacrifice;
>   And whoso suffers most hath most to give.

CHAPTER XXI

THE NEARNESS OF GOD UNRECOGNIZED

Jacob awaked out of his sleep, and he said, Surely the Lord is in this place; and I knew it not.
GENESIS 28:16.

A PREACHER OF A GENERATION AGO INTRODUCED A SERMON ON Jacob's dream by saying, "A long journey, a hard pillow, an uneasy conscience, and a heavy heart. These are the things that make men dream." If that be the natural explanation of the dream of Jacob, the supernatural value of the story is that through the medium of the dream God impressed Himself on the mind and the heart of this needy man.

I see no reason to doubt the suggestion that the dream of Jacob was very natural. After the long journey he was weary; the locality in which he halted for the night was characterized by lack of beauty, by rocky fastnesses, and barren, almost desert, expanses; the hillside swept up in terraces. As the man laid his head on the hard pillow of stone, the only kind available, what more natural than that, as he fell asleep, the strange stuff that dreams are made of should borrow the appearance on which his eyes would most likely last rest, and people the terraced hillside with angelic beings? And what more likely than that a man who believed in God as Jacob did and never ceased to do, whose father had believed in God as Isaac did and had never ceased to do, and whose grandfather Abraham had been a man of venturesome and heroic faith, what more likely than that such a man in such an hour in such a dream should imagine that God Himself stood by his side?

I say the dream is perfectly understandable and quite natural, for in every dream there is the foundation of previous experience and an added something that we cannot account for by previous experience. We can always find the first reason for our dreaming in the things through which we have been passing, and in our dreaming we always find matters introduced which seem to have no relationship to anything through which we have passed.

That recognition of the naturalness of the dream does but make it the more remarkable that God used that which was thus a perfectly natural process of the human brain, and made it the medium through which He impressed Himself on the soul of a man, and brought him to new comprehension of the fact which I venture to say he had always believed in intellectually.

It is not with the dream itself that we are proposing to deal now, but with the waking consciousness of the dreamer, especially with that aspect of it which was new and resulted from the dream. If, however, you will allow yourselves to call up this old story, which I venture to imagine is one of those which you remember most clearly, because in all probability it formed one of the foundation stones of that Biblical structure which your mothers gave you in the days of long ago—if you will recall the circumstances, you will see what I mean when I speak of the new consciousness of the man. When Jacob lay down to sleep that night he had no immediate, direct, actual consciousness of the nearness of God. When he woke in the morning he said, "Surely the Lord *is*," not *was*, "in this place; and I *knew* it not," not I *know* it not. Mark the tenses, they are all suggestive. The new consciousness was of the fact, not that God had been there the night before, not that God had visited Jacob in the night, but that

THE NEARNESS OF GOD UNRECOGNIZED 275

God was there at the moment: "Surely the Lord *is* in this place." The new consciousness, moreover, was one of Jacob's past ignorance, "I knew it not." On arriving here last night after a long and weary journey, tired and lonely, homeless and exiled, wondering and perplexed, I did not know God was here. I lay down to sleep without knowing it, without any thought of it, without it playing any part in my final resolutions or adjustments of life. "I knew it not."

Now let me invite you to follow me in a meditation on some of the thoughts suggested by this exclamation of Jacob when he awoke in the morning after the strange and wonderful dream of the night. First let us consider the fact which Jacob discovered that night, "The Lord is in this place." Second, let us consider the unconsciousness of the fact which he confessed, "I knew it.not." Third and finally, let us think of the discovery of the fact to him, how it came about, and what it meant.

First, then, as to the fact discovered. The whole matter may be stated in a very brief sentence. That night, by the impression made on his soul in a given locality and in certain clearly defined circumstances, Jacob came to discover what we speak of as the omnipresence of God. That is a phrase with which we are all familiar. It is a phrase of the theologian which has become a commonplace phrase in Christian experience. This was the hour in which Jacob came to actual, practical consciousness of the fact of the omnipresence of God, and it found expression in his case in language that spoke of God, not as omnipresent, but as being right there where he was.

That is the Biblical doctrine of God. It is impossible to conceive of the God revealed in the Bible without at once admitting the fact of His omnipresence. As is the case with every great essential truth of revealed religion, there is one classic passage in the Bible in which it is most clearly set forth. All the great doctrines and truths of revealed religion are expressed somewhere specially in the Bible; if we desire to know poetically and truthfully the relation of God to creation we turn to the book of Job and read there the theophanies of its later chapters; if we would know the value of the whole revelation of God in the sacred writings we study Psalm 119; if we would know all that can be said concerning love we turn to the thirteenth chapter of the first espistle to the Corinthians; if we would comprehend the full force of faith in the affairs of men we study the eleventh chapter of the letter to the Hebrews. So the great doctrine of the omnipresence of God is declared in that psalm which constitutes our lesson:

> Whither shall I flee from Thy presence?
> If I ascend up into heaven, Thou art there:
> If I make my bed in Sheol, behold, Thou are there.
> If I take the wings of the morning,
> And dwell in the uttermost parts of the sea;
> Even there shall Thy hand lead me,
> And Thy right hand shall hold me.
> If I say, Surely the darkness shall overwhelm me,
> And the light about me shall be night;
> Even the darkness hideth not from Thee,
> But the night shineth as the day:
> The darkness and the light are both alike to Thee.

And so on through all the majestic language of the psalm as it sets forth the omnipresence and the omniscience of God, that He is everywhere, and that no secret can be hidden from Him.

I repeat, this doctrine is the common faith, not merely of definitely Christian men and women, but of all those who intellectually receive the Christian faith as the Divine revelation to man. Yet it is a truth which men are not easily mastered by. It is a truth which is held in the upper reaches of the intellect, but which strangely fails to reach down to the volitional powers of the life, and rarely affects, even among Christian people, the emotional capacities of the life.

This fact of the omnipresence of God, what a fact it is! To state it in general terms like this is to fail to make it impressive. Even the reading of Psalm 139 is too mighty an exercise for the mind of man, and the only thing that any man can say who attempts to read that psalm is what the psalmist himself does say in the midst of its rhythmic beauty:

> Such knowledge is too wonderful for me;
> It is high, I cannot attain unto it.

To speak in general terms of the omnipresence of God, even though the mind accepts the truth, is to fail to be impressed by it.

Let us take two Biblical illustrations as illuminating the Biblical doctrine. I take the two which perpetually impress my own heart and soul. The first is in Daniel's prophecy, the story of Belshazzar's feast. It is the story of a night of carousal, drunkenness, debauchery, and ribaldry; the story of how in the midst of revelry there came the semblance of a human hand and the mystic writing on the wall, "Mene, Mene, Tekel, Upharsin." Then I listen to the prophet's interpretation of that great message to the king, and among the things he said this arrests my attention: looking fearlessly into the eyes of that drunken, debauched king, the prophet said to him, "The God in Whose hand thy breath is, and Whose are all thy ways, hast thou not glorified." I do not quote the passage at this moment to deal with the declaration that the man had failed to glorify God, but to ask you to observe the conception of God that filled the mind of the prophet. "The God in Whose hand thy breath is, and Whose are all thy ways." Belshazzar's breath at that moment was foul with drunkenness and obscenity; nevertheless, that breath was in the hand of God! To speak of the omnipresence of

God in all its vastness is to declare that which must be accepted intellectually if the doctrine of God which the Bible presents be true; but it does not impress the individual, it is too great; but when I see a drunken king, obscene and vulgar, and I watch the heaving of his breast and recognize the operation of his frame fearfully and wonderfully made, fashioned according to the plan of the most high God, and when I recognize that man's breath is in the hand of God, then I begin to understand the doctrine of the Divine omnipresence. Passing from the Old Testament into the New, I find myself in Athens with Paul and hear him saying to those Athenians—those decadent philosophers who knew nothing of a living philosophy or a vital idea, but were trading on the memory of past philosophies—that he has come to make known to them the God they ignorantly worship, and then declaring that "He is not far from each one of us: for in Him we live, and move, and have our being." Thus in language of the simplest I am brought face to face with the sublimest of all truths, and am brought face to face with that truth in such a way that the general doctrine becomes a personal arrest. It is that great doctrine of the nearness of God which became reality in the life of Jacob through that dream.

How, then, do men come to the consciousness of this truth which makes it powerful and prevailing in their lives? Take the case of Jacob. It was the consciousness of the presence of God in an unexpected place. I have already hinted at that. Let us consider a little more carefully the unexpectedness, first, as to the place itself. Jacob was near Luz. Hugh Macmillan has described Bethel thus: "At Bethel the natural landscape is so bare and exposed, that it opens no door into the supernatural." There was nothing there to suggest God to man. It seems to me there are signs in nature that must suggest God to the mind of the intelligent man. During the past week, in different parts of this country, I have looked at the autumn tints and felt as though in spite of myself I was being reminded of God, for the flaming fires of autumn, cleansing the floor and preparing for the new springing of life, seemed to me to suggest the altar fires of Deity. But there are places so barren that no such suggestion seems to be made, and Bethel was such a place. Jacob was far away from his home, far away from anything that spoke to him of religion. He said presently, "This is . . . the house of God"; but there was no temple there, for the temple was not yet erected; no tabernacle was there, for the pattern had not yet been given; there was no shrine, no altar; these he had left behind in the tents of Isaac in Beersheba. He was away from the things of worship and religion, away from everything that would be likely to suggest God to him. Yet God was there with him. That is the truth to which he awoke in this place near Luz, away from Beersheba, a place barren and bleak, away from the fruitfulness of the valley and the beauty of the hills. In this unexpected place he found God.

Take the case of Belshazzar: in the hall of sensuality and carousal God was present; He could not be excluded.

Take the parable of the rich fool, which came from the lips of the Lord Himself. He said, My fields, my fruits, my barns; and suddenly, in the midst of his calculations and his commercial enterprises, all perfectly legitimate (for I pray you notice whenever you read the story that this man was not guilty of fraudulent getting), God said, "Thou fool." God broke in upon him suddenly. Where was God? Right there in the man's fields, and in his harvests, enwrapping him more closely than the atmosphere he breathed, enabling him to get wealth. God was forgotten, but He was there.

This truth of the omnipresence of God means that God is where man is; man never escapes. My brother, you faced some stern duty to-day, and you were obedient thereto with a sense of almost unutterable loneliness possessing your soul until, perchance, you said, with Elijah, I only am left true to the ways of God. But you were not alone in that hour. When you stood firm, four-square to every wind that blew, God was with you. It may be that even to-day you have come to the sanctuary hot from sin; when you sinned you were not alone; God was with you. He is the God in Whose hand your breath is, and Whose are all your ways. There are those to-night who are in the midst of pain and suffering; they are not alone. "In this place," the chamber of physical torture, God is. "In this place" of mental anguish God is. Someone has come into this congregation lonely. Oh, the tragic, agonizing loneliness of London! Hardly a week passes over my head in this ministry but that someone talks to me of loneliness. You are alone; you know no one who sits by you to-night, you are away from home and friends and all old associations, apparently you are alone; but God is with you!

Jacob did not say, God came to me in the night, God has visited me, God was here yesternight and now has gone. He did not awake to the consciousness of a visit; He awoke to the consciousness of a presence. The thing that he found out that night was not that God visits man, but that God is with man wherever he is. We expect to meet Him in the sanctuary; but He is near us in the market place. We look for the gleaming of the glory of His face at the holy shrine; but he is as surely with us in the den of wickedness. Not alone in the sanctuary, but where the multitudes gather in defiance of His law, He is there. This is the truth to which Jacob awoke.

Consider, in the second place, this man's unconsciousness of the fact of the nearness of God. The note of tragedy in my text is this, "Surely the Lord is in this place, and *I knew it not.*" God is here, but I did not know it. How are we to account for the fact that Jacob did not know that God was there? It may be accounted for by intellectual limitation. It may be declared that he had not come to the consciousness of this great truth of the omnipresence of God. It is said by some that to these men of the past Jehovah was merely a tribal deity, one of a number of gods. That I will not argue. It may be true; but I do not believe it for a moment. I believe that what took Abraham out of Ur of the Chaldees was a conception of God as One, omnipresent, omniscient, and omnipotent.

I think we must go deeper if we are to find out why this man was not conscious of the presence of God. Not intellectual limitation only, but spiritual dullness. Remember, a man never finds God intellectually if he be spiritually dull. Man is more than matter. Man is more than mind. Man is spirit. If the spiritual fact in man's life be atrophied, dead, inactive, he cannot find God. He may be an intellectual giant. His mind may be trained perfectly, it may act with remarkable precision in every department of human life; but he never finds God. The great inquiry of the book of Job can be answered only negatively until this hour:

> Canst thou by searching find out God?
> Canst thou find out the Almighty unto perfection?

As I look back at Jacob on that night I see that he was spiritually deadened, dulled. God was there when he chose the stone on which to put his head. God was nigh when he rested his head on his chosen pillow. God was with him, but he did not know it, he had no sense of it. Intellectual limitation. No, something profounder: spiritual deadness.

But why the spiritual deadness? Because of moral failure. In the past lay trickery and baseness, meanness and deceit. Remember, this was not a man whom you can describe as godless. He was a godly man. He believed in God. The trouble with Jacob was never that he did not believe in God. The trouble was that, believing in God, he did not believe God could manage without his help. He was always trying to hurry the Divine economy by his own wit and wisdom and cleverness. That is the story of Jacob: in doing that he had descended to baseness, meanness, evil courses; and moral depravity had dulled the spiritual sense. That night he was not conscious of God.

This unconsciousness of the Divine nearness is widespread—how widespread who shall tell? In the case of men generally it is true that they do not know the presence of God. There are thousands of men to-day who, if you were to ask them as to their belief, intellectually, in God and His omnipresence, would affirm both; but they do not know God as near, they have no immediate consciousness of God, they have no commerce with God. The scientist as a mere scientist is unconscious of God. I want that statement to be correctly understood. It is quite possible for a man to be a Christian man and a scientist, and to have perpetual consciousness of God. When I speak of a scientist merely, I mean a man who is dealing with things that are of this earth, and who has no traffic with heaven. Here is the marvel of all marvels, that he will touch and handle, analyze and synthesize, examine and re-examine, investigate and reinvestigate, and continue to investigate the stuff which has come from God, and yet never recognize God, never find God. We have had a remarkable exhibition of that during this autumn in the meeting of the British Association in Dundee. If anyone shall ever refer to what President Schafer then said, let it be remembered, whatever he may have meant by it, that he declared he was dealing with *life* and not with *soul*. I think that he should always have the benefit of that admission, though I do not profess to know what he meant, and I have a shrewd suspicion that he did not know himself. One of the most highly trained scientific minds of the present day, a man of intellect, culture, refinement, reverence, is seen dealing with matter itself, recognizing the marvel of it, observing its mutations, changes, differentiations, and yet never finding God, having no consciousness of God.

It is equally true of the philosopher. That is why that

man is sorely mistaken who finds his refuge in modern philosophy. The most modern philosophy will be the laughing-stock of the philosophers of a generation yet to come. I make that affirmation in the light of the history of philosophy. Every philosophy has made its contribution, and has at last broken down, and been respectfully dismissed, while new philosophies have been introduced. This will continue so long as man is simply thinking on the level of the finite and the immediate and material. Yet here is the marvel of marvels: men will attempt to deal with wisdom, and yet be quite unconscious of God. They will argue for Him or against Him, but they do not feel Him, do not know Him, have no sense of Him.

Come to quite another illustration. There are men and women to whom I am preaching to-night to whom travel is a perpetual revelation of God; they cannot stand and gaze on the sun-capped heights of Alpine splendor without being conscious of God; they cannot cross the mighty sea and look at the wide expanse of rhythmic, orderly waters without feeling the presence of God. But there are multitudes of men who see no gleam of God's glory in the light of Alpine snows, and hear no thunder of His presence in the roar of Atlantic billows. I have crossed the Atlantic now forty times, and often have I stood and gazed over the sea, and always as I have done so, sometimes in the silence of the night, able to see little in the darkness, or at other times able to see much by the light of the moon and the stars, or as in the day I have looked at it stormy, or lying sweet and placid as though kissed to sleep—always the great word of the Bible has come back to me,

> Thy way was in the sea,
> And Thy paths in the great waters.

Then I have turned from the contemplation of the sea to the contemplation of men and women, and I have found people who have never looked at the sea for six days, they have been so busy playing bridge! God is close at hand, but they do not know it, they have no sense of it, no consciousness of it. They burn incense on Sunday, not to God, but to the respectable notion that they manifest their belief in Him by attending morning service; but they do not know Him. Yet He is there—in the sea, and in the ship, and in the cabin where they play bridge, the God in whom they live and move and have their being. Their breath is in His hand.

> Closer is He than breathing,
> Nearer than hands or feet.

But they never know it.

It may be equally true of the statesman. He may deal with national things and international things, and be busy with policies, diplomacies and arrangements; with frontiers, and readjustments, and partitions, even to-day at this very hour, and yet be entirely unconscious that God is abroad in the Balkans, and that business long deferred is being done in the resistless will and economy of God, Who will not be trifled with forever! No consciousness amid the clash of war of the presence of God and the overruling of God! "I knew it not"!

Or a commercial man watching the markets, lamenting the fall of consols, speculating on the effect that war will produce, waiting for news of the success or failure of the harvest in the distant parts of the world, may have no consciousness of God. God is there, but he does not know it.

Or even a physician, passing in and out of homes of sickness, and perpetually in the presence of pain, may not find God. God is there, but he does not know it.

Men everywhere, busy here and there through all the busy days, and wherever they are, God close at hand; but they do not know it. That is the tragedy of all tragedies. The supreme, ultimate tragedy of human life is unconsciousness of God. The supreme fact of human life is that in Him we live and move and have our being. The supreme tragedy is that we do not know it.

"I knew it not." Why not? We speak of intellectual limitation, that we cannot comprehend the fact. That is not the answer. The answer is spiritual deadness, spiritual dullness, the atrophy of the essential glory of life; for if man be spiritual he will discern the spiritual. There are very many who do discern God. In science and in philosophy and in statecraft and in every other walk of life there are men who have "endured as seeing Him Who is invisible." In these lives God is seen, and God is known, and God is recognized.

Behind all spiritual dullness are moral perversity and failure. It is sin that dims my vision of God. It is sin that atrophies my spiritual life and makes me unconscious of the nearness of God, so that I may live and move and have my being in God and yet not know Him. This is of all tragedies the supreme tragedy, that men live and move and have their being in God and do not know Him.

There for to-night I leave my message, broken off and unfinished for lack of time. We will attempt to return to it, that we may consider what that forgetfulness of God really means in human life, that we may speak of His method of discovering the fact of Himself to the soul of man, and also of what that means.

CHAPTER XXII

THE NEARNESS OF GOD DISCOVERED

Jacob awaked out of his sleep, and he said, Surely the Lord is in this place; and I knew it not.
                                                                GENESIS 28:16.

LAST SUNDAY EVENING I PREACHED FROM THIS TEXT, LEAVING my message unfinished. I return to it to-night that I may say some things which were then omitted.

In order to have sequence of thought I must briefly summarize what already has been said. The words of the text reveal the waking consciousness of Jacob after the dream in which he was brought to first-hand, practical consciousness of the omnipresence of God in discovering in that barren place and in unexpected circumstances that God was actually with him. Said he in the waking hours of the morning, "Surely the Lord is in this place; and I knew it not." In that confession two matters arrest our attention: first, the man's unconsciousness of the nearness of God; second, the discovery of the fact of God's nearness, its method and its meaning.

The first of these occupied our attention last Sunday evening: man's unconsciousness of the nearness of God. In the case of Jacob it was confessed in the hours of the morning as he looked back, "I knew it not." In all likelihood, and almost certainly, Jacob believed intellectually in the presence of God everywhere; and yet when he arrived that night after the long journey and chose for himself the only pillow available, a hard stone, and laid his head thereupon to rest, he was not conscious of the nearness of God, had not thought of God, was not engaged on a quest for God, was not seeking Him. In the morning, looking back, he said, in effect, I arrived here last night, tired and weary, chose my stone, pillowed my head thereon, and went to sleep with God; but I did not know it. This unconsciousness of God is patent in the ordinary life of men, and in the life of men who intellectually believe in the nearness of God, men whose conception of God is the Biblical conception, the Christian conception, that wherever man is found, there also is God, and that man cannot escape from Him. If a man shall ascend into heaven, God is there; or if he may descend into hell, God is there; or if he take the wings of the morning and dwell in the uttermost parts of the earth, even there God's hand holds him, supports him; if man shall say, The darkness shall hide me, even the night is light round about him, for he has to do with a God Who seeth in the darkness as well as in the light. Nevertheless, in spite of intellectual conviction, men live unconscious of the God in Whose presence they ever are.

The reasons of this unconsciousness of God are intellectual limitation, spiritual dullness, and moral failure. Intellectual limitation, for no man by searching can find out God unto perfection; He must be apprehended of the spiritual sense, and where that spiritual sense is dead, atrophied, inactive, man is unconscious of God. He may affirm the fact of God's existence, believe in His nearness, and·yet never touch Him or be conscious of His touch on his own life. Man is unconscious of God because of spiritual deadness, and all spiritual deadness in human life is the result of moral failure. "Your iniquities have separated between you and your God," said God to His people in the olden days. Because of moral failure there is spiritual deadness, and because of spiritual deadness men live and move and have their being in God, and never touch Him consciously or see Him or know Him. "Surely God is in this place; and I knew it not."

The second fact suggested by this text is the method and the meaning of discovery of the fact of the nearness of God to the soul of a man. These things are illustrated in the story in the midst of which the text is found, and for that purpose we shall again this evening make certain references thereto.

As we approach this part of our theme we have to remember not only the fact of man's prevalent unconsciousness of God, but the issues of that unconsciousness. Unconsciousness of God shows forth in the dwarfing of the life and in the corruption of the life.

Unconsciousness of God means, first, the dwarfing of the life. A man unconscious of God sees only what is near. Peter, writing to Christian souls who had deflected from the straight course, said that if a man lack the graces of the Christian character, it is because he is blind, "seeing only what is near." That is the perpetual outcome of lack of consciousness of God: man sees only the things that are near; his life is horizoned by the material; his outlook is horizontal, not vertical, as Dr. Jowett has expressed it in his recent lectures on preaching; the outlook is upon the level on which the material stands, and he sees only the thing that is near. I know well that we speak of men in the commercial world and in the world of statecraft as far-seeing men. It all depends! How far can they see? If they see but the bounds of the present world, and understand no more than its methods and its markets, its policies and its arrangements, then they are nearsighted men. Yonder old woman, poor in this world's goods, entirely illiterate, who for forty, fifty, sixty years has lived in the light of the uplifted face of God, sees farther than all commercial princes and statesmen whose outlook is bounded by time and sense and things material. The man who has lost his consciousness of God sees nothing beyond the near, the things of to-day. If a man sees only the near he can become only the little. He has lost that which appeals to life so as to lift it: the sense of the things that lie beyond the sense of the ages, of the eternities, and of the spiritual. If a man lives hemmed in by the things of to-day and the things of the material world, he himself becomes of to-day and of the material world; his long gazing thereupon, bends and stoops him downward until he is dwarfed because he is unconscious of God.

Unconsciousness of God, therefore, issues in corrupting life. Life without God is life lacking its true quality, the atmosphere for which it was created, to which in the mystic fact of its being it does finally and actually belong. It is indeed true that in trailing clouds of glory do we come from God who is our home. It is not only true that in Him "we live and move and have our being," as Paul declared on Mars Hill; it is also true as Paul also proclaimed, quoting from the Greek poets and declaring the truth of their affirmation, "We also are His offspring." To live apart from the fountain of life is to know the corrupting of life. To attempt to satisfy life on the level of the material is to debase, to degrade life. If men have no consciousness of God they are dwarfed, and presently corrupted; for there must forever remain within them the clamant cry for that for which they are made, and of which in the mystery of creation they form a part. If there be no answer to that cry, then the life is dwarfed and withered, and becomes corrupt because it turns to other sources, which do but destroy the life.

Twenty years later Jacob turned his face back again to his own land, and on his way home he had another spiritual experience. God met him in some form and semblance by the running brook Jabbok, and, wrestling with him through the night, mastered him and so changed him from Jacob, heel-catcher, to Israel, ruled by God. When the light of morning broke, Jacob said, "I have seen God face to face, and my life is healed." Men read that verse and imagine that Jacob meant, I have seen God face to face, and I am not destroyed. He meant something far finer. I have seen God, and my life is healed. Wherever the vision of God is lost the people perish. Wherever a man lacks the consciousness of God his life is dwarfed and corrupted; and as the vision heals, the absence of it destroys life.

The supreme note of the text, however, is that to this man, unconscious of the nearness of God, there came the discovery of the fact of God's nearness. Having the story in mind, let me, first of all, observe that the discovery of God to the soul of a man is always the act of God. Not only is it true that no man by searching can find out God to perfection; it is also true that man as you find him to-day is not consciously seeking God. Unconsciously, yes; in every enterprise of his life, in every enthusiasm that he allows to master him, in all the things that drive him, he is, without his knowing it, following after God if haply he may find Him. But not consciously, not willingly, does man set his face toward the face of God in the hope that it may shine upon him through the gloom. Wherever there comes to a man the actual revelation of the fact of the nearness of God, it is by the act of God. By that I do not mean to say that men may not come to intellectual apprehension of the fact of the Divine existence as the result of their own investigation. I believe men may come to that apprehension in that way. I am speaking of something more personal and immediate, more vital in the matter of life. I am speaking of the consciousness in the soul of a man of the positive fact of God; and I affirm that wherever the discovery of God is made to the soul of man it is by the act of God. God uses many ways of discovering Himself to the souls of men. I like this particular story because here it was through a dream. We emphasize the value of this story when we remember it was but a dream; there was no actual ladder, no actual angels visible to sight, no actual form of Deity standing by the side of the man: it was a dream, to be accounted for, in all probability, quite naturally. Nevertheless, through that dream of the night God made Jacob certain of Himself, so reaching Jacob's inner consciousness, so appearing to his spirit life, that when morning came—and morning is the time of disillusionment, morning is the hour in which you laugh at your dream and see the unreality of it; but in this case the man came to the morning and when the mists melted from the rough and rugged hillside and light was everywhere, and no actual thing in nature had the strange, weird appearance of something supernatural—when the morning came he said, "God is in this place; and I knew it not." So by way of a dream, explain it as you will, God rode into the consciousness of this man, and He made the dream of the night the vehicle of His approach. He came to the soul of a man by way of a dream. Let me assure you that the day for even that method of God has not passed away. Even in these days of ours, if we did but understand it, God will ever and anon appear to men in dreams, natural dreams, and through them speak to the souls of men. If you are not of that particular temperament, then God has other ways of speaking to you. The thought of God comes to you in an unexpected place and moment: some arresting thought in the midst of the busy rush of life in the city, some startling thought that possesses you while the train is bearing you sixty miles an hour to your destination, some thought born within your mind as the result of some remark made by a friend on a totally different subject. In these ways God approaches the soul. By a word spoken, by some deed, in an hour of peril, in an hour of catastrophe, in an hour of high ambition and noble aspiration, in a moment of supreme joy, God makes Himself known. These are but faulty, halting illustrations. What I would emphasize is that God discovers Himself to men, directly, immediately, setting aside the priest and the prophet and the preacher, and Himself coming to the soul. God does this in the case of every human being. The trouble is, we do not always recognize that it is God. We treat the illumination as though it had been some will o' the wisp, some wild fantasy; yet in the moment, howsoever it came, from whencesoever it came, God was a reality; and God was a reality because He Himself was breaking through upon the consciousness of man.

We of the Christian faith, of the evangelical faith, and of the evangelistic method, are greatly in danger of imagining that God comes to men only through our preaching, and because we have such vain imaginings we lose many an opportunity of leading men to walk in the gleam of light that has come to them until they find the perfect day. God makes Himself known sooner or later, most often in childhood's days, and with greatest clearness; as the years pass, the sense of God recedes, until we still intellectually affirm our belief, but emotionally and volitionally deny it. Even then God ever and anon breaks through upon us. In such hours of breaking through, an opportunity is created for the soul of man. In that hour, come when it may or how it will, whether in the sanctuary or in the market place, whether in the loneliness of our own inner chamber, or amid the multitudes of men, in that hour, in that moment, God by that breaking through creates for a man an opportunity; and in that moment the man will seize his opportunity and follow the gleam, or else refuse to walk in the light until presently—not immediately it may be, but after a lapse of time—he will laugh at the idea that God ever did speak to him. It was not very long ago that a man in public life in this country said to a great company of men in a Northern town, in what he thought was a humorous vein, You know, many years ago, I was almost converted myself! Oh, God, that he might have known the tragedy of his own confession! Many years ago God broke through the mists and shone on his soul, and he very nearly answered, but not quite; until, after the lapse of years, he looked back and laughed at the folly of the idea, the infatuation of the notion that God had touched Him. Are not some of you very nearly in that condition? God broke through when He took your child away. God impressed Himself upon you in the hour of your new joy; almost involuntarily you found yourself desiring to be a priest, that you might offer the sacrifice of praise. God broke through in the midst of tragedy, or in the rapture of the comedy. What did you do? If you followed the gleam and worshiped, then there were other revelations for the path of the just man: the true man "shineth more and more unto the perfect day."

Let me speak of such as obey after discovering this fact of the nearness of God as a great reality. What does this discovery mean to the soul of the obedient? It is, first of all, a new interpretation of life. All life is different when a man is conscious of God. I do not think we can do better than go back to the old story and take the whole of that dream, for in that dream of the night great things were suggested to the soul of the sleeping man, the power of which abode with him as the morning broke and day succeeded to day.

The ladder which he saw was a ladder whose foot was set solidly on the earth and whose top reached the heavens. These are all figures of speech, but the facts they suggest are perfectly patent. In that night Jacob saw that wonderful suggestion of interrelationship between heaven and earth, of mediation between heaven and earth. He saw angels ascending and descending, and there came to him the conception of this life, this present life, with its wounds and weariness, as ministered to by angels. The supreme fact in the new interpretation was the nearness of God and the interest of God in him, the perfect knowledge of God concerning his immediate position, and the awareness that God committed Himself to his need.

When a man becomes conscious of God he becomes conscious of the relationship between heaven and earth, conscious of the spiritual ministries all about him of which he had never dreamed, conscious of the interest of God. Two men are in a beleaguered city; without are their foes, waiting for them. One of them cries to another, Master, what shall we do? The other said, O Lord, open his eyes, and

> Lo, to faith's enlightened sight,
> All the mountain flamed with light.

He saw on the mountain heights, gathered about the place of peril, the angels of God. Someone is saying, Of course we do not believe in that! Of course not, because you do not believe in God, and you do not know God; and therefore you limit your own life to this little world, and trust to your own wit and cleverness and your own manipulation of dust; but the man who has seen God knows not only that God created us, but that other worlds and other beings are round about us, and that in the mystery of His unfathomable and unquenchable love He sends angels and spiritual forces of which we had never dreamed to minister to us and to help us. In the light of the Christ revelation the writer in the New Testament catches up the great thought and expresses it in infinite music as he says of the angels, "Are they not all ministering spirits, sent forth to do service to the sake of them that shall inherit salvation?"

To be conscious of God is immediately to have a new interpretation of life, to discover that the earth itself is more than dust, that all flowers are more than the operation of blind force; to believe with Jesus that God clothes the grass, and robes the lily as Solomon was never arrayed, that He is with the birds, and remains their comrade in their dying. All creation utters forth this great evangel when a man is conscious of God. "This is the age-abiding life, that they should know Thee the only true God, and Him Whom Thou didst send, even Jesus Christ." All life becomes new, so that the apostle will write, "If any man is in Christ,"—which is the Christian way of saying, If any man has come to knowledge of God—"he is a new creature: the old things are passed away; behold, they are become new." To be conscious of God, to know the fact of Him, to obey the revelation and to walk in the light of it, is to see every human face changed. We can no longer look with contempt on the bruised and battered face, for beneath the bruising and the battering we see the image of God. The measure in which we become conscious of God is the measure in which we cease to be narrowly patriotic, for we have come to the consciousness that "He made of one every nation of men." So flowers, birds, the sky, the earth, man, everything, becomes suffused with the glory of God when a man himself is living in the consciousness of God.

This necessarily means that a man comes to a new standard of action. His standard of action henceforth must be that of obedience to God, of co-operation with the angels. A man conscious of God has as the standard of his action the inspiration of his endeavor, a passion, all-consuming, to make this earth like unto His heaven; or, to express the thought in the older way, his passion will be that God's Kingdom shall come, that God's will shall be done, that God's name shall be hallowed on earth as it is in heaven.

This consciousness of God means not only a new interpretation of life and a new standard of action, it means also a new enablement, and that is the supreme matter and the supreme value. "God is in this place; and I knew it not."

Why? Because of some moral failure and consequent spiritual dullness, whereby I am precluded from finding God. Then God, in infinite grace, and in ways that I know not of, breaks through upon my soul, and does that for me which I never could do for myself, and I, obeying, find moral enablement. There comes to me a sense of His great mercy and His great compassion. There comes to me a sense of the forgiveness of my sins, and out of that sense, if it indeed be a true sense, there springs a hot resentment against sin, a passionate endeavor to master it; and as I start on my crusade against sin in my own life, and in the world, I find I am being empowered by mystic forces of which I never dreamed, by spiritual might which is from God. He works in me to the willing and the doing of His good pleasure. When there is moral enablement there is spiritual quickening, and I come to know the Lord, "growing up into Him in all things, which is the Head, even Christ," the horizon being put ever further back, all life widening, broadening, becomes more and more glorious. The intellectual limitation is negatived by the spiritual apprehension, and there comes that abiding certainty of God which no argument can destroy.

Finally, let us remember that of this great fact of the nearness of God the incarnation was the final unveiling. Surely that is what our Lord meant when speaking to Nathanael, the Israelite in whom there was no guile, he said, "Ye shall see the heaven opened, and the angels of God ascending and descending upon the Son of Man." In other words, all that was suggested to Jacob in the dream of the night is vindicated, and verified in the Lord Christ Himself. By incarnation God revealed His nearness to men. "In the beginning was the Word, and the Word was with God, and the Word was God . . . and the Word became flesh, and dwelt among us (and we beheld His glory, glory as of the only begotten from a Father), full of grace and truth." So opens this gospel of John in which alone is recorded the story of Christ's employment of the vision of Jacob for the suggestion of this truth. If in that incarnation the fact of God's nearness is interpreted, in what sense is God seen to be near to men? In the life of Jesus it is revealed that He is near to human circumstance and human experience of all kinds. Immediately following on the employment of the ancient story in the conversation with Nathanael three days afterward, He went to the house of joy to attend the wedding. God is near man in the hour of his joy, interested in his joy—I will say it reverently but I will say it—laughing with human joy, the merriment of the human heart causing gladness in the heart of God! Take the keynote of the Manifesto of Jesus, "Blessed," and it misses some of the music, or "happy," as some translate it, and even then you have not caught all the significance of the word the Lord did use. Not that the word "blessed" is wrong, not that the word "happy" is wrong, but that we are using them in peculiar ways; happy has become almost a flippant word, and blessed has become almost a sanctimonious word, which is worse. I venture to affirm that the word Christ used meant, well-to-do, prosperous. "Well-to-do are the poor in spirit, for theirs is the Kingdom of heaven." "Prosperous are they that mourn, for they shall be comforted." The word insufficiently translated by our word "blessed" or "happy," and ill-translated by the phrase I suggest, is a revelation of God's purpose for man, it is that of joy, gladness. The Bible tells us that He will wipe all tears away, and that sorrow and sighing shall flee away. It never tells us that He will stop humanity's laughter, or end its merriment. There is no parable in all the New Testament finer in its revelation of the Father than the parable of the prodigal. The language of the father when the son comes home is this, "Let us eat, and make merry: for this my son was dead, and is alive again; he was lost, and is found."

Jesus first went to the house of joy, near to human joy; but the last of the seven signs which John records gives us Jesus in the house of death, in the house of sorrow, God drawing near to the broken heart of humanity, and telling it the secret of the resurrection life, and illustrating the joy of the knitting up of severed friendships and reunions that are yet to be, as He gives Lazarus back to his broken-hearted sisters. Between that first sign, and that final sign, all the gamut of human emotion and experience is illustrated. The nobleman's son is sick, and God in Christ will heal him. In Bethesda's porches lies a man, eight and thirty years in the grip of an infirmity, and God in Christ will break sabbath to give that man sabbath. Five thousand folk are hungry for bread, and God in Christ knows that hunger, and supplies bread. A few souls are full of terror as the storm sweeps the sea, and God in Christ will hush the storm and give them comfort. One man blind blunders on his way, longing for the light of day, and God in Christ will open the blind eyes. Incarnation is the revelation of the God in Whose hand our breath is and Whose are all our ways.

By that incarnation He has revealed to us the purposes of His nearness. He is near to save—a great word, the most gracious word of all—to save men, to remake them in their spiritual life, and by that means to renew them in their moral life and ultimately to perfect their entire being. He is near man to save, and in order to do it He is near men to govern them.

The discovery of the nearness of God, come when it may or how it may, creates responsibility. It is possible that even now, in this evening hour, God has broken through in some life, and the sense of His nearness has come to the soul. If it has been so, follow the gleam, adjust thy life toward that light, take up the poise of soul that answers the call out of eternity, consent no longer to think of thyself as of the dust and as of to-day alone. Follow the gleam. To obey is to follow on to know more perfectly. To follow on to know more perfectly is to come to enlargement of life, and is to come ultimately to the perfecting of life. "Surely God is in this place," and let us say, We know it. If so, if ye know this thing, happy are ye if ye do all that the great truth suggests!

CHAPTER XXIII

THE PERILS OF PROCRASTINATION

As the Holy Ghost saith, To-day if ye shall hear His voice, harden not your hearts.

HEBREWS 3:7, 8.

THE LETTER FROM WHICH OUR TEXT IS TAKEN DIFFERS from the majority of the New Testament epistles in that it was written to people who had been born in the special light of revealed religion, and who had been brought into the larger, fuller, final light thereof as it came to men through Jesus Christ our Lord. It was a letter to *Hebrews*, the people who had lived in the light of hope and anticipation and confidence in a work of God to be accomplished according to covenants made with their fathers. These Hebrews were addressed by the Christian writer in the course of the letter as "holy brethren, partakers of a heavenly calling," and thus they must be counted among the number of those who had not merely had the light of the Hebrew economy of hope, but also had received that of the Messianic fulfilment of that hope. Every difficulty of those to whom the letter was addressed was one of apparent rupture between the old and the new. Profoundly convinced of the divinity of the religion of their fathers, constrained by the presentation of the evangel of the Christ to accept Him as Messiah, in the early days of their Christian experience they trembled and were afraid lest perchance they had made some mistake. That is quite understandable, for what a change was wrought by the coming of Christ! The types and shadows of the ceremonial law were all fulfilled, and gradually they were withdrawn.

The purpose of the writer of this letter, from the intellectual standpoint, was to show these people that the rupture between the old and the new was but the breaking of the shell so that men might find the kernel, the passing beyond the chrysalis stage, in order that the fully developed life might spread its wings. They made their boast in the ministration of angels in the leadership of Moses and of Joshua, in a divinely appointed priesthood and ritual; and the writer of the letter declared to them that none of these things was to be denied, but that in Christ all their suggestions had been fulfilled.

The purpose of this letter was far more than intellectual, however; it was spiritual. This wavering of faith, expressing itself as it did in disobedience, this halting in the presence of intellectual difficulty, expressing itself as it always does, sooner or later, in moral deflection, was a grave spiritual peril which the writer of these words saw threatening these Hebrew Christians. In order to bring them back again into living touch with the living forces which alone could realize the deepest in themselves and fulfil the Divine purpose, he wrote this letter; for he knew that unbelief always expresses itself in disobedience and that disobedience inevitably issues in death.

In order to discover the real force of our text it is important that we should observe that it is partly the words of the writer, and partly a quotation from a psalm. The first five words, "As the Holy Ghost saith," are the words of the writer of the letter, while the couplet which follows was a quotation:

> To-day if ye shall hear His voice,
> Harden not your hearts.

The particular purpose of this quotation from one of their own psalms was to urge on these Hebrew Christians the necessity for immediateness, and to warn them against the grave peril of procrastination. That is our theme at this time. I do not propose to dwell any further on the details of the passage of which this word of my text is the keynote. We may take the spirit of it in order to emphasize for our own times and circumstances, and for our own profit, the tremendous importance of immediate response to Divine impulses; and to emphasize also the subtle perils of procrastination in such matters.

This subject is of the widest application and might be illustrated on every plane of human activity. Here we are immediately halted and hindered by the fact that the supreme difficulty of all spiritual consideration is that men do not bring to that consideration the same acumen and earnestness and sincerity as they bring to the ordinary affairs of everyday life. In every realm of serious life we grant the absolute importance of immediateness and the grave peril of procrastination freely granted is the need for caution, that, first there must be careful consideration, the winnowing of evidence. Such sane and calculating caution is of the very soul of courage. While that is recognized in every department of life, it is also immediately conceded in political life, in commercial affairs, and indeed in all active life, that when once conviction is reached, response must be immediate. Some of the most hackneyed phrases of our common speech bear evidence of that widespread conviction: No time like the present, Never put off till to-morrow what you can do to-day. In these and many other similar proverbial utterances which pass our lips quite carelessly we express our profound conviction on the importance of immediate action in response to complete conviction.

I propose now to confine our attention to the application of this matter to the call of Christ. "To-day if ye shall hear His voice, harden not your hearts." Is not such a message necessary? What multitudes of men and women there are who lack but one thing, a personal and actual surrender to Christ! What multitudes of men and women there are who have been attracted by Him who do most honestly admire Him, and do most seriously in the deepest fact of their lives desire to be conformed to His likeness, but are disobedient, have never taken the one step of handing over their life wholly and absolutely to His control! I have said there are multitudes of such. I believe that to be true. I believe there are multitudes of such in this audience. I preach as the years run on to multitudes of men and women who I believe are exactly in that situation, reverent in their demeanor, willing to listen to the messages I endeavor to seek from God and bring to them with a patience that gladdens and strengthens my own heart. I have seen their eyes light up as the vision of the Lord Christ has come to them in many an hour of worship, and yet they are not Christian. Men and women attracted by Christ, genuinely and honestly admiring Him in that inner secret of the heart's depth, desiring to follow Him at some time, yet persistently disobedient! In this message, which it is my responsibility and holy privilege to deliver to this audience, I have but one thing to say. I want to speak of the awful peril of this prolonged postponement of decision. I shall attempt to say it in different ways. I shall attempt to illustrate the theme. By the help of the Holy Spirit, I shall, so much as in me lies, argue for the accuracy of the message I utter. But this is the one thing I now want to say:

> As the Holy Ghost saith, To-day if ye shall hear His voice, harden not your hearts.

I want to speak to-night with all love and earnestness

of the grave peril of postponing a decision which in the deepest conviction of your life you know ought to be made at once.

In attempting to understand this message, we shall consider first, necessarily, certain assumptions of this text, certain things which the words of my text take for granted. We shall consider centrally, and principally, the inferential warning of the text. Finally, we shall listen once more to the suggested gospel of the text.

First, as to the assumptions. Before I can make any appeal which is warranted by the text it is necessary that we should recognize that two things were assumed by the writer of the psalm, and by the quoter of the psalm in the letter; or may I not say, in harmony with the declaration of the text, these two things are assumed by the Holy Spirit in this text: first, that human responsibility begins with the hearing of the voice, "Today if ye shall hear His voice, harden not your hearts"; and, second, that when the voice is heard man is left free to obey or to disobey. These are the assumptions of the text which must be recognized, or we shall lose the accuracy and urgency of its appeal.

First, that responsibility begins only when the voice is heard. It is the man who knows his Lord's will and does it not who is to be beaten with many stripes. It is the disobedient man, who is the sinning man. It is not the man to whom the light has never come who is blamed for stumbling through the darkness; it is not the soul who has never heard the call who is accounted a sinner for not walking in the way which the voice indicates. Responsibility begins with the hearing of the voice. Here let us make no mistake. God speaks in many ways to human hearts as God fulfils Himself in many ways in human lives. I can imagine that a reservation such as I have made, a perfectly fair reservation—namely, that responsibility begins when the voice is heard—I can imagine that such reservation may seem to open a door of escape for some who will be inclined to say, We have not heard the voice. I pray all such to think again. How may I know when I hear the voice? It may not come to me with the articulation of human utterance. It may not come to me in any sudden blaze of glory, even mental, intellectual glory. How may I know the voice of God and the voice of Christ? The nature of the message determines the question of whose voice it is that speaks within the soul. The voice may seem to be of the mind alone; the voice may seem to man to come out of a man's own thinking. Indeed, it must come out of his own thinking. There is a sense in which, in a degree which is to my own soul growingly appalling and majestic, every human being stands absolutely separated from every other. There is a value not sometimes recognized in the great apostolic word: "Work out your own salvation . . . for it is God which worketh in you." These are blessed words of hope, for in them dynamic is added to injunction. They have another value, however: "Work out your own salvation . . . for it is God that worketh in you"; that means the inclusion of God and ourself, and the exclusion of every other human being. The voice of God never comes finally through human lips. We may have heard the voice of God in the sermon preached; we may have heard the voice of God as we have read the page; the voice may have come to us in the silence of our own home, in the loneliness of our own chamber; but it always comes ultimately in our own thinking. We may discern between the voice of God and the voice of Satan by the nature of the thought and the thing which is spoken. There came to us a call to higher life, to nobler endeavor, to the consecration of the powers of our beings to holy ventures; there came to us the voice that rebuked our sin, there came the moment of illumination when we saw the unutterable folly of our own passionate attempt to satisfy our lives with the things of dust. That is the voice of God finding utterance ultimately, as the voice of God ever must, not through the lips of the preacher, not through the written word, but in our own thinking, in our own conception. So the voice of God sounds in the soul of a man. He does in His great grace consent to use messengers whom He sends to utter truth; but we may hear sermons by the score, and never hear God. It is only when in our own souls we say amen to the truth uttered by the preacher that God has spoken to the soul. God does so speak to men.

Dare any man attempt to escape the call of this text easily by declaring that he has not heard the voice? Let him think again! Let him honestly review the years that have gone. Has not God spoken to him? Did there not come to him in a moment of wrong-doing, a high rebuke out of his own thinking? That was the voice divine. Did there not come to him some great vision of the loveliness of the Lord Christ? Did there not come to him consent of heart to the beauty of holiness? Did there not come to him a great sense of the awfulness of sin? Did there not come to him in some hour the longing to escape its power? Then by all these impressions, aspirations, desires, God has spoken to that man. These thoughts and conceptions of the human mind are divinely inspired; none of them has come from the underworld of evil, none of them has been generated within the heart of man apart from the direct illumination of God. Have not all of us at some time or other, and repeatedly, heard the voice of God speaking thus directly to our souls?

Here is another test. The voice of God always creates in the soul of a man the consciousness of responsibility. Therein is the difference between the voice of God and the voice of man, even at its best and highest. Therein, if I may say this in passing, is one of the final arguments for the divinity of this Biblical literature. We cannot study this Bible without being brought face to face with personal responsibility.

I can study Shakespeare without that sense. I can lecture on the moral drift of Macbeth, and then be immoral; and yet again on the next day lecture on Shylock and the defilement of greed, and continue myself to be covetous. I cannot preach on the word of God out of my own experience, and then disobey its teaching and continue to preach on the Word of God. That argument concerning the Bible illustrates the fact that the voice of God in the soul creates responsibility. A man stands confronting two possibilities of action in his business, in his friendships, in his recreations; a voice within says to him, That way is right, that way is wrong! That is the voice of God compelling him to see two paths stretching out before him, and convincing him that in his choosing he must choose definitely between right and wrong, light and darkness, good and evil. So we hear the voice of God, and we know it to be the voice of God by the nature of its suggestion, and by the fact that it forever creates responsibility.

The second assumption of this text is that of the freedom of the will when the voice speaks, "To-day if ye shall hear His voice, harden not your hearts." This assuredly means that we can harden them if we will; we can disobey, we can see the light and choose the darkness; we can gaze on the high and admire it, and then turn our face to the depths. It is equally true that the heart can yield, that there can be obedience. When the vision comes, if the heart of man is set on the realization of it, he will find virtue sufficient to enable him to translate the vision into victory. These are the assumptions of the text: responsibility is created by the voice of God; when the voice of God speaks, man's will is free to obey or to disobey.

Now let us solemnly attend to the warning of the text, 'To-day if ye shall hear His voice, harden not your hearts." By that initial word, "*To-day,*" which is the supreme word of the text, we are brought to a sense of the immediate, and consequently to a revelation of the peril of procrastination.

The call is heard, and he who hears intends to obey that call, but other matters are pressing and there is postponement. To obey that call will involve a change of plans. That call came to me three months ago, some man is saying; it came clearly, definitely. I heard it, felt its power, consented to its reasonableness; I determined that I would obey it, but to have obeyed it then would have been to rearrange all my life, and therefore I have not obeyed it yet.

Let us not go back. That call is coming to some man now. It has come already. While the preacher has been only arguing for the fact of the call, the voice has been heard. To obey now will be to change all the plans he has made, even for to-morrow! To obey will be to reorganize all his life around a new center. Therefore he says, There is time enough yet; I will postpone obedience. This thing must be done, it shall be done, but at some more convenient season!

Oh, my brothers, if the material walls of this sanctuary had ears and tongues what tragedies could they tell of that description! I do not think any single Sabbath passes but that within this house men and women go through this business of postponement, procrastination! I want to utter this as a personal conviction; let it be received as such, and weighed, and either rejected or accepted, according to personal conviction; I give it as personal, after over a generation of preaching; I am convinced that in this way, more men miss the highest and descend to the lowest, than in any other way. Not by antagonism to the high, but by admiration, and postponement of decision, more souls are lost, wrecked, spoiled, ruined, than in any other way I know.

In order that we may understand this let us consider carefully what are the perils of procrastination. To refuse to obey is presently to lose the sense of urgency. To fail to walk in the light of the vision is presently to fail to admire the vision. To linger when the gleam would lead us is to lose the constraint of the glory, and at last to imagine that the shining of the gleam was the creation of the imagination. Spiritual tragedies of that kind are to be found all over this land to-day. There are thousands of men who have come into the presence of Christ, who have felt the attraction of Himself and of His message, who have entertained admiration of His high ideals, who have earnestly desired to follow Him, who have determined that they would; but they have halted, waited, postponed. With what result? The attraction has passed away, and to-day they see no beauty in Him that they should desire Him; their admiration for Him has ceased, His name is but an idle story, the desire to be conformed to His high ideal is dead within the soul. And sometimes even worse, those old days are laughed at, days when they were moved toward Him.

This attitude is not always the result of the vulgarity that can be arrested by a policeman, of the bestiality which human society casts out. It is produced by procrastination, by postponement; it is the reaction on the soul of a high ideal refused, the deadening influence of disobedience to a high call. Thus the opportunity passes and the voice is no longer heard. There are multitudes of men who once were arrested by the claims of Christ, attracted by the beauty of His ideal, affrighted by the solemnity of His warnings, strangely moved by the infinite tenderness of His wooing; but to-day they are without any of these emotions; they are even cynical concerning Him, and have descended so low that they can be guilty of the vulgarity of laughing at their own experiences of long ago. In the terrific, appalling, awe-inspiring word of my text they are *hardened*. That is the peril of postponement, procrastination.

But, finally, let us hear the gospel of this text. If its argument proceeds on assumptions, and if its appeal is in itself the inference of a peril, the whole message suggests a gospel.

What is the gospel? It is all suggested in one word, *to-day*. There seems to be no music in that word. There is much, to those who know their Bible. The world's dark night is hastening on; but it has not yet come, it is still to-day.

When he made this quotation from the psalm, the writer of the letter to the Hebrews was conscious of the glorious light of the day in which he wrote, "To-day if ye shall hear His voice, harden not your hearts." The very word is full of hope. *To-day* is a gospel of immediate possibility as well as a warning of consequent peril. To-day! The voice of Christ is speaking to the sons of men. His voice is the one voice that comes clear in human articulation out of the infinite mystery of the being of God. His is the one voice that rings down the centuries of time with the finality and restfulness and strength of eternity. It is the voice of essential, eternal wisdom. The things He said are the things He says; and the things He said and the things He says are the things of truth and grace whereby, if a man live, he shall live indeed and not die; by which, if a man obey, he shall come to realization of all the infinite wonder of his own being as he finds himself led into fellowship with God and conformity to His will.

The voice of Christ does not speak speculatively to the sons of men. Christ is not suggesting to men a new philosophy which they may discuss and then receive or reject according to the calculations of their own minds. He speaks the final word with authority, with such inherent truth that when a man ceases to listen to human interpretations of the thing He says, and allows Him to speak directly to his inner life, that man immediately recognizes the authority of His word. The voice of Christ is the voice of all-sufficient might, and of final love. It is the voice which calls men to high duty, and promises the ability to obey. It is the voice which commands men to sacrifice, and provides compensation for all their losses. It is the voice that speaks to men out of perfect love.

Oh, this voice of Christ! Do not listen for it from the lips of the preacher. I mean that. I am not degrading my office. I magnify my office. I glory in my office. But do not listen for His voice from my lips. He really begins to speak when I have ceased. When my words are over, and you have properly discounted the accent and intonation of man, then the truth out of the words that gripped the heart and soul and conscience is the voice of Christ to you! The voice that tells you that you dare not do the thing of evil you had intended to do in the coming week! The voice that calls you to something higher! The voice that commands you to the Cross! The voice that says, "If thy right hand offend thee, cut it off; if thy right eye causeth thee to stumble, pluck it out." The voice that says, in the deepest secret shrine of your inner life, "Come unto Me." That is His voice. To-day if ye shall hear that voice, in the name of God, harden not your heart.

These are superlative facts. To parley is to blaspheme. To delay is to deaden the power to appreciate. Therefore there is but one reasonable time for action, and that is to-day. Oh, there is infinite music in that word *to-day!* It is still called to-day! The voice is speaking; heed it, answer it. Your first steps may falter through mists, but the pathway you begin to tread if you obey that voice will shine more and more unto the perfect day.

You may have listened to me and by that very activity be in danger of missing the Voice. Let Him speak! He is speaking! What He is saying to you generally I know right well. What He is saying to you particularly I cannot tell; but you know. I know what He is saying generally. He appeals to you: "Follow Me." But there is some particular secret between Himself and your soul. To the young ruler it was, "Sell all that thou hast, and distribute to the poor . . . and come, follow Me." Not to every man does He say that. What is He saying to you? Almost invariably there is at the crisis one last thing between a man and a decision. What is it in your life? I do not ask to know. I do not want to know. I will not be a confessor. Ah, but you know. He has put the finger of His justice and His mercy on the thing that must be abandoned, on the new duty that must be faced, on the new attitude that must be assumed, on the restitution that must be made. "To-day if ye shall hear His voice, harden not your hearts."

CHAPTER XXIV

THE CRIPPLING THAT CROWNS

And He said, Thy name shall be called no more Jacob, but Israel: for thou hast striven with God and with men, and hast prevailed.
GENESIS 32:28.

TAKEN IN ALL ITS SIMPLICITY, IT WILL READILY BE GRANTED that this old and very familiar story is, nevertheless, most remarkable. To summarize with almost brutal bluntness, it is the story of God crippling a man, the story of God Himself taking the form of a man in order to lay His hand on a man, and that in order to cripple him.

This is not the story of Jacob's triumph over God, save in a secondary and yet a very spiritual sense. This is primarily the story of God's triumph over Jacob. Old as it is, familiar as it is, I propose to give a little careful attention to it, for it is one of those Bible stories which has made a most profound appeal to the heart of humanity. I venture to suggest to you that our very fondness for it has led us to accept interpretations which I cannot characterize in any way but as superficial. Gradually, by the transmission of these interpretations, slightly modified as they have been transmitted, we have been in danger of missing the deepest thing in the story.

Just a word in an aside; perhaps this word is a sort of open secret for my brethren in the ministry who may be here. I suppose that at some time or another all of us who have been preaching for any number of years, say a generation, have preached from the words, "I will not let Thee go, except Thou bless me," in order to prove what wonderful power there is in prayer. I certainly have done so. Now, I do not think that idea is here at all. I have no doubt the sermon on prayer was true, but it did not properly belong to this text. That, I fear, is rather a common trouble with sermons. That confession, which is good for my soul, if not for yours, will help me to say that I have returned to this story, and after further consideration, I want to utter, so far as God shall help me, the things it has been saying to my own soul.

Let us first remind ourselves of the story of this man up to this point. I will omit all the things of his earlier years, and simply take the happenings of the twenty years prior to this event. At seventy years of age Jacob left home, a keen, hard man, intellectually convinced of God, but self-reliant, and at that moment defeated and disgraced. After twenty years, the story sees him returning wealthy, embittered, hardened; still intellectually convinced of God, still self-reliant, but afraid, haunted with a strange sense of fear. This particular day, to which we are brought in this chapter, and the happenings of which are so closely related to our text, was a day of hosts. Behind Jacob was Laban's host departing, returning after a bitter interview between the men. Then, somehow, to Jacob, in that very day, there came a vision of angels; he saw hosts of angels passing before him. It does not at all matter for the moment whether we say that this was simply a reminiscence of the days when he started away, and had a dream of angels and a ladder; or whether we believe that God in that moment gave him an actual vision of some great company of angels. The fact that abides is that to this man, hard, astute, by no means emotional, there came the sense of the angels' presence. He saw a vision of angels, and said, This is Mahanaim, or, to translate, The place of two hosts. And, moreover, there was another host. His servants returning to him, brought him this news, "We came to thy brother Esau, and moreover he cometh to meet thee, and four hundred men with him." Thus it was a day of hosts, the hosts of Laban returning from him, the hosts of Esau approaching, and God's host of angels round about him.

Jacob set himself with characteristic carefulness to arrange for the coming of Esau. He was still the self-reliant man, arranging for the presence of Esau by sending him presents. We see the man if we read the story fully and carefully. See how he arranged. He divided his present into parts, and gave his servants strict instructions, When you come to Esau, if he receive you, well; if not, give him the first instalment of the present, but do not give him more than you can help; if that does not help matters, bring up the next instalment, and so on.

That is the revelation of the man, a wonderfully clever man. I am perfectly sure he would have been a most successful business man in London or New York!

But there was more in the man than all that cleverness. There was haunting fear, a fear which would not have been there if he had not been a man of faith. Contradictory as that may appear, it is certainly true. There was a feeling in his heart that everything was not done, although he had done everything. There was a consciousness that something was left unattended to, something which he could not do alone. Therefore, as in that Eastern land the sun suddenly sank to its rest, he sent across the Jabbok the vast companies of his household, and he was left alone. That which happened in the hour of that loneliness is the theme of our meditation; that which led up to the word spoken to him as the next day broke, "Thy name shall be called no more Jacob, but Israel;

for thou hast striven with God and with men, and hast prevailed." No more Jacob, heel-catcher, but Israel, governed by God. What led to that word spoken to the man?

We shall notice three things. First, Jacob's need as he himself felt it and his need as God saw it. Second, the struggle of the night, that strange happening, which always fascinates us, however often we may return to the story. Finally, the blessing as it is crystallized into speech in the words, "Thy name shall be called no more Jacob, but Israel."

The need: first of all as Jacob saw it. We have tried to pass over the ground and to watch him up to that moment of loneliness. We have spoken of a haunting fear, a mystic sense that everything was not done, that took possession of him. Let us look a little more carefully at the man, and attempt to enter into his consciousness at that moment. I think we may do so by saying that he was looking back, and looking on, and looking round about, at the immediate. As he looked back, what did he see? Those twenty years. There can be no question but that as he looked back over those twenty years he had a sense of great satisfaction. They had been years of wonderful success. I am warranted in saying all this by the prayer which he had offered earlier in the day, when in the presence of the God of his father Isaac and of Abraham, he had recognized how wonderfully successful he had been. To our Western ears the words "With my staff I passed over this Jordan; and now I am become two companies" have very little of meaning; yet we know, if we take time to think, that in these words we have the expression of great and wonderful success, of a fortune twice amassed in those twenty years. As he looked back Jacob was conscious of victory, of success. I cannot help saying—for I am trying to understand the man on the human level, on the level of my own humanity—that he was conscious of a pardonable sense of satisfaction in that he had proved himself too strong for

THE CRIPPLING THAT CROWNS

all the cunning of Laban. Read at your leisure the story of the conversation with Laban. Jacob reminded Laban that during those years he had ten times changed his wages, yet, nevertheless, in spite of all Laban's trickery, this man had moved through to a great and assured success, and such a success—do not forget this—that when talking to Laban about it he could say that Laban could bring no charge of dishonesty against him; he had never robbed Laban; he had only outwitted him. He had the knowledge of twenty years of success wrung out of adverse circumstances. A man is always permitted some amount of satisfaction as he looks back over twenty years of that kind. That was the backward look.

Ah, but that is not quite far enough back! Why those twenty years in Laban's country? The answer would remind him of that business of the blessing, and that business of the birthright! Over all the twenty years of success was the haunting shadow of meanness and baseness and wrong. Jacob knew those years. There in the loneliness of that night, with the Eastern sunset and darkness round about him, or only the light of the stars overhead, while the little Jabbok murmured on its way down to the Jordan, he was thankful and pleased about the success; but there was Esau! Phantoms of the past were floating in front of him. He shook them off and looked on!

What was ahead? The land, the land promised, and therein faith was operating. That land was not fairer than the land he had been dwelling in. Why did he desire it? Because God had sworn to give it to Abraham and to Isaac and his seed, because the possession of that land was within the Divine economy, because Jacob knew, however much through base deceit and meanness he had interfered, hindered, postponed the Divine purpose rather than helped it, Jacob knew that in the purpose of God he was a link in the chain of the Divine economy, moving ever on toward high purpose. He returned to the land because God had called him, because it was in God's purpose to create a continuity: Abraham, Isaac, Jacob; but the phantoms of the past were the terrors of the future. Esau was in possession in that land, and was traveling toward him with four hundred men.

After the backward look and the forward look, the look around at circumstances followed. Everything was done that could be done; presents were sent to Esau which were in themselves confessions of a sense of wrong done in the long ago and evidence of Jacob's desire to placate his brother. The mother and the children were guarded, so far as he could guard them. What now? One thing he needed, he thought, and what was it? That God should help him. Is not that perfect? Is it not exactly what a man ought to feel at such a point? Let us leave our inquiry and find our answer in the sequel.

Now, with all reverence I approach what seems to me to be, in the way of exposition, the more difficult part of the subject, that which must be approached with reverence. As I read the story itself, up to this point I see Jacob's sense of need. How did God see that hour? What was God's vision of that man? How did God understand his need? How near together, or how far apart, were Jacob's sense of need and God's knowledge of it? I affirm that God saw a man whom He knew to be a believer in Himself. It is impossible carefully to study this story of Jacob without seeing that. Criticize him as we may, and we surely shall do so, as we find out how much he is like ourselves; nevertheless, through the story from beginning to end we are conscious of the fact that deep down in the profoundest things of his life this man believed in God and never wavered in that belief. God saw him as a man profoundly believing in Himself. He saw him, moreover, as a man who believed in the Divine purpose, and who desired to come into line with the Divine purpose, to cooperate with the Divine purpose. He saw him as a man who, in a wonderful degree, had entered into the appreciation of the master principle of faith in the spiritual, which had made his grandfather Abraham a man of strong initiative, and his own father Isaac a man strong in the quietness of passive faith. He had entered into this great inheritance; he believed in God and His purpose, and he passionately desired to be in line with it, to co-operate with it, and so to fulfil his destiny.

God saw this man not only as a believer in Himself, not only as a believer in His purpose, and not only desiring to co-operate therein; He saw him self-reliant. He saw this man as one who felt himself able to help God, who felt that it was necessary in certain conditions for him to manipulate events in order to bring about the Divine consummation. That had been the story of all the past, the story of every blunder he had made. There is no single tale of infidelity in the life of Jacob. There is no story of hours of deflection from the pathway of desire to co-operate with God. His failure lay in the fact that he had said, in effect, It is God's desire that I should have the birthright; I will help God by taking advantage of Esau's hunger to obtain it; it is God's purpose that I should have the patriarchal blessing; I will clothe myself in these skins and go and help God by cheating my father. Every blunder had as its motive the desire to help God. This self-reliance made him imagine that it was necessary for him to hurry God, to manipulate events so that they should minister to the speedy realization of the Divine consummation.

God saw that what Jacob supremely needed was first to discover his own weakness, and that in order that he might discover, as he never had done before, the power of the God in Whom he believed. On the threshold of possession of the land he must be brought to that attitude of soul in which he would be willing to receive the possession as the gift of God rather than imagine that he had gained it by his own cleverness and his own wisdom.

I believe there are those who are listening to me, brethren and sisters in comradeship of faith, who are really in revolt against this presentation of this story, those who are saying, Is it not the right thing for a man to work out his own destiny on the basis of his own belief in God? There is a sense in which that is true; but there is a deeper truth, and in order to discover it we need to ponder this story most carefully in the light of the whole movement of this man's history. In order that we may be preserved from the crippling, it is good that we should do so in the days before we come to the sense of weakness that will drive us back to it. Let it not be forgotten, Abraham was never crippled. With all reverence, if I may say it of One Who was more than man and yet was very man, Jesus never passed through such an hour as this in order to perfect His faith. However much we may be in revolt against this way of stating the story, let us consider it before we dismiss it. This is the lesson that God would teach Jacob, this is the need as God saw it: that Jacob should understand that a man can enter into possession of God's inheritance and destiny only as he receives it as a gift from God. He never can enter on the Divine destiny merely on the basis of intellectual assent to the fact of God and by means of his own cleverness.

That will be further illuminated if we take a step forward and glance, in the second place, at the story of the struggle. "There wrestled a man with him until the breaking of the day." That is so easily read, and yet it is so impossible of interpretation by a preacher in the pulpit; but I know that there are men and women in this house who in their own experience understand it. Through the long, long night there wrestled a man with him. God was limiting His own strength

THE CRIPPLING THAT CROWNS

in order to create a consciousness of it to Jacob. God incarnate, that is the story. God—to use Charles Wesley's daring phrase—was contracted to a span, limiting Himself to the level of humanity, a man facing a man, yet infinitely more than man! God stooped to the level of man and put on the man Jacob the hand of man in the night. What for? To bring into play all Jacob's force, that it might express itself to the uttermost, and so learn its limit and its weakness.

As I watch the long struggle of that night I am more than ever amazed at Jacob; how wonderful a man he was. He knew, of this there can be no doubt, that the touch was supernatural, even though it was the touch of another man. As I watch him through the night I see the old character manifesting itself, the determination to make the most of an opportunity. It is not said that Jacob wrestled with the man, but that the man wrestled with Jacob. There is no question that Jacob wrestled too; but the beginning of the struggle was on the side of God: it was the man who wrestled with Jacob.

When the first sudden flush of the new day shot up the Eastern sky the man who had wrestled said to Jacob, "Let me go, for the day breaketh." This was said after that strange, and wonderful, and appalling touch which crippled Jacob. I cannot explain it any further. The man might have crippled Jacob at the beginning of the night; but he did not. He might have done it at any point; but not until Jacob had wrought out all his own strength in answering the strength of God did God touch him and cripple him. It was when Jacob discovered that his strength was ebbing away, and that he could no longer resist the power that was laid upon him that the strange, wonderful thing happened. Jacob replied to the voice of his Master, "I will not let thee go, except thou bless me." We could not know what the man said unless we heard him say it, and caught the tone and accent. The spirit of a man is never in the words he utters, but in the tone in which he speaks. How did he say it? I am always so thankful that what seems to me to be the Divine interpretation of the story was given long centuries afterwards. I turn to the prophecy of Hosea and listen to the great prophet as he was denouncing Ephraim for his sins, and from that denunciation I am going to read only a few words:

> Ephraim feedeth on wind, and followeth after the east wind: he continually multiplieth lies and desolation; and they make a covenant with Assyria, and oil is carried into Egypt. The Lord hath also a controversy with Judah, and will punish Jacob according to his ways; according to his doings will He recompense him.

So far, the prophet was dealing with the people about him; then in a flash he went back to the actual Jacob of long ago: "In the womb he took his brother by the heel; and in his manhood he had power with God: yea, he had power over the angels, and prevailed: *he wept, and made supplication unto him.*" It was not by tremendous courage that he won the victory, but by the sob and sigh, by the agony and the utter sense of defeat. It was an appeal out of helplessness. He said it with tears, with a sob, in a moment when all the resoluteness of the years was breaking down. He came to a sense of weakness and inability, and out of that hour of defeat he rose into higher strength and greater majesty than he had ever achieved: "I will not let thee go,"—he hardly had strength to finish it; I think his voice was choked with tears—"except thou bless me"! It was the last sob of a defeated man. The last sob of the defeated man, the man defeated by God, is the first note in the triumph song of the selfsame man: "I will not let thee go, except thou bless me." "What is thy name?" My name is Heel-catcher. That is not so poetic as Jacob; but it is well to be truthful. Every Jew will read that every time he reads Jacob. "Thy name shall be called no more Jacob, but Israel, for thou hast striven with God and with men, and hast prevailed," so reads the text. We discover that there is difficulty in this text; the translations of the Revised and Authorized versions are different. I venture to suggest to you that the words may have meant, as I certainly believe they did mean, not that Jacob had struggled with God and had prevailed over God—there is a secondary sense in which that is true—but rather that Jacob had striven with God and God had prevailed, and therefore that God had striven with man and God had prevailed. I do not believe that the reference was to past victories over men; but rather that it was a prophecy of the new type of victory over man in that hour when, paradox of the faith-life, he had won his victory over God through defeat by God. If a man will prevail with God he will do so in the hour in which he is mastered by God.

What was the blessing? We have already touched on it; let us but return to it for a moment. "Thy name shall be called no more Jacob, but Israel; for as a prince hast thou power," said the old version, and that has been the reason of the persistent declaration that Israel means prince. It means nothing of the kind; neither does it mean one who has power with God, save as that may be a deduction from what it really does mean. These Hebrew words occur all through the Bible, made up in some way with the name of God ending them. Isra-el means God-governed, a God-mastered man.

The sun had risen now, and Jacob was going back to join his company. I cannot help it if you charge me with imagination. I never go back with him. I prefer to be with the company that met him. On the other side of the Jabbok I am waiting in imagination with his friends, wondering what has happened, why he does not come. At last, there he is, he is coming. See him? But can that be the man who went down last night? He has had an accident; he is limping; he is a cripple! I hasten to meet him, and I ask, What has happened? Why are you limping? I think he would have said, Do not call me Jacob, I have a new name; and there is no need for anyone to draw any special attention to this limp in the way of commiseration or pity; this limp, this halt as I walk, which will go with me to the end of my days, is a patent of nobility.

Presently he entered the land. And how did he enter the land? what of Esau? Esau ran to meet him and embraced him and kissed him. "Thou hast striven with God; and with men hast prevailed." Because in the strife with God thou hast been mastered, Jacob, therefore hast thou risen into co-operation with the forces of God that can disarm your brother and bring him to you with kisses and tears. That is the lesson of all lessons. Do not misunderstand me. This man had a great deal to do and a great deal to learn, as subsequent history teaches; but he had learned the central lesson, and all its values and experiences would now be wrought out into his own experience, line upon line, precept upon precept, here a little and there a little.

You say that this is a very old story, and that times and customs and conditions are all changed. Why bring this story to men in these modern times? Why go back there? For the simple reason that if it be true that times and customs and conditions have changed, God has not changed, and man has not changed. If for a moment you were inclined, in a kindly way, to criticize me for leading you back to Genesis, you have surely discovered that there is wonderful comradeship between you and Jacob. God has not changed, man has not changed; therefore the values are permanent. What are they?

Let me attempt to gather them up. Granted the principle of faith—and I am speaking only to believing men and women—then God will perfect it by teaching us our dependence on Himself. Happy indeed are we if we yield to the truth at the beginning, as did Abraham; or as did Joseph even more perfectly; but so many of us are like Jacob, we struggle independently of the God in Whom we believe. We do believe in Him. We do desire to be conformed to His will, and to co-operate with His purpose; and then we struggle and make our plans and we succeed wonderfully; but inevitably, sooner or later, there comes a crisis, not necessarily in circumstances, though sometimes in circumstances; but some crisis, in which by the direct act of God He lays His hand on us and we are brought to the appalling sense of our own incompetence and weakness. That is a great hour, an hour of overwhelming disappointment merging to despair; to some, let it be carefully said at once, an hour of actual, personal affliction as the result of which we shall never again be what we were, but shall go softly all our days, shall always halt by the way, and in certain senses be cripples.

Let us look carefully at such hours. I may be speaking to some man or woman in the midst of such an hour. Consider it carefully, and try to find out what God means. Is He not saying to thee this morning, clever, astute, capable man: Always hast thou believed in God, yet always hast thou manipulated thine own life, made thine own arrangements with wonderful success; suddenly thou art crippled, broken? God is saying to you, What is thy name? Is there not the strange, new light on the eastern sky that foretells a day of triumph? You may go softly all your days, you may never walk quite as you walked before. Shall I ever forget that hour when I heard a friend of mine, whose name I will not mention here, preach as I had never heard him preach before; when, going into the anteroom afterwards, I took him by the hand and said, Man, what has happened to you? Quite literally he walked his vestry with a limp, and as I looked at him I saw that this magnificent man was crippled for life, and he said, By that limp I live! In that hour of his unmaking he was made.

To gather up everything as I see it and feel it, let this story say this one thing: When God cripples, it is in order to crown. May we learn the secret and rise to the place of power by yielding ourselves to Him.

CHAPTER XXV

GRACE AND LAW

Fear not: for God is come to prove you, and that His fear may be before you, that ye sin not.
EXODUS 20:20.

IN THOSE WONDERFUL DAYS OF THE EMANCIPATION OF THE Hebrew people and their realization of the constitutional national life Moses twice uttered these words, "Fear not." In each case they were addressed to the people when they were filled with fear. In the first case the fear was fear of Egypt; in the second, it was fear of God.

The fear of Egypt was born of what appeared to be imminent and inevitable destruction. The Hebrews were encamped before Pi-hahiroth, caught in a trap, the sea before, the foe behind, and they themselves unarmed and undisciplined for war. In their terror they cried out against Moses, and complained that he had brought them away from Egypt, and he replied, "Fear ye not, stand still, and see the salvation of the Lord, which He will work for you to-day: for the Egyptians whom ye have seen today, ye shall see them again no more for ever. The Lord shall fight for you, and ye shall hold your peace."

In the second case, that of our text, the Hebrews' fear was fear of God. After three months' journeyings they had encamped beneath Sinai. There God had spoken to them through Moses, first in terms of tender grace and then in terms of law. The giving of the law had been accompanied by manifestations of majesty and might, thunders and lightnings, a thick cloud covering the guarded mount, and the voice of a trumpet exceeding loud. The people trembled and stood afar off, and besought Moses that they might not hear the voice of God, and to that sense of fear he uttered these words, "Fear not: for God is come to prove you, and that His fear may be before you, that ye sin not." These words, then, are supremely valuable in revealing the meaning of law.

First, they describe the true attitude of men toward the law in the words, "Fear not," which relate the law of God to the grace of His heart; second, they describe the method of the law of God in the words, "God is come to prove you, and that His fear may be before you"; and, finally, they reveal the purpose of grace and of law in the words, "that ye sin not." This is a consideration full of importance. Innately man is an anarchist; experientially, that is as the result of observation, he admits the necessity for law, and he is always anxious that the other man should submit to it. But for himself he desires freedom from it. Restraint is irksome. We would fain go our own way without any reference to law. This attitude of mind colors our thinking of the law of God, and strangely persists even in the life and the experience of Christian men and women. Unconsciously to ourselves, we think of the law of God as hard and severe, the opposite of love and of grace; and we perpetually quote certain words in the New Testament in a tone of voice which reveals a false conception of contrast between law and grace. I refer to words occurring in the first chapter of John which we render thus: "The law was given by Moses; grace and truth came by Jesus Christ." That intonation—which by the way cannot be printed—is a commentary on the text and a revelation of our misconception of it. We read the earlier declaration, "The law was given by Moses," in a tone of thunder and severity; then suddenly our voice melts into tenderness as we read, "grace and truth came by Jesus Christ." In doing so we prove that we understand neither the law which came by Moses nor the grace and truth which came through Jesus Christ. The law of God is the expression of the love of God, and its giving, even in the midst of the old economy, was as certainly an activity of the grace of His heart as was the coming into this world of His Son. Law expresses the rules of conduct for a man and for all time; truth is the essential integrity out of which all such expression comes. It is in the discovery of this fact, that law is the expression of grace, that is found the inspiration of obedience which prepares the way for that final and further operation of grace whereby a man is enabled to obey the law. To know that the law of God is the language of love is to exclaim, "Oh, how love I Thy law! It is my meditation all the day." Until a man is brought to recognition of the excellency of the law of God he will never yield himself to the redeeming power of God. In this sense also it is true that the law is our custodian to lead us to the faith; for it arrests us, and compels us toward God, and so prepares the way for that activity by which He rescues us and enables us to do His bidding.

Our theme this evening, then is the relation between grace and law; and I propose that we consider law, first in its inspiration, which is grace; second, in its method, which is that of revelation; finally, in the purpose, which is purity; and all this as preliminary to a consideration of the fact that there are things that the law cannot do, but which grace is able to do.

That grace is the inspiration of law cannot be more perfectly illustrated than in the context. Everyone knows the content of the twentieth chapter of the book of Exodus.

But how many are familiar with the nineteenth chapter? The twentieth chapter cannot be accurately read unless the nineteenth chapter has been read. They are closely and intimately related; they form parts of one great whole; they constitute a contrast and a harmony. To read the nineteenth without the twentieth is to read an unfinished fragment; to read the twentieth apart from the nineteenth is to read that which standing alone is indeed full of error. "In the third month after the children of Israel were gone forth out of the land of Egypt, the same day came they into the wilderness of Sinai." So the nineteenth chapter begins. It is the story of Pentecost, that is, the story of fifty days after emancipation. Fifty days after emancipation the children of Israel found themselves in the wilderness of Sinai. There they pitched their camp, and God, through the mediator Moses, began to deal with them in order to give them their national constitution. Now let us summarize chapter nineteen. We have, first, the terms of grace. These were immediately followed by the answer which the people gave to the message of grace. The chapter closes with the response of law to the answer of man. In the twentieth chapter the order is reversed. It opens with the terms of law, the Ten Words of the Decalogue. Immediately following we have the answer of man to these terms of law. The chapter closes with the response of grace.

This is the account of God's first messages to this emancipated people, half vulgarized as the result of the long process of slavery. They were now to be organized into national life, a life of peculiar character. In God's dealings with the world they were to constitute a theocracy, a nation through which He would reveal Himself to other nations for their healing and blessing. The story records, first, God's terms of grace, the Hebrews' answer, and His immediate response in law; then His terms of law, their answer, and His final response in words of grace.

The terms of grace in chapter nineteen are remarkable:

> Thou shalt say to the house of Jacob, and tell the children of Israel, Ye have seen what I did unto the Egyptians, and how I bare you on eagles' wings, and brought you unto Myself. Now therefore, if ye will obey My voice indeed, and keep My covenant, then ye shall be a peculiar treasure unto Me from among all peoples; for all the earth is mine.

Mark that interjection. At the very beginning of their history God reminded this people that they were not His peculiar people in the sense of the rejection of other peoples: "All the earth is Mine"—and "ye shall be unto Me a dynasty of priests, and an holy nation." These were the terms of grace. I think no one will quarrel with that definition when I remind them of the fact that we find in the New Testament that when Peter wrote his letter for the strengthening of trembling souls, he climbed no higher height in his description of the Christian Church than that of these words. The words thrill with the tenderness of a great love. They constitute the revelation of the infinite purpose of the heart of God.

They answered, saying, "All that the Lord hath spoken we will do." Then, if we were reading this chapter for the first time and could have that inestimable blessing of coming to it with a fresh mind, we should inevitably be impressed by the change in the language. The Lord said, "Lo, I come unto thee in a thick cloud, that the people may hear when I speak with thee." Let the people not come nigh! Set bounds and fences round about the mountain so that no beast shall touch it! This was God's response to man's answer to His terms of grace. Then followed the giving of the Ten Words, the terms of law amid the thunders and the lightning, out of the darkness and the cloud; and then men answered, "Speak thou with us, and we will hear; but let not God speak with us, lest we die." To that cry of fear the response of God through Moses was, "Fear not: for God is come to prove you, and that His fear may be before you, that ye sin not." This was followed by instructions concerning an altar, and sacrifices, and the promise of God, "I will come to you."

The opening note was that of grace: I have "brought you unto Myself"; the final note was also of grace: "I will come unto thee and I will bless thee." Between the two we find man's arrogance, God's unfolding of law, and man's trembling. Fear not! God's purpose is that of grace, and therefore His plan must be that of law.

Let us glance at this matter from a slightly different standpoint, that of law as a method of grace. The ready answer of these people, which I have already described as the answer of arrogance, demonstrates to us how little they knew of their own hearts. They said, "All that the Lord hath spoken we will do." This is not to condemn them for saying this. I hope nothing I have said, even this description of their words as words of arrogance, would convey that impression. When these people said, "All that the Lord hath spoken we will do," they were uttering the deepest thing of their lives. They were speaking out of the very depth of their souls. Surely He had brought them out of Egypt, surely He had borne them on eagles' wings, surely He had shown His power, and now in terms of infinite grace He had spoken to them: I have brought you unto Myself, to make you a dynasty of priests, for all the earth is Mine, and you are to be a blessing to all nations. To this they replied, Yes, we will fulfil that high vocation, we will be obedient, and do anything that God says. This was the voice of noble aspiration, but they did not know what lay between them and realization; they had not found the measure of their own incapacity; they had not learned their weakness. Therefore law was given, revealing God to them, and themselves to themselves as in the presence of God. The function of law was that of revelation, never that of salvation. In the words of Paul in his Galatian letter, one little sentence reveals the truth concerning law, "The law is not of faith."

Law is a revelation. It was a revelation to these men, first of life according to the will of God. It was a revelation to men of the standards of life in the economy of God. As the first ten words were uttered they constituted a revelation of holiness in human life. They are words which define man's relationship to God and man's relationship to his fellow man: broad foundation words, on which all future codes were to be erected. They discovered God in His purity, in His holiness, in His justice, in His righteousness. The first four revealed man's relation to God as the foundation of all morality; the last six revealed man's relationship to his fellow man as the expression of his obedience to the first four. From these words of the law there shone upon men the light, the awful light of the holiness of God.

That revelation of holiness was in the hearts of the men who heard it inspiration, the creation of desire, or of admiration of the ideal. Perhaps as Paul became the most remarkable illustration in the apostolic records of incarnate Christianity, so also Saul of Tarsus was the most remarkable revelation in the Bible of incarnate Hebraism. In his Roman letter Paul declared that after the inward man, he delighted in the law of God; he knew its glory, he knew its beauty. That is the first thing that the law does for a man. Men who break the law with apparent ease and wicked persistence, nevertheless do know in the deepest of their lives the glory and the beauty of the law they break. The most depraved and immoral man—and herein lies the heinousness of his sin—knows the excellency of the ideal to which he will not conform. Strange paradox of human consciousness, but undoubtedly true. The law reveals God and reveals holiness, and carries to the souls of men inevitable conviction as to its height, its nobility, and its grandeur.

If the law is thus a revelation of God it necessarily becomes to the men who receive it a revelation of themselves. When the light of the law flamed on these men they knew their failure, and they knew their weakness; and so while it is true that law becomes an inspiration, the final word is that law becomes a condemnation. It is the revelation of failure. Because in the light of the requirement of the law I learn how I fail and how weak I am, it rests on me as a perpetual condemnation and denunciation. The law, then, is a revelation which inspires and creates admiration for goodness in the soul of a man; but as it reveals it condemns, making a man conscious of how far he has come short and of how appallingly weak he is. Grace declares a purpose beneficent and beautiful, and man says, I will obey. The law then reveals to him the conditions on which he may enter on the purpose beneficent, and he is filled with fear; but the language of law is the language of grace.

Thus we come to the final note: "That ye sin not." There are many words in our Bible translated "sin" in both Hebrew and Greek, but the common word in the Hebrew and the common word in the Greek have exactly the same significance. Sin is missing of the mark, failure to realize; and that whether it be wilful or ignorant. If we are dealing with sin as guilt, then the sin of ignorance brings no guilt with it. It is wilful sin that brings guilt. But if we are dealing with man, and attempting to see his place in the economy of God and the purpose of heaven for the true realization of life, then sin is failure. If a man comes short of the highest fulfilment of his own life, that is sin. The law was given that men may not sin, that they may not miss the mark, that they may not fail to realize the real meaning and purpose of their own lives. In what sense does law minister to that end? Only as it reveals to man the standard, as it brings to him the measurement of his own life, as it unfolds before him the possibilities of his life, and reveals to him the conditions on which it shall be possible for him to fulfil those possibilities.

In this connection we must take a wider view of law than Exodus affords. We go back to the beginning of human history as the Bible records it, and there we find law, not the law which was here uttered, but human life conditioned in the will of God, God uttering His own word, a commandment laid on man as a safeguard and revealing to him his relation to a supreme authority. That is law. Leave these earlier records and come to the New Testament, and in the teaching of Jesus we find law; but the Master goes to deeper depths, searching the profound things of human life, no longer merely conditioning external conduct, but setting up His standard in the inner recesses of motive and desire. The broadest conception shows that law is a revelation to man of himself, made by the grace of the Divine love; a kindly and tender declaration of the path in which he should go, that he may not miss his way; statement of the principles that govern his life, that he may not violate them. In Christ men are set free from the law which is Hebrew; but they are brought under the law of the Spirit of life. Thus in the new economy we have a yet clearer unfolding of the truth that law is the language of love. God bending over a nation or bending over a man says to it or to him, "Thou shalt have no other gods before Me." That is not the language of hardness, of severity, of unkindness. It is love showing the nation or the man that life must be adjusted to the supreme things in order that it may rise to the height of its possibility.

This is true of every one of the ten words; and it is equally true of the words of Jesus. They are severe, they are awe-inspiring, they search and scorch and frighten the soul, if men will listen to them. Nevertheless they are the words of infinite compassion, of infinite tenderness; they are words uttered to my soul in order that I may know the way wherein I should go, if I am not to miss the meaning of my life, if I am to realize it in its height, its breadth, its depth, its glory. Jesus said that He did not come into the world to condemn the world, but that the world through Him might have life. Bear in mind that great declaration, and then hear me while reverently I say that He did condemn the world. That is not to contradict the word of the Lord, it is to attempt to understand it. Jesus is not in this assembly to condemn; but how He does condemn! The purpose of His heart is not condemnation; but if I remit my soul to His inquiry, to His investigation, then I lay my hand on my lip, and say, Unclean, unclean! He condemns me.

That, however, is not the ultimate fact. The condemnation of His scorching law is in order that I may be driven closer yet to Him for salvation. Grace utters the law, that man may discover sin, and, remitting himself to its measurement, may find his failure.

If law is the expression of grace, it is not its final word. Law brings man to a consciousness of his sin, and has no more that it can do. What will grace say to a man who stands condemned by this uttering of law? Let us first remember this. Grace does not deny that man's sin. The business of grace is not to hide sin or cloak it over or deny the reality of it. Let us remember, in the second place, that grace does not excuse the sinning man. Nevertheless, in some infinite mystery of love, grace operates in such a way that the sin of sinning man may be forgiven and the sinning man himself be conformed to the very ideal of purity and beauty which the law has revealed. To go back to the illustration in Exodus, grace first says God's purpose is to bring man to Himself, and man agrees. Law then discovers to man his own weakness, and man is afraid, and says, "Let not God speak." Has grace no more to say? Grace then says, "Fear not." There is a way of approach. It is the way of an altar, the way of a sacrifice. The central word of grace is that of God, "I will come to thee." That is what grace says to the man condemned under the law; it draws near with healing, with renewal.

If you ask me how grace can accomplish this, I point you to the Cross and ask you to listen to the words of inspiration as you gaze on the profound mystery. "God was in Christ reconciling the world unto Himself, not reckoning unto them their trespasses." Or again, "God commendeth His love toward us in that while we were yet sinners Christ died." By an infinite transaction in the very Being of God, grace, having spoken in the law and thereby revealed to me my failure, reaches me, captures me, holds me, remakes me, energizes me; and all this in order that I may become that which law has revealed to me I have failed to be.

If again you ask me for an illustration of how this can be, I shall take you to the simplest figure in the New Testament used by Christ and His holy apostles, realizing that it is but a figure, realizing that it is a figure that we do not often make use of in this regard, and yet convinced that it is one of the most illuminative in all the New Testament. I mean the figure of the forgiveness of debt. What is it to forgive debt? Remember, in the first place, that no man can forgive debt except the man to whom the debt is owed. Let me reverently place the illustration on the commonplace level of the currency. Here is a man who owes to another man a hundred pounds. He has nothing to pay, he is bankrupt. The man to whom it is owed, in grace forgives it. Has he a right to do it? No one will question the right. How does he do it? By himself suffering the loss. That is the principle of the Cross. He bore our sins, He carried our sins, He made Himself responsible for our moral debts. He Himself took over our suffering. Grace is set upon the perfection of man. Grace initiates the law whereby the man may be made perfect, and reveals to man his imperfection and his weakness. Then grace confronts the bankrupt soul and says, I forgive by suffering the loss. I know the frailty and the imperfection of all this illustration. I would not use such a figure if it were not a figure in the New Testament. Yet this is exactly what God does. He forgives by suffering loss. The very grace that is set on my perfecting and has given me the law that I may know what perfection is, and thereby has revealed to me my imperfection, steps into the breach, gathers into itself the infinite loss, cancels the bond, and so gives me forgiveness and life.

Think once more in the realm of that illustration. On the level of human interrelationships the illustration may break down in ninety-nine cases out of a hundred, but in the one-hundredth it is fulfilled in the sense in which I now use it. Let us go back to the two men. The one owes the other. The other forgives his debt, himself suffering the loss of that which is owed. What happens? The forgiven man goes out to begin again, freed from encumbrance, freed from the burden. In the passion born of gratitude for the act of grace he gives himself no rest until a day comes when he pays his debt.

I do not hesitate to use the illustration now. So will it be with all the truly ransomed. He Who met me, and revealed to me my failure, and made known to me how far I am in debt, He Who then in infinite grace bore the loss Himself, and uttered the word of freedom, He, at last, by the inspiration of the love and gratitude of my heart, by an operation of power given to me in the economy of that grace, will present me faultless before the throne of God; He shall see of the travail of His soul and be satisfied.

Law is beneficent, the language of love, and yet it condemns. The grace that utters law has other things to say, and by virtue of what it is in itself brings to men more than law. It brings the pardon and power by which at last, measured by the standards of law, they will be perfect in the sight of God.

CHAPTER XXVI

GOD-GOVERNED LIFE

The Lord our God spake unto us in Horeb, saying, Ye have dwelt long enough in this mountain.
DEUTERONOMY 1:6.

THE SOJOURN OF THE PEOPLE OF GOD AT MOUNT HOREB had been a most vital one. There they had received the law, an expression of the Divine grace. There the national constitution had been perfected, so that they were in very deed a theocracy, a people subject to the throne of God. There the system of worship had been given, a perpetual symbol of their distance from God by reason of their sin and of the possibility of their approach to Him by the way of sacrifice.

All this being accomplished, the word was spoken which called them to the practical realization of the fact that they were a people God-governed: "The Lord our God spake unto us in Horeb, saying, Ye have dwelt long enough in this mountain." They heard the Divine message, obeyed the Divine command, and marched through the great and terrible wilderness to the margin of the land of promise. The sequel, as we know, was one of failure, and of consequent discipline, the story of which is told in the book of Numbers. After forty years they were brought again to Kadesh-barnea, and there Moses, the great leader, ere leaving them, uttered these farewell discourses which have been preserved for us in the book of Deuteronomy. The words of our text were the opening words of the first of these discourses. As he stood and confronted these people whom he had been privileged to lead for forty years through varied experiences, the first words that fell from his lips were those reminding them of that hour when there came to them, in their corporate national capacity, the first command of God, "The Lord our God spake unto us in Horeb, saying, Ye have dwelt long enough in this mountain."

Spoken thus after the experience of forty years, while yet referring to the first command uttered to the nation in its corporate capacity, they introduce us to the subject of the Divine government of human life, help us to understand its method, purpose, and issue, and suggest to us what our relationship to that government should ever be.

My reference to the government of God is not now to that wider fact which embraces all creation. As we have often reminded ourselves, no man can escape from the government of God. No part of the universe is beyond the authority and power of God. That is a wider aspect of truth, with which at the moment we are not dealing. It is well, however, that we remind ourselves of this fact, for both our comfort and our warning. For our comfort let us remember that God has never vacated His throne, never handed over the affairs of the universe, or the smaller matters of this world of ours, to any other authority. It is perfectly true that men and nations may condition their experience of the Divine government by their attitude thereto, but escape it they cannot. A man can fling himself against the bosses of the shield of God and be broken in pieces, or he may nestle beneath the panoply of God and know the rest of the heart of God; but he cannot escape God. Lucifer, son of the morning, may say, "It is better to reign in hell than serve in heaven"; but he cannot reign in hell. God reigns in hell. Nations may throw off restraint and laugh at God; but He will have them in derision, and will laugh when their day of calamity comes. That is the wider aspect of this truth of Divine government.

I want this evening to speak more particularly of the government of God in the case of those who recognize it, yield themselves to it. How does God govern in the case of such?

The first matter to be emphasized is that God does govern. I think I need not stay to argue it. I do, however, desire to remind you of it. Sometimes I think that even we as Christian people do need to be reminded of the actuality of the government of God. We are a little in danger of treating God as though He were some infinite, marvelous abstraction; or as though He were seated afar off in some distant heaven, unacquainted with the actual experience of these little human lives of ours; or as though He had formed and fashioned us in some mysterious creation, and one day, at the end of a period of loneliness, he would meet us again and call us to account. All such conceptions of God are unwarranted by the Biblical revelation, and are untrue to the profoundest things of our Bible.

Let us then remind ourselves that the Bible reveals the actual, immediate government by God, of the lives of His own people. Let us further remind ourselves that this government of God is autocratic. He never consults us as to what He will do with us. The government of God is absolute; He permits no compromise. The government of God is inclusive; He exempts no territory. All that produces no fear in the hearts of men and women who know the government of God; for if the government be autocratic, so that He never consults me; absolute, so that He permits no compromise; inclusive, so that He exempts no territory—it is the government of God, and God is love, and God is wisdom. It is the government of the One Who fashioned me in answer to the impulses of His own love. It is the government of One Who knows my thought afar off and understands the sobbing desire that underlies all the failure, and Who will be infinitely patient with me until He has perfected that which concerneth me. But it is government, direct, immediate, absolute, autocratic.

Let us consider the nature of this government. Falling back on the text, and using all the background of the story for the purpose of illustration, there are three things I desire to say concerning the nature of that government. First, the government of God is a disturbing element in human life. Second, the government of God is a progressive element in human life. Finally, the government of God is a methodical element in human life.

First, then, let us consider the fact that the government of God is a disturbing element in human life, for it always is so. Traveling back beyond the moment in which this word came, take the story to the beginning of the history of that wonderful people. How did the people who were that day disturbed come into being? The nation came into being as the result of one human life being disturbed by God. In Ur of the Chaldees a man saw a vision of God and a vision of the purpose of God, and in some mystic, wonderful communion was brought into the place of great familiarity with God. He was a man of substance and position in Ur of the Chaldees. To that man suddenly there came a voice, the voice of God: "Get thee out of thy country, and from thy kindred, and from thy father's house, unto the land that I will show thee." "And he went out, not knowing whither he went." He was disturbed by God. The history of the people, from that first movement until this very hour when the voice of God came to them, was a history of perpetual, persistent disturbance. Disturbed in Ur of the Chaldees, Abraham moved into the land. Presently there came an hour when his grandson Jacob and his sons were driven out of the land by the Divine command and sent down to Egypt. Centuries ran their course, and the seventy souls who went down to Egypt multiplied into a great host; and again the Divine disturbance came: they were moved from Goshen and Egypt and encamped at Pihahiroth, hemmed in by enemies and the sea; they were then led out of danger, and across the highway of the dried sea, into the wilderness; they encamped beneath Sinai, a ransomed people, freed from bondage, escaped from slavery, resting at last amid the quietness and peace of the magnificent solitudes of the mountain. For a year and a month, free from all oppression, they realized the peace and blessedness of the Divine government, and then came the voice, "Ye have dwelt long enough in this mountain," and immediately all engagements had to be canceled, every tent had to be struck. The next picture we have is that of marching hosts moving forward, leaving the place of peace, tramping the dreary, desolate wilderness with faces set toward the goal of the Divine purpose. They were a disturbed people from beginning to end.

It is ever thus. To be governed by God is to be constantly disturbed, to have human arrangements interfered with. Here is a man whom God has called to some definite piece of work, and in the place of his service, he is conscious of the Divine presence, the Divine blessing. It may be that after a period of toil and travail everything is coming into adjustment and the golden radiance of harvest is on all the field. Then suddenly to the soul of the man comes the voice of God: "Ye have dwelt long enough in this mountain"; the work must be left, the location changed, and all the experience of the past apparently contradicted. The man is disturbed, and that by the Divine government. Or in other ways God disturbs us; crosses the threshold of the home of peace and quietness, and breaks it up, and we are no longer in the place of peace as we were, because God has disturbed our lives; some close earthly friendship in which comrade ministered to comrade in all things high and noble, sweet and strong, is suddenly broken in upon, and the friends are separated as far as the poles geographically. God is disturbing two lives; hopes and aspirations that gleamed and inspired, are suddenly put out, and all the movement of the years towards the goal seem to end in defeat. These are the common experiences of the saints. They are the problems of the saints. They are the problems of the men who observe the saints. Again and again they have been made the reason of ridicule of the saints. Along the avenue of these experiences Satan has ridden with all his host to assault the faith of the believer: If God loved you would He allow you thus to be disturbed? If God really loved you, would He not have left you that sacred, holy companionship? If God were really governing your life would He move you while your work seems to be successful? God is always doing it. Divinely governed souls are always sojourners in tents, pilgrims. "Let your loins be girded about, and your lamps burning; and be ye yourselves like unto men looking for their Lord," was the word of the Master Himself, indicating to the men who would follow Him that their true attitude should ever be that of expecting disturbance and change and alteration. Beneath the height of God's mount we are encamped, impressed by its majesty and its glory, comforted by the great words of law which proceed from the heart of grace for the conditioning of our lives, seeing the mosaic of the Divine arrangement manifest itself in constitution and ritual, in beauty and in order. Surely now at last, the long bondage over, we are finding a place of peace and quietness. When, lo, suddenly the word is spoken: Let the tents be struck, the baggage packed, "ye have dwelt long enough in this mountain."

If the Divine government of human lives be a disturbing element, it is a progressive element. Why were these people disturbed? I go back to the actual text, and I will now read a little more than the text:

The Lord our God spake unto us in Horeb, saying, Ye have dwelt long enough in this mountain: turn you, and take your journey, and go to the hill country of the Amorites, and unto all the places nigh thereunto, in the Arabah, in the hill country and in the lowland, and in the south, and by the sea shore, the land of the Canaanites, and Lebanon, as far as the great river, the river Euphrates. Behold, I have set the land before you: go in and possess the land which the Lord sware unto your fathers, to Abraham, to Isaac, and to Jacob, to give unto them and to their seed after them.

That reading of the context seems to make a defense of the disturbing almost unnecessary so far as this story is concerned, for thereby the light of the Divine purpose flashes on the fact of the Divine disturbance, and we see that the purpose of the disturbance was the possession of the land. The place of silent solitude is to be left, and the way of the wilderness is to be trodden; but why? That the land which lies beyond may be possessed. Progress is not necessarily pleasant. When Moses described the journey a little later in this same discourse, he speaks of it thus—the first journey, remember, not the subsequent journey of discipline— "We . . . went through all that great and terrible wilderness."

Here again the picture is a parable and the teaching is patent. God's dealings with a man to-day are always in the interest of his perfecting to-morrow. God's disturbance of human life is always in order that the life may climb to a higher height and come to fuller realization.

Now let all my exposition end as I take you to another of these discourses, yet hardly a discourse, the great song Moses was commanded to write. Listen to this:

> The Lord's portion is His people;
> Jacob is the lot of His inheritance.
> He found him in a desert land,
> And in the waste howling wilderness;
> He compassed him about, He cared for him,

> He kept him as the apple of His eye:
> As an eagle that stirreth up her nest,
> That fluttereth over her young,
> He spread abroad His wings, He took them,
> He bare them on His pinions.

In that exquisite figure we have the merging of the elements of disturbance and progress. May I take it for granted that all the adults in my congregation understand that figure? Well, for the boys and girls here I want to explain it; the others can take a rest. It is a very Eastern picture. We in England can hardly understand this picture of the eagle. Even in Scotland it can hardly be appreciated. We must get right away to the East if we would interpret its suggestiveness. Let us go and see what is happening. Yonder is an eagle's eyrie on the rocky ledge far up the heights. There the eagle has built her nest; there she has brought her young into being by her maternal brooding, and there she feeds them and guards them. The eaglets are in their nest on that rocky ledge, to which none can climb and to which none can descend in perfect safety; and the eagle watches over her young, and broods over them. Living somewhere in the neighborhood, let us imagine, we have watched this process from day to day, until there comes a day when something happens that is full of surprise. The mother bird that has seemed to be so tender and careful is doing the strangest of things. She is flinging those eaglets out of the nest, herself turning them out, beating them out. As I watch, I see the eaglets in the air, struggling, falling in the element which is strange to them. All the peace and safety and the restfulness of the nest is gone. "As an eagle stirreth up her nest."

Yes, but let us carefully watch. What next? The eagle spreads her broad pinions over the birds as they fall, and then suddenly, with the swiftness of the lightning, swoops beneath them and catches them on her broad wings. It seemed as though they must be destroyed. They are not destroyed. She bears them back on her wings to the ledge, and with a great sense of relief the eaglets struggle back into the nest. They are so glad to be back! To-morrow she will do it again, and the next day she will do it again; until one day as I watch I notice that one of the eaglets, perhaps a little stronger than the rest, when flung out of the nest and beginning to fall, puts out its wings and tries to use them. Then the purpose of the disturbance is seen. That will go on from day to day, until one day those eaglets will not struggle in the air, will not fall, but will spread their wings and fly with the mother bird sunward.

> As an eagle that stirreth up her nest,
> That fluttereth over her young,

so the Lord disturbs with progressive disturbance in order to realize life in all its fulfilment. Leave the eaglet undisturbed in the nest on the rocky height and it will fail of the very powers that are resident within it. Fling it out into the unaccustomed air, show it how to use its wings, catch it in its falling, bear it back again, give it a rest, disturb it again, and it will fulfil the meaning of its own life.

"Ye have dwelt long enough in this mountain." Leave that sphere of work which you love so well; be severed from that comrade without whom you feel you cannot live; know the breakup of home. What is God doing with you? Developing the powers of your own life, enabling you to discover the things in you which are of Himself, bearing you on His pinions in the moment of your utterest weakness, until presently He teaches you to use the wings He has given you. A disturbing element, but a progressive element.

Finally, this government of God is a methodical element in human life. The provision is made. "Behold, I have set the land before you." The course is marked out. Notice how particular are the instructions. Take your map of Palestine and mark the country out, and you will discover that these people never reached their destination; nor have they yet. God's limit was beyond anything they ever arrived at. Never did they stretch the bounds of their habitation as far as the great river Euphrates. I have read that to show that God had a plan for them which was possible for Him to express in terms of geography.

But there is something else in this chapter I want you to notice:

> Thy God bare thee, as a man doth bare his son, on all the way that ye went, until ye came unto this place. Yet in this thing ye did not believe the Lord your God, Who went before you in the way, to seek you out a place to pitch your tents in, in fire by night, to show you by what way ye should go, and in the cloud by day.

There are things in this Bible I would to God I knew how to read as they ought to be read. Oh, the poetry there is in that! There is no poetry in the way I read it. Read it for yourselves and find the poetry. God went before you in the way to seek you out a place in which to pitch your tents. We sing to-day, and the sentiment is true and beautiful, "We nightly pitch our moving tent a day's march nearer home." Then let us remember that the pitching of the tent at night is not accidental, for God has been before us. Think of it. I arrive nowhere but that God has been ahead of me. It may be that for the moment most of this congregation will be only reverently patient; but there is some man here, some woman, some youth, or some maiden, buffeted, broken, perplexed, lonely, almost mad with the agony of life. Just where you are, God was ahead of you. Out of the terror of the hour He is creating forces of triumph in your life which would always have been missing had you not pitched your tent right there where He has appointed the place. God is not making any experiments with you. There are some texts that we of a weaker generation hardly dare preach about. I will tell you one;

you will find it in Samuel, in the last psalm that David wrote ere he died: "An everlasting covenant, ordered in all things, and sure." Yes, you say, that is all very well for David. But read more, and you will find that David was describing what God's king ought to be, and he said:

> Verily my house is not so with God;
> Yet He hath made with me an everlasting covenant,
> Ordered in all things, and sure.
> For it is all my salvation, and all my desire
> Although He maketh it not to grow.

When David sang of the "covenant ordered in all things, and sure," he sang out of his disappointment, out of his sense that he had failed. He saw even his failure as within the Divine government. In his great letter to the Ephesians Paul reminds us in infinite music that "we are His workmanship," and not merely that we are His workmanship, but that "we are His workmanship, created in Christ Jesus for good works, which God afore prepared that we should walk in them." To the man who is truly God-governed the morning breaks and there is in his heart the consciousness that nothing can merely happen, in the infidel sense of the word. There can be no accident. Yes, I may suffer, I may suffer some physical evil, some mental trouble, some assault on the soul; I may pass through the great and terrible wilderness; but the covenant is ordered in all things, and sure. God cannot be surprised. Exigency, contingency, are very useful words for you and for me; but God has no need of them. No exigency surprises Him. No contingency baffles Him. He sees the end from the beginning, and all the affairs of the universe are under His control. The man God-governed is a man who lives at the very heart of method and order.

What, then, is our true relationship to this government? The answer is the simplest of all answers. Our true relation to the government of God is that of obedience, immediate and unconditional. What are the conditions of such obedience? Confidence in the method because it is the method of God, even when I cannot see its value; keeping forever in view the ultimate purpose in me and through me, and being forever ready to be disturbed. I love the paradoxes of faith. Here is one: the only man who is never disturbed is the man who is always ready to be disturbed. "Let your loins be girded about, and your lamps burning," ready to be disturbed; then when the call comes you will not be disturbed. It is when I allow my life to be anchored to friend, home, church, that if God wants me to do without this friend, break up this home, leave this church, I am disturbed. When my life is anchored in God, then no disturbance can disturb. That is the philosophy of life of the men who really live in the Divine government.

Oh, the unutterable folly of doing what these people did! They started well, they struck their tents, they came to the borderland; then they appointed a commission to find out about the land God told them to possess. That commission published two reports, the majority and minority reports; and then, as ever since, the minority was right. The people halted with fear, they went back; then they presumed and tried to go in without God, and fought the Amalekites and were defeated. Then followed forty years of discipline. "Forty years was I grieved with this generation." Consider in the light of this history what God does with people with whom He is grieved. He bare them as a man bears his son, with infinite patience and tender compassion, waiting for them.

Someone has heard the disturbing call of God, it may be within the last four and twenty hours. If so, I think this sermon is for you. What are you going to do? Go forward, counting no cost in your obedience? There are giants there. Yes, for you to slay. There are walled cities there. Yes, for you to take. There are rough ways ahead. Tramp them, they lead to peace. But there is awful loneliness. Welcome it, it admits you to the comradeship of God. The only thing we must not do, if God says we have tarried long enough, is to tarry. Some of you heard that voice long ago, and you disobeyed, and you have had a long weary wilderness; but tonight you are once again on the margin of the land. I pray you remember that all the wilderness has been in His government. This is the method of our God. He ever gives men a second time. The second time on the margin of the land. The word of the Lord came to Jonah the second time. If the vessel be marred in the hand of the Potter He will make it again a second time. All the years that the cankerworm hath eaten, He will restore them. He is plenteous in mercy and compassion,

> For the love of God is broader
> Than the measures of man's mind,
> And the heart of the Eternal
> Is most wonderfully kind.

Some man listening to me quite reverently says, I do not understand all this. I never hear a voice like that disturbing me. No, my brother, you are living in Egypt, in bondage: garlics, leeks, fleshpots! God-forsaken men are not disturbed. Yet listen. God is calling even you, and at this moment some of you have heard Him asking you to readjust your lives from this moment to make them kingdoms of God. You have tarried long enough in Egypt! At God's call arise and follow, and He will perfect that which concerneth you.

www.ingramcontent.com/pod-product-compliance
Lightning Source LLC
Chambersburg PA
CBHW052142300426
44115CB00011B/1486